거의 모든 상태 표현의 영어

서영조
한국외국어대학교 영어과, 동국대학교 대학원 연극영화과를 졸업했다. 영어 교재 출판 분야에서 유익한 영어 학습 콘텐츠를 개발해 왔고, 전문 번역가로서 영어권 도서들과 부산국제영화제를 비롯한 여러 영화제 출품작들을 번역해 왔다. 저서로《영어 회화의 결정적 단어들》,《영어 문장의 결정적 패턴들》,《여행 영어의 결정적 패턴들》,《거의 모든 행동 표현의 영어》,《디즈니 OST 잉글리시》,《디즈니 주니어 잉글리시 - 겨울왕국》 등이 있고, 번역서로《브레인 룰스》,《조이풀》,《철학을 권하다》,《일생에 한 번은 가고 싶은 여행지 500》 등이 있다.

거의 모든 상태 표현의 영어

지은이 서영조
초판 1쇄 인쇄 2025년 4월 25일
초판 1쇄 발행 2025년 5월 9일

발행인 박효상 **편집장** 김현 **기획·편집** 장경희, 오혜순, 이한경, 박지행 **디자인** 임정현
마케팅 이태호, 이전희 **관리** 김태옥

기획·편집 진행 김현
본문·표지 디자인 고희선

종이 월드페이퍼 **인쇄·제본** 예림인쇄·제본

출판등록 제10-1835호 **발행처** 사람in **주소** 04034 서울시 마포구 양화로 11길 14-10 (서교동) 3F
전화 02) 338-3555(代) **팩스** 02) 338-3545 **E-mail** saramin@netsgo.com
Website www.saramin.com

책값은 뒤표지에 있습니다.
파본은 바꾸어 드립니다.

ISBN
979-11-7101-156-8 14740
978-89-6049-936-2 세트

우아한 지적만보, 기민한 실사구시 사람in

미묘한 감정, 맛, 성격, 환경까지 딱 말하고 싶은 영어 표현이 온다!

서영조 지음

사람in

'행동'에 이어 '상태'까지 영어로 자유롭게

몇 년 전《거의 모든 행동 표현의 영어》를 출간하여 많은 사랑을 받았습니다. '한 다리로 서다', '커피를 내리다', '지하철을 놓치다', '유튜브 채널을 구독하다' 등 우리가 하는 거의 모든 행동을 영어로 어떻게 표현하는지를 망라한 책이었지요. 그 책이 영어 단어는 많이 알아도 일상의 행동을 영어로 표현하는 데 어려움을 겪는 영어 학습자들에게 적지 않은 도움을 주었으리라 생각합니다.

그런데 우리의 일상은 행동으로만 이루어져 있지는 않습니다. 우리는 끊임없이 머리로 생각하고, 다양한 감정을 경험하고, 여러 가지 감각을 느낍니다. 아울러 사회 속에서 살아가면서 다양한 상태와 상황에 처합니다. 이런 생각과 감정, 감각, 상태, 그리고 우리가 속한 사회의 온갖 현상, 우리를 둘러싼 자연 현상까지, 동작이 아닌 것들도 우리 삶을 구성하고, 그런 것들에 대해서도 우리는 많은 이야기를 하며 살아가지요. "나 지금 너무 초조해.", "그 사람은 눈치가 없어.", "저는 마른 비만이에요.", "스웨터에 보풀이 일었네요.", "이 애플파이는 겉바속촉이군요!", "이 거리는 무척 한적하군요." 같은 말들을요.

이번에는 그런 말들을 영어로 어떻게 표현하는지를 한 권에 정리했습니다. 그 광범위한 표현들을 '상태 표현'이라고 칭합니다. 상태 표현은 행동 표현과 함께 우리가 하는 말, 우리가 나누는 대화를 구성합니다. 따라서《거의 모든 행동 표현의 영어》와 함께 이 책《거의 모든 상태 표현의 영어》만 있으면 일상에서 나누는 대부분의 이야기를 영어로 할 수 있습니다. 영어 실력이 뛰어나지 않아도 두 책에 수록된 표현들만 익히면 우리가 하는 행동과 우리와 이 세상의 상태를 영어로 자유롭게 표현할 수 있습니다. 따라서 이 두 책은 영어 회화의 지름길을 제시하는 책이라고 할 수 있습니다.

지름길이 되고자 하는 책인 만큼《거의 모든 상태 표현의 영어》는 우리와 우리를 둘러싼 세상의 상태를 이야기할 때 꼭 필요한 표현들, 우리가 일상 대화에서 자주 쓰는 표현들을 엄선해서 수록했습니다. 이 책에 실린 표현들 가운데에 일상에서 흔히 사용하지 않는 표현은 없을 거라고 자부합니다.

대부분의 사람들이 영어를 잘하고 싶어 합니다. 영어를 잘한다는 것에는 여러 기준이 있을 수 있지만, 가장 기본은 하고 싶은 말을 막히지 않고 잘하는 것이겠지요. 이를 위해 《거의 모든 상태 표현의 영어》는 영어 회화에 꼭 필요한 상태 표현들을 주제에 따라 '사람의 몸과 마음', '사물', '의식주', '일과 생활', '사회', '자연과 환경' 등 여섯 개 범주로 나누어 제시합니다. 의미의 이해를 돕는 그림들은 공부한다는 부담감을 덜어 주고 내용을 이해하고 기억하는 데 도움을 줄 것입니다. 표현들을 보다 보면, '이런 감정은 영어로 이렇게 표현하는구나.', '이런 상태는 영어로 이렇게 말하면 되는 거네!' 하고 감탄하는 순간들이 적지 않을 것입니다.

이 책은 순서대로 공부할 필요는 없습니다. 모든 표현을 다 외우겠다는 욕심은 버려도 됩니다. 이 페이지 저 페이지 관심 가는 곳을 펼쳐 보면서 학습하세요. 궁금한 표현이 있으면 책 뒤의 인덱스에서 찾아보세요. 그렇게 학습하다 보면 어느새 상태를 나타내는 많은 영어 표현들이 여러분의 것이 되어 있을 것입니다.

여러분의 즐거운 영어 학습과 영어 회화 실력 향상을 응원합니다!

서영조

이 책은 총 6개 파트, 22개 챕터로 이루어져 있습니다. PART 1은 사람의 몸과 마음을 나타내는 상태 표현을, PART 2는 사물을 설명하는 상내 표현을, PART 3는 의식주와 관련한 상태 표현을, PART 4는 일과 일상생활 속 상태 표현을, PART 5는 우리 사회를 나타내는 상태 표현을, 마지막으로 PART 6는 자연과 환경을 나타내는 상태 표현을 소개합니다.

이 책은 처음부터 끝까지 순서대로 학습해야 하는 책은 아닙니다. 물론 앞에서부터 차근차근 학습하셔도 좋습니다만, 그렇게 하지 않아도 됩니다. 목차를 보고 눈길이 가는 부분이나 어떤 내용일지 궁금한 부분을 펼쳐서 먼저 공부하고, 또 다른 궁금한 부분으로 넘어가서 학습하면 됩니다. 그리고 궁금한 표현이 있다면 언제든 책 뒤에 실린 인덱스에서 찾아보면 됩니다.

첫술에 배부를 수 없다는 건 영어 공부에서도 절대적인 진리입니다. 이 책은 한 번 읽었다고 끝이 아니라 여러 번 반복해서 읽어야 합니다. 이미 알고 있는 표현이라면 확인만 하고 넘어가고, 모르던 표현일 경우에는 여러 번 반복해서 읽어 자기 것으로 만들어야 합니다. 이때 머릿속으로만 읽지 말고 입으로 소리 내어 읽는 게 훨씬 효과적입니다. 손으로 써 보기까지 하면 더 좋습니다.

추천하는 학습 방법은 각각의 한글 표현을 읽고 영어로는 어떻게 말할지 생각해 본 다음 책에 나와 있는 영어 표현을 확인해 보는 것입니다. 학습이 어느 정도 이루어졌다는 생각이 들면 인덱스에 있는 한글 표현을 보면서 영어로 말해 보는 훈련을 해 보세요. 영어 상태 표현을 온전히 자기 것으로 만드는 과정이 될 것입니다.

왼쪽의 QR코드를 스캔하시고 '바로듣기'를 탭하세요.
해당 도서의 음원을 바로 들으실 수 있습니다.
반복 재생과 속도 조절도 가능합니다.

영어 회화 실력 향상에 꼭 필요한《거의 모든 상태 표현의 영어》는 다음과 같이 구성되어 있습니다.

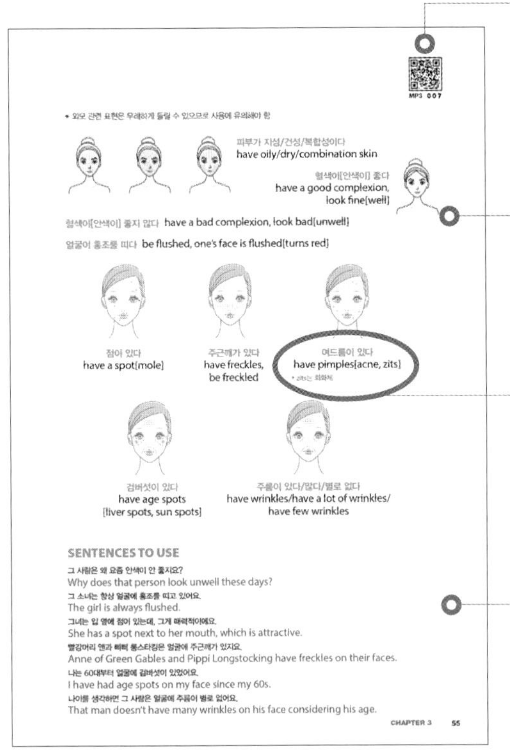
MP3 007

* 외모 관련 표현은 무례하게 들릴 수 있으므로 사용에 유의해야 함

피부가 지성/건성/복합성이다
have oily/dry/combination skin

혈색이[안색이] 좋다
have a good complexion, look fine[well]

혈색이[안색이] 좋지 않다 have a bad complexion, look bad[unwell]

얼굴이 홍조를 띠다 be flushed, one's face is flushed[turns red]

점이 있다
have a spot[mole]

주근깨가 있다
have freckles, be freckled

여드름이 있다
have pimples[acne, zits]
* zits는 회화체

검버섯이 있다
have age spots [liver spots, sun spots]

주름이 있다/많다/별로 없다
have wrinkles/have a lot of wrinkles/have few wrinkles

SENTENCES TO USE

그 사람은 왜 요즘 안색이 안 좋지요?
Why does that person look unwell these days?
그 소녀는 항상 얼굴에 홍조를 띠고 있어요.
The girl is always flushed.
그녀는 입 옆에 점이 있는데, 그게 매력적이에요.
She has a spot next to her mouth, which is attractive.
빨강머리 앤과 삐삐 롱스타킹은 얼굴에 주근깨가 있지요.
Anne of Green Gables and Pippi Longstocking have freckles on their faces.
나는 60대부터 얼굴에 검버섯이 있었어요.
I have had age spots on my face since my 60s.
나이를 생각하면 그 사람은 얼굴에 주름이 별로 없어요.
That man doesn't have many wrinkles on his face considering his age.

CHAPTER 3 55

본문의 영어 표현과 SENTENCES TO USE의 영어 문장을 원어민이 정확한 발음으로 녹음했습니다.

본문은 우리말-영어 표현 순으로 제시됩니다. 표현에서 have oily/dry/combination skin처럼 /는 have oily skin, have dry skin, have combination skin처럼 같은 위치의 단어를 해당 단어로 대체하면 다른 의미의 표현이 된다는 뜻입니다.

have pimples[acne, zits]는 have pimples, have acne, have zits로 다른 단어를 대입해도 의미가 변하지 않는 걸 의미합니다.

SENTENCES TO USE는 위에서 배운 표현이 실제 회화 문장에서 쓰이는 예를 보여 줍니다.

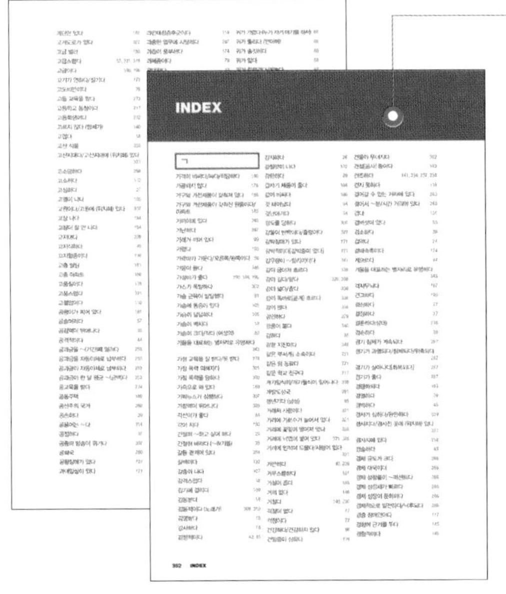

어느 정도 학습이 되었다고 판단되면 인덱스의 한글 부분을 보면서 영어 표현을 말해 보세요. 이렇게 하면 여러분의 영어 실력이 몰라볼 만큼 성장할 것입니다.

차례

PART 2 사물

CHAPTER 1 사물의 외형

CHAPTER 2 사물의 성질

PART 3 의식주

CHAPTER 1 의복

CHAPTER 2 음식

CHAPTER 3 주거

PART 4 일과 생활

CHAPTER 1 일과 업무

CHAPTER 2 관계, 소속

PART 1

사람의 몸과 마음

CHAPTER

1

사람의 마음

UNIT 1

긍정적인 감정

기분이 좋다 feel good[fine, nice, happy, great], be in a good mood, be in high spirits, be happy

기쁘다 be[feel] happy[glad, pleased, delighted]

* glad와 pleased는 중간 수준의 행복감, delighted가 좀 더 높은 행복감, happy는 가장 일반적인 표현

무척 기쁘다, 황홀하다 be[feel] overjoyed[thrilled]

행복하다 be[feel] happy

~하는 것은[~하면, ~해서] 기쁘다 it's a pleasure to 동사원형[동사ing]

~하는 것은[~하면, ~해서] 즐겁다 it's fun to 동사원형[동사ing]

설레다, 들뜨다, 신나다 be[feel] excited, ~ make(s) one's heart flutter(시적이고 낭만적인 표현)

SENTENCES TO USE

힘든 하루를 보내고 따뜻한 욕조에 몸을 담그고 있으면 기분이 좋아요.
I feel good when I soak in a warm bath after a hard day.

그 사람에게서 오랜만에 연락을 받아서 기뻤어요.
I was glad to hear from him after a long time.

그녀는 장기자랑대회에서 상을 받아 무척 기뻤어요.
She was overjoyed to win a prize in a talent contest.

나는 밤하늘의 별자리를 찾아보는 게 즐거워요.
For me, it's fun to look for constellations in the night sky.

파리로 여행 간다는 생각에 너무 설레서 잠이 오지 않았어요.
I couldn't sleep because I was so excited at the thought of traveling to Paris.

~(하는 것)에 만족하다, ~해서 만족스럽다
be satisfied[content] with 명사[동사ing]
be content to 동사원형, be satisfied that 주어+동사

걱정이 없다 be carefree, be free from worries

느긋하다, 여유롭다, 태평하다 be relaxed [laid-back, easygoing, carefree]

* laid-back, easygoing은 성격적 특성을 나타냄

~해서 안도하다 be relieved to 동사원형

마음이 편안하다 be[feel] at ease, feel comfortable, feel at home, have peace of mind

~해서 다행이다 it's good that 주어+동사, it's a relief[blessing] that 주어+동사(relief 뒤에는 걱정했던 것과 상반되는 내용이, blessing 뒤에는 운 좋은 사건이 나옴), be glad that 주어+동사

SENTENCES TO USE

그는 자신의 소박한 일상에 만족합니다.
He is satisfied with his simple daily life.

복권에 당첨된 후 그는 현재 여유로운 생활을 즐깁니다.
After winning all that money in the lottery, he now enjoys a carefree lifestyle.

그들은 탑승자 전원이 구조되었다는 소식에 안도했습니다.
They were relieved to hear that all the passengers had been rescued.

그녀는 업무 방식이 느긋해서 그녀의 팀에서 일하면 내 마음이 편합니다.
She has a laid-back approach to work, so being on her team makes me feel at ease.

수술이 성공적이어서 다행입니다.
It's a relief that the operation was a success.

UNIT 1

(사람)이[에게]/~에 대해 고맙다, 감사하다 be thankful[grateful] to 사람/for ~(고마운 내용)

(사람)에게 ~에 대해 고맙다, 감사하다 be thankful[grateful] to 사람 for ~(고마운 내용)

~해서[~한 데 대해] 고맙다, 감사하다 be thankful[grateful] to 동사원형[that 주어+동사]

~에/~해서 감명받다, 감동받다, 감격스럽다 be moved[touched, impressed] by 명사/to 동사원형
* moved와 touched는 감정적으로 영향을 받은 것이며, impressed는 감탄과 존경의 뜻을 내포함

~가/~한 것이 자랑스럽다 be[feel] proud of 명사/동사ing

~해서 뿌듯하다 feel great to 동사원형(만족감, 행복감), be proud to 동사원형(성취나 행동에 대한 뿌듯함)

가슴이 벅차다 be overwhelmed, one's heart is filled with joy(시적인 표현)

~해서 흐뭇하다 be pleased[delighted, content, happy] to 동사원형

~에 희망을 품다, ~을 기대하다 be hopeful about[of] 명사

~하리라는 희망을 품다, ~하리라고 기대하다 be hopeful that 주어+동사

~을/~일 거라고 낙관하다
be optimistic about[of] 명사/be optimistic that 주어+동사

활기가 넘치다 be[feel] exuberant

SENTENCES TO USE

나를 걱정해 준 친구가 고마웠어요.
I was grateful to my friend who worried about me.

나는 십 대 때 그 작가의 수필을 읽고 감동을 받았어요.
I was moved to read the writer's essay when I was a teenager.

그는 예전에 음악을 가르친 학생이 유명 가수가 된 걸 보니 뿌듯했어요.
He was proud to see his former music student become a famous singer.

그녀는 종양이 다 사라졌다는 소식을 듣고 가슴이 벅찼습니다.
She was overwhelmed to hear that all the tumors had disappeared.

수확한 포도를 보고 있노라니 그 농부는 흐뭇했습니다.
The farmer was pleased to see the harvested grapes.

~에/~하는 데에 관심이 있다, 흥미가 있다
be interested in 명사/동사ing

자유롭다 be free

~에/~하는 데에 자신 있다 be confident in 명사/동사ing,
have confidence in 명사/동사ing

~을/~할 것을 확신하다
be convinced[confident, certain] of 명사/동사ing,
be sure of[about] 명사/동사ing

~라고 확신하다
be convinced[confident, sure, certain] that 주어+동사
* sure와 certain은 흔히 부정문, 의문문에 쓰임
* sure의 경우, 의심의 여지 없는 확신을 나타낼 때는 보통 quite sure로 씀

(기분이) 상쾌하다, 산뜻하다
be[feel] refreshed

짜릿하다 be so exhilarating

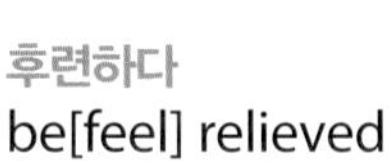

후련하다
be[feel] relieved

SENTENCES TO USE

그는 월급 외에 가욋돈을 버는 데 관심이 있습니다.
He is interested in making extra money in addition to his main salary.

어렸을 때는 온라인 게임에서 이길 수 있다는 자신이 더 있었어요.
When I was younger, I was more confident in my ability to win online games.

30분 동안 달리고 나서 샤워를 하면 기분이 상쾌해요.
I feel refreshed when I take a shower after running for 30 minutes.

그 팀이 역전승을 거둔 것이 너무나 짜릿했어요.
It was so exhilarating that the team came from behind and won.

그 엄청난 과제를 제출하고 나니 후련했어요.
I felt relieved after handing in that giant assignment.

UNIT 2

부정적인 감정

안 좋은 기분

MP3 002-1

기분이 나쁘다 feel bad[awful, terrible], be in a bad mood, be[feel] unhappy

불행하다 be[feel] unhappy

마음이 불편하다 be[feel] uncomfortable, be ill at ease, feel uneasy

(~이) **불만스럽다** be[feel] dissatisfied (with ~)

(~에) **실망하다** be[feel] disappointed (in ~)

(~이) **불쾌하다**, (~에) **기분이 상하다** be[feel] displeased (with ~), be[feel] offended (by[at] sth, with sb)

* offended는 상대의 무례함 등으로 모욕감을 느끼는 것

불안하다 be[feel] uneasy[anxious, nervous]

* anxious, nervous는 uneasy보다 더 큰 불편과 걱정을 암시

SENTENCES TO USE

내가 말하는 동안 그가 계속 스마트폰만 봐서 기분이 나빴어요.
I felt bad because he kept looking at his smartphone while I was talking.

데이비드에게 그가 시험에 불합격했다는 소식을 전하려니 마음이 불편했어요.
I felt uncomfortable telling David that he had failed the exam.

오늘 택배가 오지 않아서 실망했어요.
I was disappointed that the package hadn't arrived today.

손님이 돈을 카운터에 던졌을 때 빌은 불쾌했습니다.
Bill was displeased when the customer threw money on the counter.

꿈자리가 나빠서 종일 조금 불안했어요. 다행히도 아무 일 없었어요.
I had a bad dream, so I felt a little anxious all day. Fortunately, nothing bad happened.

MP3 002

화, 짜증

MP3 002-2

당황스럽다 be[feel] embarrassed[baffled, panicked], be in a panic
* panicked, in a panic은 자제력과 판단력을 잃을 정도로 당황한 상태에 씀

속상하다 be[feel] upset

짜증 나다 be[feel] annoyed[irritated]

좌절하다, 낙담하다 be[feel] discouraged[frustrated]

심술 나다 be[feel] grumpy

화가 나다(상태) be[feel] angry, be mad

분노하다 be[feel] outraged[furious]

분하다, 분개하다 be[feel] resentful[bitter]

억울하다 feel aggrieved[unfairly treated, wronged]

SENTENCES TO USE

내 스스로가 갑자기 화가 나서 당황스러웠어요.
I was embarrassed by my own sudden anger.

나는 친구가 또 늦어서 짜증이 났어요.
I was annoyed since my friend was late again.

그녀는 20대에 큰 병에 걸렸지만 좌절하지 않았습니다.
She suffered a serious illness in her 20s, but she was not discouraged.

사람들은 그 정치가의 막말에 분노했습니다.
People were outraged by the politician's rude remarks.

그는 자신에 대한 편향된 판단에 억울함을 느꼈어요.
He felt aggrieved by the biased judgments made against him.

UNIT 2

슬픔, 우울, 걱정

MP3 002-3

우울하다 feel blue,
be[feel] depressed[gloomy](depressed가 gloomy보다 좀 더 심한 상태),
be in a gloomy mood

슬프다 be[feel] sad[sorrowful]
* sorrowful은 대개 문예체, 격식체에 쓰임

걱정이다 be worried about[over] 명사,
be worried that 주어+동사

괴롭다 be painful[in pain],
be[feel] agonized[distressed],
find it painful to 동사원형

상처받다 be hurt
* 신체적, 정신적 상처를 다 나타낼 수 있음

속상하다 be[feel] distressed[upset]

허무하다 feel empty[hollow],
feel that ~ is futile

SENTENCES TO USE

그녀는 비만 오면 왠지 우울해져요.
She tends to feel gloomy for some reason whenever it rains.

그는 속 좁은 사람처럼 보일까 걱정이었어요.
He was worried that he would seem narrow-minded.

그 사람하고 한 사무실에서 일하는 게 괴롭네요.
I find it painful to work in the same office with him.

그녀는 아끼던 목걸이를 잃어버려서 속상했어요.
She was upset because she lost her favorite necklace.

우울증 치료를 받기 전에 나는 항상 너무 허무했습니다.
Before I got help for my depression, I always felt so empty.

무력감을 느끼다 be[feel] helpless

비참하다 be[feel] miserable[wretched]

외롭다, 쓸쓸하다 be[feel] lonely[lonesome]
* lonesome은 주로 미국과 캐나다에서 쓰임

소외감을 느끼다 feel left out[alienated, isolated, excluded]

단절감을 느끼다 feel cut off[disconnected]

(집이나 고향에) 향수를 느끼다 feel homesick

(과거에) 향수를 느끼다 feel nostalgic

SENTENCES TO USE

그는 그녀를 위해 아무것도 할 수 없다는 사실에 무력감을 느꼈어요.
He felt helpless that he couldn't do anything for her.

그녀는 가족도 없고 친구도 없는 자신의 현실이 비참하게 느껴졌어요.
She felt miserable about her reality of having no family and no friends.

나이가 들수록 자꾸 외로워요.
I often feel lonely as I get older.

나는 마을 사람들에게서 소외감을 느꼈어요. 그들은 십 년 넘게 서로 알고 지냈거든요.
I felt left out by the villagers who had known each other for over a decade.

그는 고국을 떠나고 몇 년 뒤부터 향수를 느꼈어요.
He felt homesick a few years after leaving his home country.

UNIT 2

무서움, 충격, 죄책감

MP3 002-4

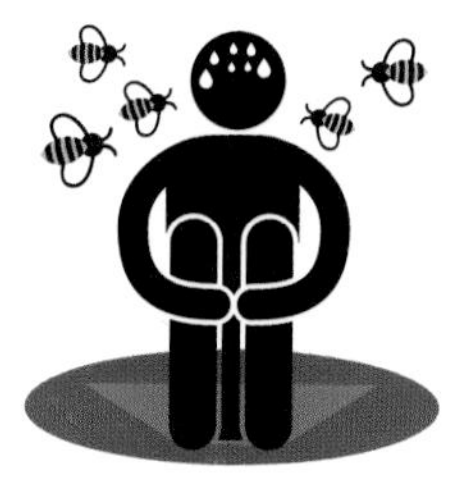

부끄럽다, 창피하다 be[feel] ashamed[humiliated, embarrassed]

겁먹다 be[feel] scared[terrified, horrified]

* scared가 일반적인 의미, terrified가 가장 심하게 겁먹은 상태,
horrified는 공포와 충격이 섞인 감정

두렵다 be[feel] afraid[scared, fearful], dread

* fearful은 격식체로, 많이 안 쓰임,
동사 dread는 발생할지도 모를 상황에 대한 두려움을 표현

무섭다, 무서워하다 be[feel] scared[frightened, terrified]

놀라다 be[feel] surprised

깜짝 놀라다, 충격을 받다 be shocked[frightened, shaken]

* frightened는 공포의 느낌을 수반,
shaken은 충격적인 사건으로 화난 상태를 암시

죄책감을 느끼다 feel guilty

양심의 가책을 느끼다 have a guilty conscience

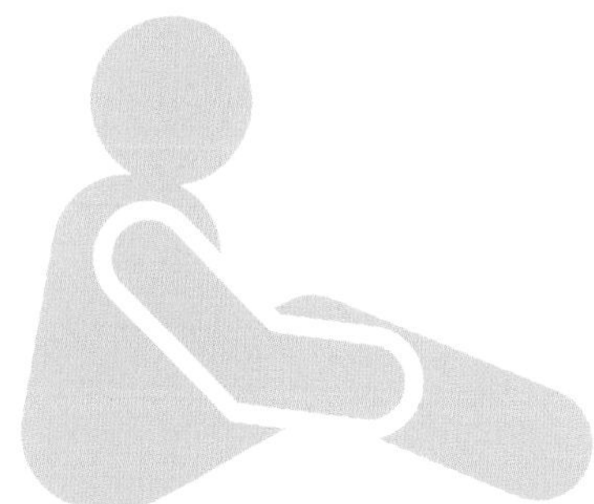

SENTENCES TO USE

사람들 앞에서 눈물을 보여서 창피했어요.
I was embarrassed to show tears in front of people.

교통사고를 겪고 나서 한동안은 운전하기가 두려웠어요.
After the car accident, I was afraid to drive for a while.

나는 그 사람이 미국에서 유학했지만 영어를 잘 못한다는 사실에 놀랐어요.
I was surprised that he studied in the United States but did not speak English well.

그와 그녀가 한때 결혼했었다는 소식에 모두가 충격을 받았습니다.
Everyone was shocked at the news that he and she were once married.

답답함, 아쉬움

MP3 002-5

압박감[중압감]을 느끼다 feel pressured

답답하다 be[feel] frustrated

따분하다 be[feel] bored

초조하다 be[feel] anxious[nervous]

부담스럽다 사람 be[feel] burdened, 상황 be burdensome

~해서 안타깝다 it's a pity that 주어+동사,
it's regrettable that 주어+동사(더 격식을 갖춘 표현)

~해서 아쉽다 it's too bad that 주어+동사,
it's a shame that 주어+동사

~해서 유감이다 be sorry that 주어+동사,
it's regrettable that 주어+동사,
be sorry to 동사원형, regret to 동사원형

* regrettable, regret이 더 격식을 갖춘 표현

~해서 섭섭하다, 서운하다 be sorry[disappointed] that 주어+동사,
regret that 주어+동사

SENTENCES TO USE

그녀는 마감일이 빠듯한 새 프로젝트를 맡은 후 중압감을 느끼고 있어요.
She is feeling pressured after taking on a new project due to tight deadlines.

나는 그가 말을 너무 느리게 해서 답답했어요.
I was frustrated because he spoke so slowly.

취업 면접에서 내 차례가 다가오니 초조했어요.
I was nervous as my turn approached at the job interview.

그가 시도 때도 없이 너무 자주 연락해서 부담스러워요.
I feel burdened because he keeps in touch too often.

그녀와의 사이가 예전 같지 않아서 유감이에요.
I'm sorry that my relationship with her is not the same as before.

UNIT 3

생각, 심리

~라고 생각하다 think (that) 주어+동사, consider (that) 주어+동사

A를 B라고 생각하다, 여기다 think of A as B(명사),
consider A(명사) (to be/as) B(명사), regard A(명사) as B(명사)

~라고 느끼다 feel (that) 주어+동사

~임을 깨닫다, 알아차리다 realize (that) 주어+동사,
notice (that) 주어+동사, become aware that 주어+동사

~임을 지각하다, 인지하다
perceive (that) 주어+동사, be aware that 주어+동사

~임을 감지하다, 느끼어 알다 sense (that) 주어+동사

~을 알고 있다, 의식하고 있다
be aware of 명사, be aware that 주어+동사,
be conscious of 명사, be conscious that 주어+동사

(보거나 듣고서 누구인지/무엇인지) 알아보다
recognize 명사, recognize (that) 주어+동사

SENTENCES TO USE

많은 사람이 그녀의 행동은 부적절하다고 느꼈어요.
Many people felt that her behavior was inappropriate.

그레고르 잠자는 자신의 몸이 거대한 벌레로 변했다는 것을 깨달았습니다.
Gregor Samsa realized that his body had transformed into a huge insect.

그는 뭔가 일이 잘못되어 가고 있다는 것을 인지했어요.
He perceived that something was going wrong.

경찰 고위 관리들은 사고의 위험성을 잘 알고 있었습니다.
Senior police officials were well aware of the danger of accidents.

나는 그 사람이 사기꾼이라는 걸 진작에 알아봤죠.
I recognized early on that he was a swindler.

(존재를, 진실성을) 인정하다
recognize 명사, recognize (that) 주어+동사

A를 B라고 인정하다 recognize A(명사) as B(명사)

~에 대해 숙고하다
consider 명사, think over 명사, ponder (on[over, upon]) 명사

~에 대해 고심하다
think hard about 명사, struggle with 명사

~하기로 결정하다, 결심하다 decide[determine] to 동사원형, make a decision to 동사원형

~인지 아닌지 궁금해하다
wonder if 주어+동사

누가/왜/어떻게/언제/어디서 ~하는지 궁금해하다
wonder who/why/how/when/where 주어+동사

SENTENCES TO USE

UN무역개발회의는 2021년에 대한민국을 선진국으로 인정했습니다.
UNCTAD recognized South Korea as an advanced country in 2021.

그는 시골로 이사 가는 것을 결정하느라 오랫동안 고민했어요.
He struggled for a long time with the decision to move to the countryside.

제 조카는 대학교에서 심리학을 전공하기로 결정했습니다.
My niece decided to major in psychology at university.

그녀는 몇 가지 일자리 선택지들을 놓고 숙고했지만 결정을 못 내렸습니다.
She considered her various job options but couldn't make a decision.

나는 그가 그때 왜 그런 결정을 했는지 정말 궁금해요.
I really wonder why he made that decision then.

UNIT 3

~을 원하다 want 명사

~하기를 원하다 want to 동사원형

~을 바라다, 소망하다 hope for 명사

~하기를 바라다, 소망하다
hope (that) 주어+동사, hope to 동사원형

~을 염원하다, 간절히 바라다 long for 명사

~하기를 염원하다, 간절히 바라다 long to 동사원형, aspire to 동사원형, be eager to 동사원형

~가 좋다 like 명사, love 명사(무척 좋아한다는 의미)

~하는 게 좋다 like 동사ing[to 동사원형], love 동사ing[to 동사원형](무척 좋아한다는 의미)

~가 싫다 hate 명사, dislike 명사(hate보다 순화된 느낌)

~하는 게 싫다, ~하기 싫다 hate 동사ing[to 동사원형]

~에 질리다, 싫증 나다
be sick of 명사[동사ing], be tired of 명사[동사ing]

~에 신물이 나다 be sick and tired of 명사[동사ing], be fed up with 명사[동사ing]
* 이 표현들이 바로 위의 표현들보다 더 짜증스러움과 불만을 나타냄

SENTENCES TO USE

현대 사회에서는 많은 사람들이 물질적 성공을 원합니다.
In modern societies, many people want material success.

많은 이들이 2022년에 시작된 그 전쟁이 어서 끝나기를 소망합니다.
Many hope that the war which began in 2022 will end soon.

그 소녀는 핀란드의 산타클로스 마을에 간절히 가고 싶어 해요.
The girl is eager to visit Santa Claus Village in Finland.

그는 밝은색 옷을 입는 것을 싫어해서 주로 검은색이나 회색 옷을 골라요.
He hates wearing bright clothes and usually chooses black or gray ones.

나는 그녀가 자기 남자 친구 얘기하는 거 듣는 데 질렸어요.
I'm tired of hearing her talk about her boyfriend.

~을 존경하다 respect 명사, have respect for 명사, admire 명사

~을 존중하다 respect 명사

~을 동경하다, 그리워하다 yearn for 명사
* 얻기 힘든 것을 동경하고 갈망함

간절히 ~하고 싶어 하다, ~하기를 열망하다 yearn to 동사원형
* 성취하기 힘든 일을 열망함

~에 감탄하다, 탄복하다 admire 명사

~을 추앙하다, 숭배하다 idolize 명사(비판 없이 극도로 애정하고 추앙함), revere 명사(마음속 깊은 곳에서 존경함), worship 명사(주로 종교적, 은유적 관점)

~을 혐오하다 detest 명사, loathe 명사, abhor 명사(좀 더 격식체)

~을 무시하다 ignore 명사(의도적으로 무시하는 것),
neglect 명사(의도적인 무시는 아니고 소홀히 하는 것),
pass over 명사(못 보고 넘어가는 것)

~을 무시하다, 업신여기다 look down on 명사

~을 경멸하다, 멸시하다 despise 명사, disdain 명사,
scorn 명사, look down on 명사

SENTENCES TO USE

자녀들에게 존경받는 부모가 되는 건 쉽지 않습니다.
It is not easy to be a parent who is respected by their children.

그 팀장은 팀원들의 의견을 존중해요.
The team leader respects her team members' opinions.

요즘 많은 어린이들이 유명인이 되기를 갈망합니다.
Many children these days yearn to become celebrities.

왜 그런 사이비 교주를 추앙하는 사람들이 있는지 나는 이해가 안 가요.
I don't understand why there are people who worship a cult leader like that.

안타깝지만 성소수자들을 혐오하는 사람들이 적지 않게 있습니다.
Unfortunately, there are quite a few people who abhor LGBTQ individuals.

CHAPTER

2

사람의 성격, 성품, 태도

UNIT 1

성격, 성품, 태도 – 긍정적인 표현

착하다, 선량하다 be nice[good-natured]

좋은 사람이다 be a good person

인간성[인성]이 좋다
have a good personality

온화하다
be gentle[mild-mannered]

따뜻하다, 정이 많다
be warm[warm-hearted, kind, kind-hearted]

친절하다 be kind

다정하다, 상냥하다
be friendly[kind, nice]

마음이 넓다
be big-hearted[broad-minded, tolerant], have a big heart

동정심이 많다
be compassionate[sympathetic], have a lot of sympathy

자애롭다, 자비롭다
be benevolent[gracious, merciful]

SENTENCES TO USE

톰슨 씨는 좋은 사람이에요. 친구도 많아요.
Mr. Thompson is a good person. He has lots of friends.

그들의 아버지는 온화하고 가정에 헌신적이셨어요.
Their father was gentle and devoted to his family.

그 교수님은 참 따뜻하고 친절하세요. 그러니 학생들이 좋아하죠.
The professor is very warm and kind. That's why students like him.

그녀는 동정심이 많아서 길고양이들을 돌보기까지 해요.
She is so compassionate that she even looks after stray cats.

성모 마리아는 가톨릭 신자들에게 자애로운 어머니 같은 존재로 여겨집니다.
The Virgin Mary is considered a benevolent mother by Catholics.

이해심 있다 be understanding

포용력 있다 be tolerant[understanding, broad-minded]

공감력이 뛰어나다 have great empathy,
be good at empathizing

너그럽다, 관대하다, 아량 있다
be tolerant[magnanimous]
* magnanimous는 특히 경쟁자나 적에게 너그러운 것을 나타냄

(인심이) 후하다, 너그럽다, 관대하다 be generous
* 주로 물질적으로 잘 베푼다는 의미

사려 깊다 be considerate[thoughtful]

믿을 수 있다, 신뢰할 수 있다
be reliable[trustworthy]

책임감 있다
be responsible

(~에) 헌신적이다
be devoted[committed, dedicated] (to ~)

SENTENCES TO USE

나는 다정하고 이해심 있는 사람을 만나고 싶어요.
I want to meet someone who is kind and understanding.

포용력이 있다는 게 리더로서 그 사람의 장점이에요.
Being tolerant is his strength as a leader.

그녀는 공감력이 뛰어나서 사람들은 그녀에게 자기들 문제를 자주 이야기합니다.
She has great empathy, so people often tell her about their problems.

폴은 인심이 후해서 친구들과 이웃들에게 밥을 자주 사요.
Paul is generous and often treats his friends and neighbors to meals.

프랭크는 믿을 수 있는 사람이니, 빌린 돈은 갚을 거예요.
Frank is trustworthy, so you know he will pay back the money he borrowed.

UNIT 1

긍정적이다
be positive[upbeat]
* upbeat는 회화체

낙천적[낙관적]이다
be optimistic,
be happy-go-lucky

마음이 열려 있다
be open-minded

융통성 있다 be flexible

성실하다 be faithful[honest, sincere]
* faithful은 충실하고 헌신적이라는 의미,
honest와 sincere는 진실하고 진심이라는 의미

정직하다, 솔직하다 be honest[frank, straightforward]
* honest는 성품과 언행이 정직하고 거짓 없다는 의미,
frank는 가식이 없고 노골적일 정도로 솔직하다는 의미

순수하다 be pure

차분하다, 침착하다
be calm[composed, self-possessed],
have a calm personality

느긋하다, 태평스럽다
be easygoing[laid-back]

SENTENCES TO USE

그녀는 늘 긍정적이에요. 나도 그러면 좋겠어요.
She is always positive. I wish I were more like her.

그는 사려 깊으면서 정직해요. 필요한 말만 하죠.
He is thoughtful and honest. He only says what he needs to say.

그 소설의 주인공은 순수했지만, 현실을 직면하면서 점차 변해 갔어요.
The heroine of the novel was pure, but gradually changed as she faced the realities.

그 배우는 겉모습과 다르게 성격이 차분하다고 합니다.
Contrary to his appearance, the actor is said to have a calm personality.

나는 늘 조바심을 내는데, 그런 모습이 싫어요. 좀 더 느긋해지고 싶어요.
I'm always anxious, and I hate it. I want to be a little bit more laid-back.

밝다 be bright

유쾌하다, 쾌활하다, 명랑하다
be bright[cheerful, joyful]

정력적이다, 원기 왕성하다
be energetic

적극적이다, 활동적이다
be active

사교적이다 be sociable

생기 넘치다, 활기차다 be full of life, be lively

열정적이다 be passionate[enthusiastic]

에너지가 넘치다
be energetic

자신감이 있다
be confident[self-assured],
have confidence

SENTENCES TO USE

그 아이는 무척 밝아서 함께 있으면 기분이 좋아요.
The girl is very bright, and I feel good when I'm with her.

그녀는 항상 자원봉사를 하고 지역 사회에서 매우 적극적으로 활동합니다.
She volunteers all the time and is very active in her community.

그는 무척 사교적이어서 어디를 가든 친구를 사귀어요.
He is so sociable that he makes friends wherever he goes.

그는 늘 활기차고 품위가 있는데, 그 모습이 매력적이에요.
He is always both lively and dignified, which is attractive.

무슨 일을 하든, 자신감이 있는 건 큰 강점이죠.
No matter what you do, being confident is a great strength.

UNIT 1

매력적이다, 매력 있다
be attractive[charming, appealing]

유머 감각이 있다 be humorous,
have a (good) sense of humor
* a (good) sense of 뒤에 감각이 있는 대상을 써서 확장 가능
ex) have a (good) sense of fashion 패션 감각이 있다

재미있다 be funny[interesting]
* funny는 웃음 유발, interesting은 호기심과 흥미 유발

호기심이 많다
be curious

두뇌 회전이 빠르다, 머리가 잘 돌아가다
be quick-witted, have quick wits[quick perception]

눈치가 빠르다
be good at reading the room,
be good at reading people
* 분위기나 사람의 마음을 잘 파악하는 것

눈치 있다 be tactful
* 눈치가 있어서 다른 사람의 기분을 상하게 하지 않는 것

세심하다, 섬세하다 be sensitive
* 남의 기분을 헤아리는 데 세심하고 섬세하다는 뜻

꼼꼼하다, 세심하다
be meticulous[detailed, precise]
* precise는 정밀하고 정확한 느낌

SENTENCES TO USE

그녀는 유머 감각이 있는데, 이게 회의 분위기를 화기애애하게 만드는 데 일조합니다.
She has a good sense of humor, which contributes to the positive vibe of the meeting.

그는 호기심이 많아서 뉴스도 잘 알고 관심 분야도 많아요.
He is curious, so he follows the news and has a lot of interests.

그는 두뇌 회전이 빨라서 말싸움에서 절대 안 져요.
He's quick-witted, so he never loses an argument.

그녀는 세심해서 사람들의 기분을 잘 헤아리고 말을 조심스럽게 해요.
She is sensitive, so she understands people's feelings and speaks carefully.

우리 팀 막내 직원은 꼼꼼해서 이 업무를 믿고 맡길 수 있습니다.
The youngest member of our team is meticulous, so we can trust her with this task.

(~에) 통찰력이 있다
have insight (into ~)

합리적이다, 분별 있다, 지각 있다
be reasonable[sensible]

공정하다
be fair

편견이 없다
be unbiased[impartial, unprejudiced]

신중하다 be careful[prudent, discreet]

* careful은 실수를 막기 위해 조심하는 것, prudent는 결정할 때 현명하고 조심스러운 것, discreet는 타인의 감정을 다치지 않도록 말과 행동에 조심하는 것

진지하다 be serious

독립적이다 be independent[self-reliant]

참을성 있다 be patient[persevering, long-suffering]

* persevering, long-suffering은 힘들어도 과정을 계속하거나 참을성을 보이는 것

위엄 있다, 품위 있다
be dignified

SENTENCES TO USE

스텔라는 아직 젊지만 세상사를 꿰뚫어 보는 통찰력이 있어요.
Although Stella is still young, she has insight into worldly affairs.

우리 상사는 합리적이고 직원들에 대한 기대치가 너무 높지 않습니다.
My boss is reasonable and does not have too high expectations of the staff.

내가 기억하기에 그 시절의 그는 편견이 없고 열린 마음을 가지고 있었어요.
As far as I remember, he was unbiased and open-minded back then.

그녀는 신중해서 지키지 못할 약속은 하지 않아요.
She is careful, so she doesn't make promises that she cannot keep.

그녀는 사소한 일에 너무 진지한데, 그게 좀 거슬릴 수 있어요.
She's so serious about the smallest things, which can get tiresome.

UNIT 1

강하다 be strong

* 신체적, 정신적으로 회복력이 강한 것을 의미

용감하다 be brave[courageous]

카리스마가 있다 be charismatic, have charisma

똑똑하다 be smart[clever, bright, intelligent]

재능 있다, 재능이 많다 be talented[gifted]

창의성[창의력] 있다
be creative

상상력이 풍부하다
be imaginative, be full of imagination,
have a rich[a lot of] imagination

말을 잘하다 be a good[great] talker,
be a good[great, smooth] speaker,
have a silver tongue, speak well

야망이 있다 be ambitious

SENTENCES TO USE

그녀는 카리스마가 있어서 사람들이 그녀를 따르죠.
She is charismatic, so people follow her.

그 부부의 어린 아들은 똑똑하고 피아노 연주에 재능이 있어요.
The couple's young son is smart and talented at playing the piano.

그녀는 창의력이 있고 상상력도 풍부해요. 기획부서에 아주 딱입니다.
She is creative and full of imagination. She is a perfect fit for the planning department.

말을 잘하는 사람보다 잘 듣는 사람이 더 귀합니다.
A person who listens well is more valuable than a person who speaks well.
(= A good listener is more valuable than a good speaker.)

그는 야망이 있어서 지금 자리에 만족하지 않을 거예요.
He is ambitious and will not be satisfied with his current position.

근면하다, 부지런하다
be hardworking[industrious, diligent]

검소하다
be frugal[thrifty, careful with money]

소탈하다, 털털하다
be free and easy

시간을 잘 지키다 be punctual

진심이다, 성의가 있다 be sincere[earnest]

이타적이다
be altruistic[selfless]

겸손하다
be modest[humble, unassuming]

예의 바르다, 공손하다
be polite[courteous]

협조적이다
be cooperative

SENTENCES TO USE

그 사람은 근면하고 검소했으며 소박한 삶을 살았습니다.
The man was hardworking, frugal, and led a simple life.

그는 처음에 소탈해 보였는데, 저는 그게 마음에 들었어요.
He looked free and easy at first, and I liked that.

시간을 잘 지키는 것은 다른 이들의 기분을 신경 쓴다는 걸 보여 주는 거라고 생각합니다.
I think being punctual shows that you care about other people's feelings.

완벽한 팀원은 이타적이고 협조적입니다.
A perfect teammate is both altruistic and cooperative.

그 유명인사는 예의 바르고 겸손했는데, 그 모습이 다소 놀라웠어요.
The celebrity was polite and humble, which was somewhat surprising.

UNIT 2

성격, 성품, 태도 – 부정적인 표현

MP3 005-1

못되다
be mean[evil, wicked]

* 불퉁거리고 악의적인 행동을 하는 것은 mean, 도덕적으로 잘못된 행동을 하는 것은 evil, wicked

성격이 나쁘다, 괴팍하다
be grumpy[bad-tempered]

사악하다, 악랄하다
be evil[wicked, malicious, vicious]

거만하다, 오만하다 be arrogant[haughty]

자만심이 강하다 be conceited[vain]

무례하다 be rude[impolite, insolent]

성급하다, 충동적이다 be impetuous [rash, hasty, impulsive]

다혈질이다, 화를 잘 내다, 욱하는 성격이다
be quick-tempered[short-tempered, hot-tempered],
have a quick[short, hot] temper,
have a short fuse

신경질적이다 be irritable

SENTENCES TO USE

신데렐라의 의붓언니들은 성격이 못됐고 끊임없이 신데렐라를 괴롭혔어요.
Cinderella's stepsisters were mean and constantly harassed her.

그 노인은 괴팍하다고 생각했지만, 알고 보니 따뜻한 사람이었습니다.
The old man was thought to be grumpy, but it turned out that he was warm-hearted.

그 사람은 돈을 좀 벌고 나서 거만해지더니 사람들을 무시했어요.
After making some money, he became arrogant and looked down on people.

그녀는 성급해서 일을 그르칠 때가 가끔 있어요.
She is impetuous and sometimes makes a mess of things.

그는 다혈질이라 작은 일에도 짜증을 내곤 합니다.
He is hot-tempered and gets irritated over small things.

변덕스럽다 be unpredictable[capricious, fickle]

무관심하다, 무심하다 be indifferent

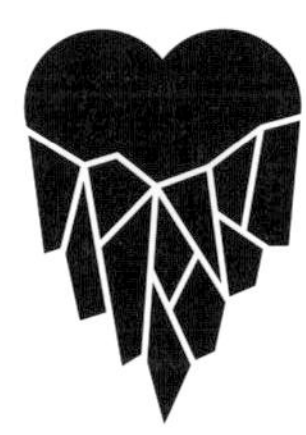

냉정하다, 무정하다
be cold[cold-hearted]

이기적이다, 자기중심적이다
be self-centered
[selfish, egoistic]

독선적이다
be self-righteous

제멋대로다
have one's own way

자기애가 강하다, 자기도취에 빠져 있다 be narcissistic

허영심이 강하다 be vain

속물적이다 be snobbish

부도덕하다 be immoral

SENTENCES TO USE

그 여자는 변덕스러워서 예고 없이 마음이 바뀌어요.
She is fickle and changes her mind without warning.

많은 사람들이 남들의 고통이나 고민에는 무관심합니다.
Many people are indifferent to other people's pain or worries.

그는 냉정해서 직원이 갑자기 세상을 떠났을 때도 눈 하나 깜짝하지 않았습니다.
He's cold-hearted and never batted an eye when his employee suddenly died.

그는 자기중심적이고 남을 전혀 생각하지 않기 때문에 사람들은 그를 좋아하지 않습니다.
He is self-centered and never thinks about others, so people don't like him.

그녀는 너무 속물적이라 모든 것을 돈과 권력에 따라 평가합니다.
She is so snobbish that she evaluates everything based on money and power.

UNIT 2

소극적이다, 수동적이다
be passive

소심하다
be timid

우유부단하다
be indecisive

속이 좁다, 옹졸하다
be narrow-minded

부주의하다, 덜렁대다 be careless

산만하다, 침착하지 못하다 be scatterbrained

교활하다 be cunning[crafty, sly, sneaky]

음흉하다, 엉큼하다 be sneaky[sly, devious]

질투심이 많다 be jealous

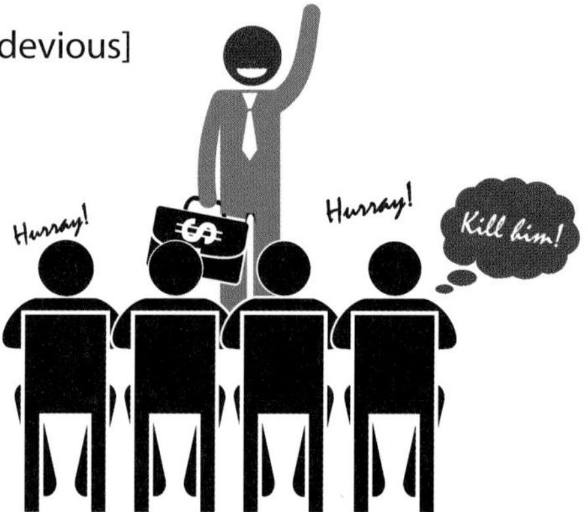

SENTENCES TO USE

그는 너무 소심해서 낯선 사람에게 말을 못 걸어요.
He is too timid to talk to strangers.

그녀는 우유부단해서 칫솔 하나 사는 데도 시간이 오래 걸려요.
She is indecisive and takes a long time to buy even a toothbrush.

내가 그렇게 중요하지 않은 일에 화낼 정도로 속이 좁지는 않아요.
I'm not narrow-minded enough to get angry over something so unimportant.

그 사람은 교활해서 당신은 그를 상대하기가 힘들 거예요.
He's cunning, and you'll have a hard time dealing with him.

그녀는 참 엉큼해서 무슨 생각을 하는지 도무지 모르겠어요.
She's so sneaky that I never know what she's thinking.

(감각이, 머리가) 둔하다 be thick

~ 센스가 없다 have a poor sense of ~

* 뒤에 humor, fashion, direction 등의 관련 대상이 옴

눈치가 없다 be tactless,
be bad at reading people, be bad at reading the room

* tactless는 눈치 없는 말과 행동으로 상대의 기분을 상하게 하는 것

부정적이다 be negative

* 상황의 나쁜 면만 고려하는 것

비관적이다, 염세적이다 be pessimistic

* 앞으로의 일이 잘 안 될 거라 생각하고 모든 일을 부정적으로 보는 것

No, this is half empty.

의심이 많다
be suspicious

직설적이다
be blunt

* 조금 부정적이고 무례한 느낌

(지나치게) 예민하다
be (overly) sensitive

감정적이다
be emotional

SENTENCES TO USE

그녀는 둔해서 친구가 머리 자른 것을 눈치채지 못했어요.
She was thick and didn't notice her friend's haircut.

그는 눈치가 없고 부적절한 질문을 해서 상황을 어색하게 만드는 경우가 잦아요.
He's tactless and often asks inappropriate questions, creating awkward situations.

그 사람은 매사에 부정적이라 함께 있기가 불편해요.
That person is negative toward everything, so it's uncomfortable to be around him.

톰은 지나치게 예민해서 그와 대화할 때는 조심스러워요.
Tom is overly sensitive, so I am cautious when talking to him.

그녀는 너무 직설적이어서 사람들을 기분 나쁘게 하는 경우가 적지 않아요.
She is so blunt that she often offends people.

UNIT 2

요구가 많다
be demanding

공격적이다
be aggressive[belligerent]
* belligerent가 더 강한 적대감을 나타냄

까다롭다, 까탈스럽다 be picky

(~에게) 적대적이다
be hostile[belligerent] (to[towards] ~)

짓궂다
be mischievous[impish, naughty]
* mischievous와 impish는 장난스러운 걸 의미하고, naughty는 행동거지가 나쁘고 복종하지 않는다는 의미를 내포

게으르다 be lazy

무기력하다
be spiritless[lethargic, low on energy], feel low

어리석다 be stupid

SENTENCES TO USE

그 팀장은 이것저것 요구하는 게 많아서 그 밑에서 일하기가 쉽지 않아요.
The team leader is so demanding that it is not easy to work for him.

그 사람은 평상시에도 말투가 다소 공격적이었어요.
The person's tone was somewhat aggressive even under normal circumstances.

그녀는 먹는 것에 까다로워서 최고로 신선한 재료들만 골라요.
She is picky about what she eats and only chooses the freshest ingredients.

그는 자기 작업을 비판하는 사람은 누구에게든 적대적이에요.
He is hostile to anyone who criticizes his work.

그 남자아이는 너무 짓궂어서 여자아이들은 그 애랑 같이 놀기를 꺼려요.
The boy is so mischievous that the girls are reluctant to play with him.

탐욕스럽다 be greedy

인색하다 be tight with one's money

약다, 영악하다 be astute[clever]

수다스럽다
be talkative

진중하지 못하다, 경박하다 be frivolous

경솔하다 be indiscreet[careless](부주의한 느낌), be rash[hasty](성급한 느낌)

순진하다
be naive

고지식하다 be rigid[inflexible]

융통성이 없다
be inflexible[unadaptable, rigid]

SENTENCES TO USE

그 소설의 여자 주인공은 이기적이고 탐욕스럽습니다.
The female protagonist of the novel is selfish and greedy.

그는 약아서 늘 자기가 손해 볼 일이 없게 하지요.
He is astute and always makes sure he doesn't lose anything.

그 남자는 진중하지 못해서 책임자 자리에는 적합하지 않아요.
The man is frivolous, so he's not suitable for a leadership position.

그곳 사람들은 순진해서 그 광고 문구를 그대로 믿었어요.
The people there were so naive that they believed what the advertisement said.

그 사람은 너무 고지식해서 이런 일에는 타협하지 않을 겁니다.
The person is very rigid and won't compromise on this matter.

UNIT 2

중립적 표현

MP3 005-2

외향적이다
be outgoing[extroverted]
* '외향적인 사람'은 an extrovert

내향적이다, 내성적이다
be introverted
* '내향적인 사람'은 an introvert

조용하다 be quiet

민감하다, 예민하다 be sensitive

수줍다, 낯을 가리다 be shy[afraid of strangers]

SENTENCES TO USE

그녀는 외향적이어서 사람들과 어울리는 것을 좋아해요.
She is outgoing and likes to mingle.

그는 내향인이라 집에 혼자 있는 것을 좋아하지요.
He is an introvert and likes to be home alone.

그 사람은 워낙 조용해서 모임에서 눈에 잘 안 띕니다.
He is so quiet that it's hard to notice him in meetings.

그녀는 내성적이고 예민해서 상처를 잘 받는 편이에요.
She is introverted and sensitive, so her feelings tend to get hurt easily.

저는 수줍음이 많은 성격이라서 모르는 사람들이 있는 곳에 가는 것을 안 좋아해요.
I'm shy, so I don't like going to places where there are people I don't know.

THE OLD MAN WAS THOUGHT TO BE GRUMPY,

BUT IT TURNED OUT THAT HE WAS WARM-HEARTED.

CHAPTER

3

사람의 외형

UNIT 1

얼굴 전체, 인상

* 다른 문화권의 사람들에게는 얼굴형을 언급하는 것이 민감한 일일 수 있으니 조심해야 함

얼굴이 길다
have a long face,
one's face is long

* 문맥에 따라 have a long face는 '우울한[시무룩한] 얼굴을 하다'라는 뜻으로도 쓰임

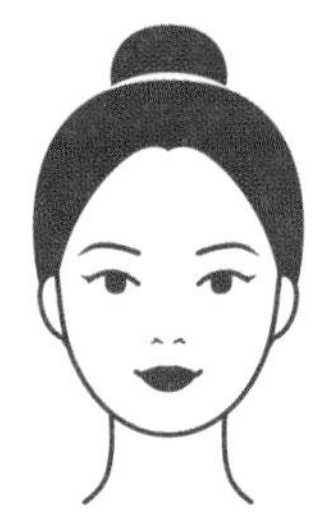

얼굴이 둥글다, 동그랗다
have a round face,
one's face is round

얼굴이 달걀형이다
have an oval-shaped
[egg-shaped] face

얼굴이 갸름하다 have a slim face, one's face is slim,
have a thin face, one's face is thin

* slim은 갸름하고 예쁘다는 뜻, thin은 살이 빠지고 말라서 갸름하다는 뜻

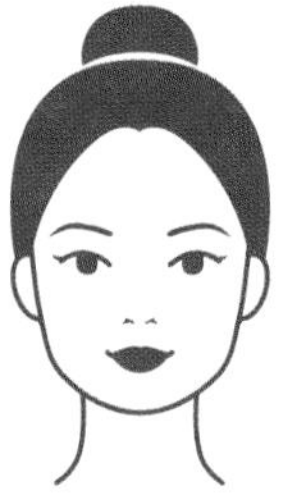

얼굴이 네모나다, 사각형이다
have a square face,
one's face is square

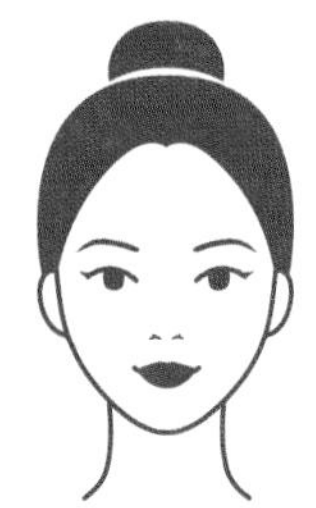

얼굴이 역삼각형이다
have a face like an inverted triangle

SENTENCES TO USE

나는 얼굴이 동그래서 브이넥 상의가 잘 어울려요.
I have a round face, so I look good in V-necks.

우리 언니는 얼굴이 달걀형이고 피부가 하얗습니다.
My sister has an oval-shaped face and fair skin.

그는 살이 빠져서 얼굴이 갸름해졌어요.
He has lost weight and his face has become thinner.

그녀는 얼굴이 네모나서 짧은 머리가 잘 어울립니다.
She has a square face, so short hair suits her.

* 외모 관련 표현은 무례하게 들릴 수 있으므로 사용에 유의해야 함

이마가 넓다 have a broad forehead, one's forehead is broad

이마가 좁다 have a narrow forehead, one's forehead is narrow

귀가 크다/작다 have big/small ears, one's ears are big/small

광대가 튀어나왔다
have high cheekbones, one's cheekbones are high, one's cheekbones stick out[protrude]

광대가 납작하다 have small[flat] cheekbones, one's cheekbones are small[flat]

볼이 통통하다 have chubby[plump] cheeks, one's cheeks are chubby[plump]

볼에 살이 없다
have flat cheeks, one's cheeks are flat

볼이 푹 꺼졌다
have sunken cheeks, one's cheeks are sunken

보조개가 있다 have dimples

턱선이 각지다 have an angular jawline

사각턱이다 have a square jaw

이중턱이다 have a double chin

SENTENCES TO USE

이마가 좁은 게 그 사람 콤플렉스예요.
Having a narrow forehead is a source of insecurity for him.

그 사람 귀는 부처님 귀를 닮아서 아주 커요.
He has very big ears, resembling Buddha's.

그 여성은 광대가 보기 좋게 튀어나왔어요.
The woman's cheekbones stick out nicely.

나는 살이 빠지면서 얼굴 살도 빠졌어요. 그 결과 볼이 푹 꺼졌어요.
As I lost weight, I also lost facial fat. As a result, my cheeks became sunken.

그 여배우는 각진 턱선이 매력 포인트예요.
The actress has an angular jawline that makes her attractive.

* 외모 관련 표현은 무례하게 들릴 수 있으므로 사용에 유의해야 함

예쁘다 be pretty[lovely]

아름답다 be beautiful

귀엽다 be cute

* 외모에서 성적 매력을 느낄 때도 씀

잘생겼다 be handsome[good-looking]

* good-looking은 얼굴이 매력적이라는 뜻으로, 남성과 여성 모두에게 쓸 수 있음

매력적이다, 매력 있다 be attractive[appealing]

* attractive는 외모가 매력적이며 아울러 성격도 좋음을 나타내고, appealing은 태도나 분위기가 매력적인 것을 나타냄

매력 없다 be unattractive

* 외모가 매력 없음을 나타냄

못생기다 be homely[ugly, plain]

* ugly는 무례한 표현이므로 사용에 유의
* plain은 주로 여자의 외모가 수수하고 평범한 것을 나타냄

동안이다, 나이보다 어려 보이다 look young for one's (actual) age, look younger than one's (actual) age

나이 들어 보이다 look old for one's (actual) age, look older than one's (actual) age

SENTENCES TO USE

그 여배우는 60살이 넘었지만 여전히 아름다워요.
The actress is over 60, but still beautiful.

월드컵 경기에서 두 골을 넣은 그 축구 선수는 잘생기기까지 했어요.
The soccer player, who scored two goals in a World Cup match, was handsome as well.

미나는 얼굴이 판에 박은 듯이 예쁘지는 않지만 그래도 매력적이에요.
Mina doesn't have a conventionally pretty face, but she is still attractive.

그는 잘생기지는 않았지만 자신감이 있어서 매력 있어 보여요.
He is not good-looking, but his confidence makes him appealing.

그녀는 동안이에요. 실제 나이보다 열 살은 어려 보여요.
She looks young, about 10 years younger than her actual age.

* 외모 관련 표현은 무례하게 들릴 수 있으므로 사용에 유의해야 함

인상이 좋다, 좋은 인상을 풍기다
make a good impression

인상이 푸근하다, 푸근한 인상을 풍기다
make a warm impression

인상이 날카롭다, 날카로운 인상을 풍기다 make a sharp impression

인상이 나쁘다, 나쁜 인상을 풍기다 make a bad impression

인상이 험하다, 험한 인상을 풍기다 make a rough impression

세련되다, (스타일이) 멋지다, 고급스럽다
be classy[stylish, sophisticated]

우아하다, 기품 있다
be elegant[graceful]

빈티가 나다 look poor[shabby]

옷태가 나다 look good in everything one wears

지적으로 보이다
look intelligent

사랑스럽다
be lovely[sweet, lovable, adorable]

SENTENCES TO USE

우리 학교 앞 분식집 사장님은 인상이 푸근했어요.
The owner of the snack bar in front of our school made a warm impression.

그는 좋은 사람인데 인상이 험해서 오해를 자주 받아요.
He is a nice person, but he makes a rough impression and is often misunderstood.

그 남자는 새 턱시도를 입으니 무척 세련되고 멋져 보였다.
The man looked very classy wearing his new tuxedo.

그녀는 지적으로 보이는데, 그게 그녀의 매력 중 하나입니다.
She looks intelligent, and that's one of her charms.

그 소녀는 밝고 사랑스러워서 모두가 좋아해요.
Everyone likes the girl because she is bright and lovely.

UNIT 2

피부, 안색

* 외모 관련 표현은 무례하게 들릴 수 있으므로 사용에 유의해야 함

피부가 좋다 have good[great, beautiful] skin, one's skin is good[great, beautiful]

피부가 안 좋다[나쁘다] have bad skin, one's skin is bad

여드름성 피부다
have acne-prone skin

피부가 백옥같이[눈처럼] 희다 have skin as white as snow, one's skin is as white as snow

피부가 까무잡잡하다 have dark skin, one's skin is dark

피부에 잡티가 많다
have a lot of blemishes on one's skin

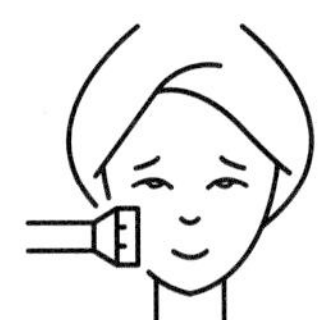

피부가 부드럽다
have soft skin, one's skin is soft

피부가 탱탱하다[탄력 있다]
have firm skin, one's skin is firm

피부가 거칠다 have rough skin, one's skin is rough

피부가 건조하다 have dry skin, one's skin is dry

피부에서 광이 나다
have shiny skin, one's skin is shiny

SENTENCES TO USE

그녀는 피부가 무척 좋아서 많은 이들이 부러워합니다.
She has such great skin that many people envy her.

나는 여드름성 피부라 얼굴에 여드름이 자주 나요.
I have acne-prone skin, so I often get pimples on my face.

그녀는 피부가 눈처럼 하얘서 백설공주라고 불렸습니다.
She was called Snow White because her skin was as white as snow.

나는 피부가 부드럽긴 한데 점과 잡티가 많아요.
I have soft skin, but I have a lot of moles and blemishes.

그는 피부가 건조한데, 특히 가을과 겨울에 그래요.
He has dry skin, especially during fall and winter.

* 외모 관련 표현은 무례하게 들릴 수 있으므로 사용에 유의해야 함

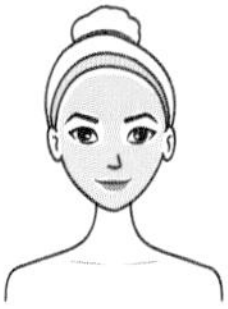

피부가 지성/건성/복합성이다
have oily/dry/combination skin

혈색이[안색이] 좋다
have a good complexion, look fine[well]

혈색이[안색이] 좋지 않다 have a bad complexion, look bad[unwell]

얼굴이 홍조를 띠다 be flushed, one's face is flushed[turns red]

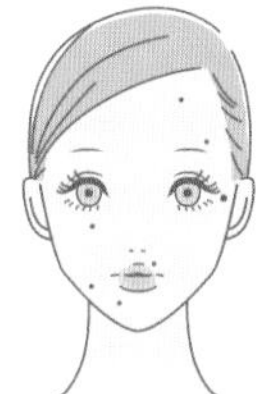

점이 있다
have a spot[mole]

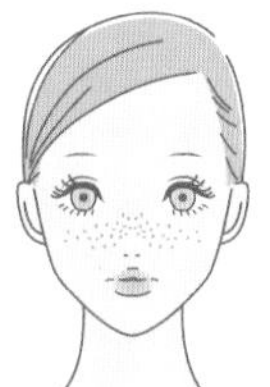

주근깨가 있다
have freckles, be freckled

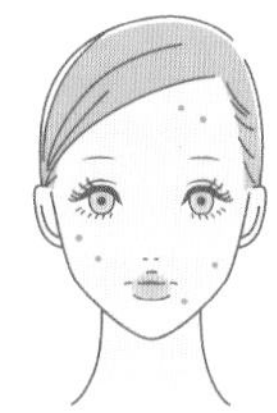

여드름이 있다
have pimples[acne, zits]
* zits는 회화체

검버섯이 있다
have age spots [liver spots, sun spots]

주름이 있다/많다/별로 없다
have wrinkles/have a lot of wrinkles/ have few wrinkles

SENTENCES TO USE

그 사람은 왜 요즘 안색이 안 좋지요?
Why does that person look unwell these days?

그 소녀는 항상 얼굴에 홍조를 띠고 있어요.
The girl is always flushed.

그녀는 입 옆에 점이 있는데, 그게 매력적이에요.
She has a spot next to her mouth, which is attractive.

빨강머리 앤과 삐삐 롱스타킹은 얼굴에 주근깨가 있지요.
Anne of Green Gables and Pippi Longstocking have freckles on their faces.

나는 60대부터 얼굴에 검버섯이 있었어요.
I have had age spots on my face since my 60s.

나이를 생각하면 그 사람은 얼굴에 주름이 별로 없어요.
That man doesn't have many wrinkles on his face considering his age.

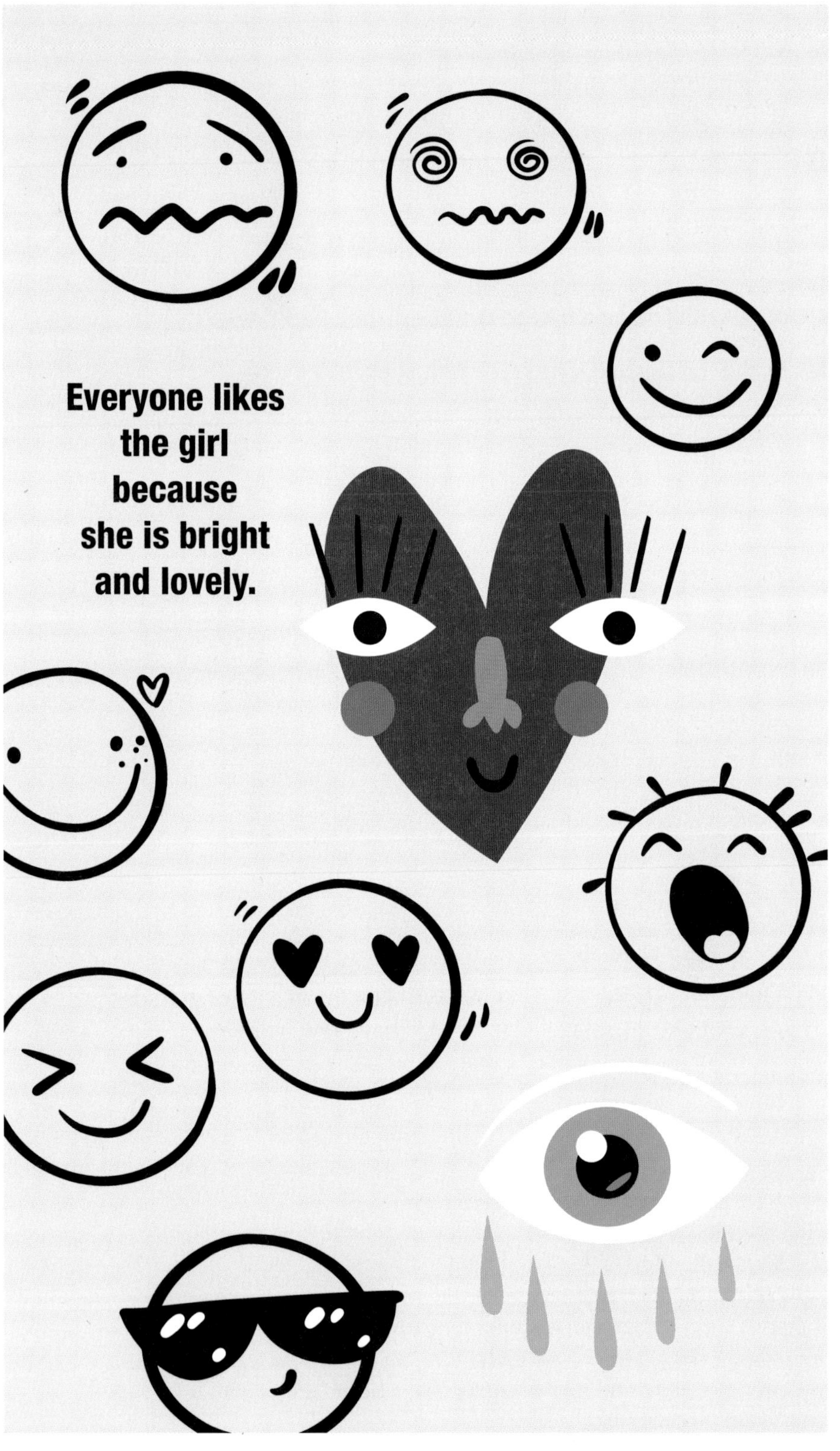

Everyone likes the girl because she is bright and lovely.

UNIT

3 두발, 헤어스타일

MP3 008

* 외모 관련 표현은 무례하게 들릴 수 있으므로 사용에 유의해야 함

머릿결이 좋다, 부드럽다 have silky (smooth) hair,
one's hair is silky (smooth),
one's hair is in good condition

머릿결이 안 좋다 one's hair is in bad condition

머릿결이 건조하다, 푸석하다 have dry hair,
one's hair is dry

머리에 윤기가 나다, 머리가 찰랑거리다 have shiny hair,
one's hair is shiny

직모다 have straight hair,
one's hair is straight

머리카락이 가늘다 have fine hair,
one's hair is fine

머리카락이 굵다 have thick strands of hair,
one's hair strands are thick

곱슬머리다 have (naturally) curly hair,
one's hair is (naturally) curly

흑인 같은 곱슬머리다 have textured hair
* 흑인 커뮤니티에서 주로 쓰이며, 민감한 사항이므로 사용에 유의

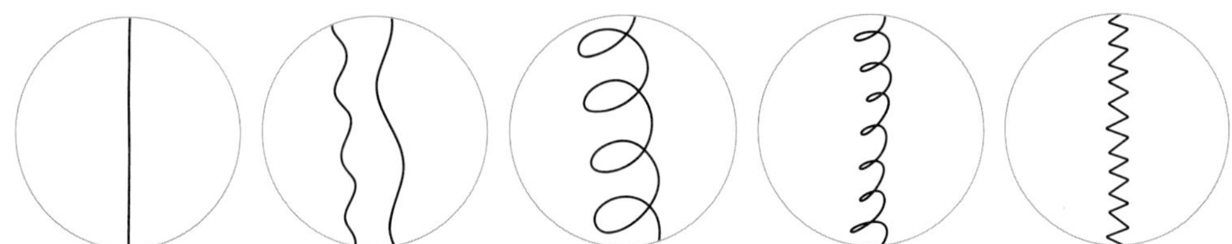

SENTENCES TO USE

그 소녀는 피부도 하얗고 머릿결도 좋아요.
The girl has fair skin and silky smooth hair.

그녀는 머릿결이 안 좋아서 머리카락 관리에 공을 많이 들입니다.
Her hair is in bad condition, so she puts a lot of effort into taking care of it.

그 여자는 늘 윤기 나는 긴 생머리를 하고 있었어요.
That woman always had long, shiny hair.

내 머리카락이 점점 가늘어지는데, 그게 탈모의 증상 중 하나예요.
My hair has become finer, which is one of the symptoms of hair loss.

그 사람, 파마한 것 같지만 사실 곱슬머리예요.
It looks like he had a perm, but he actually has naturally curly hair.

UNIT 3

* 외모 관련 표현은 무례하게 들릴 수 있으므로 사용에 유의해야 함

머리숱이 많다 have a lot of hair, have thick hair

머리숱이 적다 don't have a lot of hair, one's hair is thin

* one's hair is thin은 탈모로 숱이 줄어든 상태를 의미

~ 머리가 잘 어울리다 look good with ~ hair

머리가 길다
have long hair, wear one's hair long, one's hair is long

머리가 짧다
have short hair, wear one's hair short, one's hair is short

단발머리다
have a bob haircut

컷트머리다
have short hair, have a pixie cut (여성에게 사용)

스포츠머리다 have a crew cut

민머리다, 삭발한 머리다 have a shaved head, have one's head shaved

파마머리다 have permed hair, have a perm

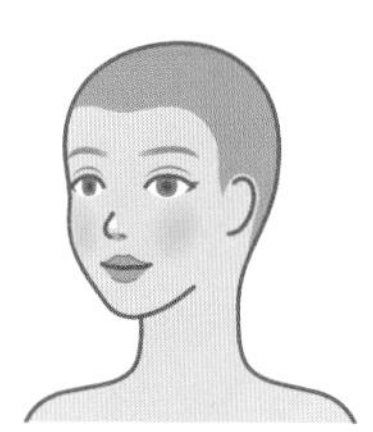

SENTENCES TO USE

젊어서는 머리숱이 많았는데, 나이가 들면서 머리숱이 줄었어요.
I had a lot of hair when I was young, but as I've gotten older, my hair has thinned.

나는 머리숱이 적어서 스타일링하기가 힘들어요.
Since I don't have a lot of hair, it's hard for me to style it.

오드리 헵번은 짧은 머리가 잘 어울렸죠.
Audrey Hepburn looked good with short hair.

그 여성 아나운서는 단발머리인데, 잘 어울리네요.
The female announcer has a bob haircut, and it suits her well.

그 남자는 민머리에 늘 모자를 쓰고 다닙니다.
The man has a shaved head and always wears a cap.

* 외모 관련 표현은 무례하게 들릴 수 있으므로 사용에 유의해야 함

앞머리가 있다 have bangs

머리가 어깨까지/가슴까지/허리까지 오다
one's hair reaches[comes down to] one's shoulders/chest/waist
* come down to는 캐주얼한 회화에 사용, reach가 더 정확한 의미를 전달

가르마가 가운데다/왼쪽이다/오른쪽이다
one's hair is parted in the middle/on the left/on the right

2 대 8 가르마를 하다 one's hair is parted into 2 to 8 parts[in a 2 to 8 ratio], one's hair has a 2 to 8 part

흰머리가 있다 have gray hair

흰머리가 많다 have a lot of gray hair

머리가 반백이다 one's hair is gray[salt and pepper], have salt-and-pepper hair

대머리다 be bald

머리가 빠지다, 탈모가 진행되다 be losing one's hair, one's hair is thinning

헤어라인이[앞이마가] M자다 have a widow's peak, have an M-shaped hairline, one's hairline is M-shaped * 주로 남성에 사용

SENTENCES TO USE

그녀는 지금 앞머리가 있는데, 그래서 더 어려 보여요.
She has bangs now, which gives her a younger appearance.

요즘 머리가 어깨까지 와요. 여름이라 잘라야 할 것 같아요.
My hair reaches my shoulders these days. It's summer, and I think I need a haircut.

그 남자는 항상 2 대 8 가르마를 하고 머리에 기름을 바르고 다녀요.
His hair is always parted into 2 to 8 parts, and he applies oil to it.

그는 40대 초반인데도 흰머리가 많아요.
Although he is in his early 40s, he has a lot of gray hair.

그녀는 40대 초반부터 탈모가 진행되고 있어요.
She has been losing her hair since her early 40s.

그는 20대 초반인데, 벌써 헤어라인이 M자더라고요.
He is in his early 20s, and his hairline is already M-shaped.

UNIT 3

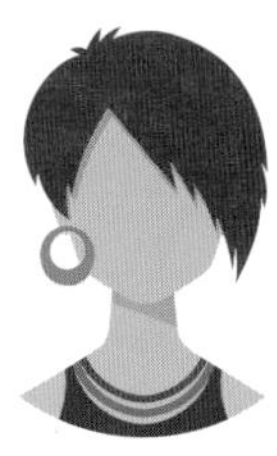

염색하다(상태) have dyed hair, one's hair is dyed

~색으로 염색하다(상태) one's hair is dyed ~

탈색하다(상태) have bleached hair, one's hair is bleached

머리핀을 꽂다(상태) have a hairpin in one's hair

머리를 묶다(상태) have one's hair tied up

머리를 포니테일로 묶다(상태) have one's hair tied in a ponytail

똥머리를 하다(상태) have one's hair pulled up into a bun

양갈래 머리를 하다(상태) have one's hair in pigtails

(양갈래로) 머리를 땋다(상태) have one's hair braided (on both sides), wear one's hair in (two) braids

머리띠를 하다(상태) be wearing a headband

머리를 (묶지 않고) 풀다(상태) let one's hair down, have one's hair untied

SENTENCES TO USE

그녀는 머리를 파란색으로 염색한 상태였어요.
Her hair was dyed blue.

그 소녀는 멜빵 치마를 입고 머리를 포니테일로 묶고 있었어요.
The girl was wearing a suspender skirt and had her hair tied in a ponytail.

그녀는 똥머리를 하고 있었어요.
She had her hair pulled up into a bun.

빨강머리 앤은 머리를 양 갈래로 땋고 있었죠.
Anne of Green Gables wore her hair in two braids.

앞머리가 자꾸 걸리적거려서 그는 머리띠를 하고 있어요.
His bangs kept getting in his way, so he's wearing a headband.

MORE

MP3 009

머리 색

머리가 ~색이다
one's hair is 색깔
have 색깔 hair

검은색의 black

검은색 머리 black hair

칠흑같이 검은 jet black

칠흑같이 검은 머리 jet-black hair

새까맣고 윤이 나는 머리 raven hair

* 문학적인 표현. One's hair is raven.이라고는 쓰지 않음

갈색의 brown

갈색 머리 brown hair

짙은 갈색의 dark brown, brunet, brunette

* brunet, brunette은 머리나 눈 색에만 쓰는 단어

짙은 갈색 머리 dark brown hair

짙은 갈색 머리에 갈색 눈, 까무잡잡한 피부를 가진 서양인 brunet(남), brunette(여)
* 실제로는 남성에게 brunet은 잘 쓰지 않음

금발의 blond(남성을 묘사할 때), blonde(여성을 묘사할 때)

금발 머리 blond hair

금발인 사람 blond(남), blonde(여)

빨간색의 red

빨간 머리 red hair

불그스름한 갈색의 ginger

불그스름한 갈색 머리 ginger hair
* 영국에서 주로 쓰임

불그스름한 갈색 머리인 사람 ginger

UNIT 4 눈, 눈썹

눈

MP3 010-1

* 외모 관련 표현은 무례하게 들릴 수 있으므로 사용에 유의해야 함

눈이 크다 have big eyes, one's eyes are big * 영어 원어민에게는 비정상적으로 큰 눈으로 해석됨

눈이 작다 have small eyes, one's eyes are small

눈꼬리가 처졌다
have downturned eyes,
one's eyes are downturned

눈꼬리가 위로 올라갔다
have upturned eyes,
one's eyes are upturned

눈이 동그랗다
have round eyes,
one's eyes are round

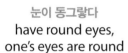

눈이 아몬드 모양이다
have almond-shaped eyes,
one's eyes are almond-shaped

외꺼풀이다, 쌍꺼풀이 없다 have monolid eyes[monolids, mono eyelids]

쌍꺼풀이 있다 have double eyelids

눈이 튀어나왔다 have protruding eyes, one's eyes are protruding

눈이 움푹[깊이] 들어가 있다 have deep-set[sunken] eyes, one's eyes are deep-set[sunken]

* deep-set은 중립적이고 긍정적인 의미, sunken은 피곤함이나 질병을 암시

SENTENCES TO USE

그는 눈이 처져서 상냥해 보여요.
He has downturned eyes and looks friendly.

그녀는 눈꼬리가 위로 올라갔는데, 그게 매력적이에요.
She has upturned eyes, which are attractive.

그 소녀는 눈이 아몬드 모양인데 웃을 때마다 그 눈에서 따뜻함이 느껴져요.
The girl has almond-shaped eyes, which radiate warmth whenever she smiles.

몽골 인종은 눈이 외꺼풀이에요.
Mongolians have monolid eyes.

그녀는 눈이 깊이 들어가 있어서 신비로운 매력을 발산합니다.
She has deep-set eyes, giving her a mysterious allure.

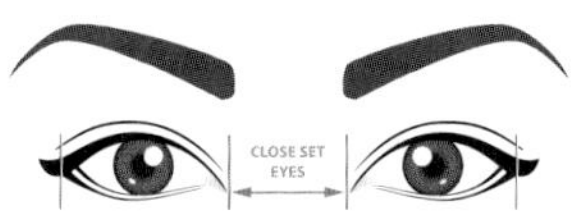

두 눈 사이가 좁다
have close-set eyes,
one's eyes are close together

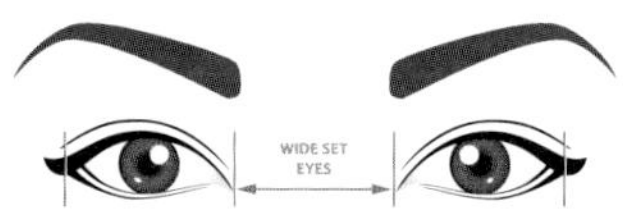

두 눈 사이가 넓다
have wide-set eyes,
one's eyes are wide apart

눈이 반짝거리다
one's eyes are sparkling

눈빛이 깊다 have deep eyes

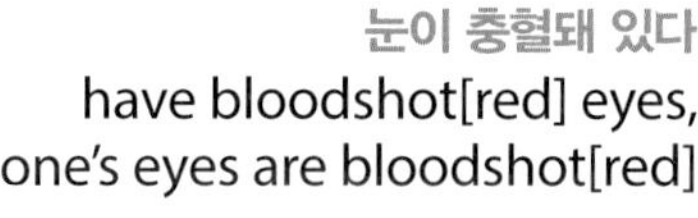

눈이 충혈돼 있다
have bloodshot[red] eyes,
one's eyes are bloodshot[red]

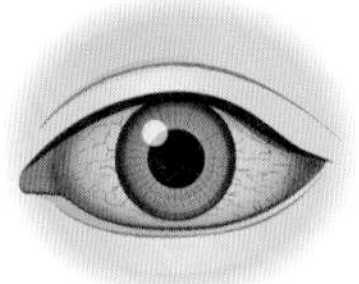

눈이 침침하다
have blurry vision, one's eyes are blurry

시력이 좋다/나쁘다
have good/bad eyesight

시력이 나빠지다
one's eyesight is getting worse

노안이다
be farsighted due to old age, need reading glasses

SENTENCES TO USE

그녀는 두 눈 사이가 넓어서 좀 멍해 보여요.
She has wide-set eyes, which make her look a little silly.

그 아이는 눈이 맑고 반짝거리죠.
The child's eyes are clear and sparkling.

어젯밤에 너무 늦게까지 안 자고 깨어 있었더니 눈이 충혈됐어요.
My eyes are bloodshot because I was up so late last night.

요즘 시력이 나빠졌는지 눈이 좀 침침해요.
My eyes are a little blurry these days maybe because my eyesight has gotten worse.

나는 40대 중반에 노안이 돼서 안경을 써야 책을 읽을 수 있어요.
I became farsighted in my mid-40s, so I have to wear glasses to read books.

눈썹

MP3 010-2

* 외모 관련 표현은 무례하게 들릴 수 있으므로 사용에 유의해야 함

눈썹이 진하다
have thick eyebrows,
one's eyebrows are thick

눈썹이 연하다
have light eyebrows,
one's eyebrows are light

눈썹 문신을 했다(상태) have tattooed eyebrows

12 mm

속눈썹이 길다
have long eyelashes,
one's eyelashes are long

5 mm

속눈썹이 짧다
have short eyelashes,
one's eyelashes are short

속눈썹을 붙였다(상태) wear false eyelashes

속눈썹이 위로 올라갔다(상태)
one's eyelashes are curled up

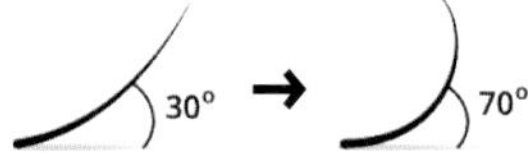

속눈썹이 처졌다(상태) have droopy eyelashes,
one's eyelashes are droopy

속눈썹이 눈을 찌르다 one's eyelashes poke one's eyes

SENTENCES TO USE

그 배우는 눈썹이 진한 걸로 유명했죠.
The actor was famous for having thick eyebrows.

그녀는 지금은 눈썹 문신을 한 상태고, 원래는 눈썹이 무척 연했어요.
She has tattooed eyebrows now, and her eyebrows were originally very light.

요즘엔 아이들 대부분이 속눈썹이 길더라고요.
Most children these days have long eyelashes.

그녀는 속눈썹이 짧아서 인조 속눈썹을 붙이는 경우가 잦아요.
She has short eyelashes, so she often wears false eyelashes.

그는 속눈썹이 처져서 가끔 속눈썹이 눈을 찌르기도 해요.
He has droopy eyelashes, and they sometimes poke his eyes.

UNIT 5

코

MP3 011

* 외모 관련 표현은 무례하게 들릴 수 있으므로 사용에 유의해야 함

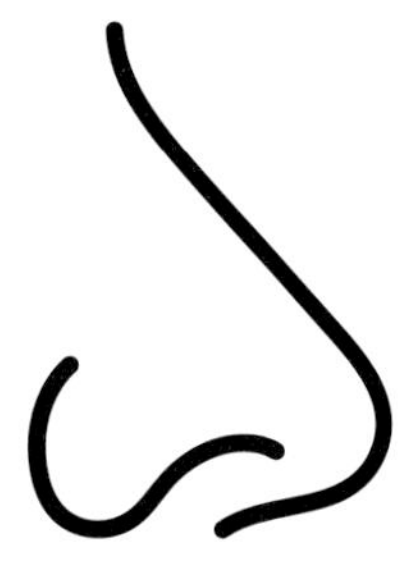

코가 크다 have a big[large] nose, one's nose is big[large]

* large가 중립적이고 격식을 갖춘 느낌

코가 작다 have a small nose, one's nose is small

코가 길다 have a long nose, one's nose is long

코가 짧다 have a short nose, one's nose is short

코가 작고 둥글다 have a button nose

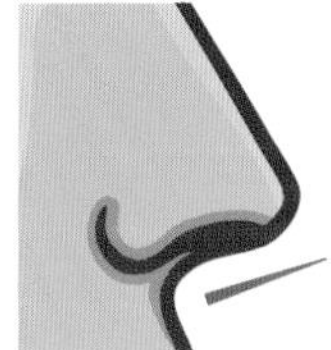

코가 높다, 코가 오똑하다
have a high-bridged nose,
one's nose is high-bridged,
one's nose bridge is high

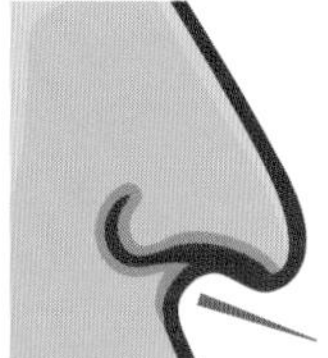

코가 낮다
have a flat[low-bridged] nose,
one's nose is flat[low-bridged],
one's nose bridge is low

매부리코다
have a hawk nose

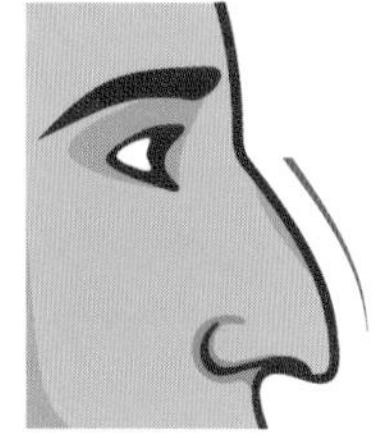

SENTENCES TO USE

프랑스의 시인이자 검객 시라노 드 베르주락은 코가 컸습니다.
Cyrano de Bergerac, a French poet and swordsman, had a large nose.

코가 길면 나이가 들어 보인다고 생각하는 사람들이 있어요.
Some people think that if you have a long nose, you look older.

그녀는 코가 작고 둥글어서 귀엽고 어려 보여요.
She has a button nose, which makes her look cute and young.

부모님은 두 분 모두 코가 낮은데 그는 코가 오똑합니다.
Both of his parents have flat noses, but he has a high-bridged nose.

매부리코를 가진 사람은 성격이 강하다는 오해를 받기 쉬워요.
A person who has a hawk nose is often misunderstood as having a strong personality.

UNIT 5

* 외모 관련 표현은 무례하게 들릴 수 있으므로 사용에 유의해야 함

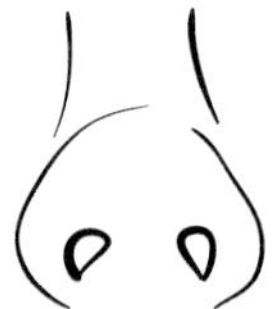

들창코다, 코끝이 들렸다
have an upturned nose,
have a turn-up[snub, pug] nose

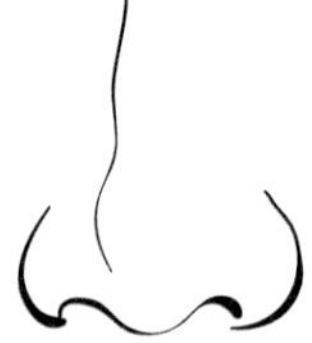

코가 휘었다
have a crooked nose,
one's nose is crooked

코가 빨갛다, 딸기코다 have a red nose, one's nose is red

주먹코다 have a bulbous[potato] nose

콧구멍이 크다 have big[wide] nostrils,
one's nostrils are big[wide]

콧구멍이 작다 have small[narrow] nostrils,
one's nostrils are small[narrow]

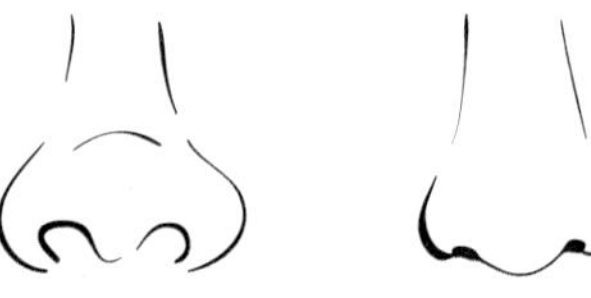

(관용 표현) 콧대가 높다
be high-nosed[toffee-nosed, arrogant]
* toffee-nosed는 주로 영국에서 사용

SENTENCES TO USE

그는 코가 휘어서 수술을 받았어요.
He underwent surgery because his nose was crooked.

그 남자는 매일 술에 취해 있어서 늘 코가 빨갛죠.
The man is drunk every day, so his nose is always red.

그는 주먹코이고 얼굴에 여드름도 많아요.
He has a bulbous nose and has a lot of acne on his face.

콧구멍이 큰 게 제 콤플렉스예요.
I'm self-conscious about my big nostrils.

그녀는 콧대가 너무 높아서 웬만한 남자한테는 관심도 주지 않아요.
She is so high-nosed that she doesn't pay attention to most men.

UNIT 6 귀

MP3 012

MP3 012-1

귀가 크다 have big ears, one's ears are big

귀가 작다 have small ears, one's ears are small

귓불이 크다/넓다/두툼하다 have big/wide/thick earlobes, one's earlobes are big/wide/thick

귓불이 작다/좁다/얇다 have small/narrow/thin earlobes, one's earlobes are small/narrow/thin

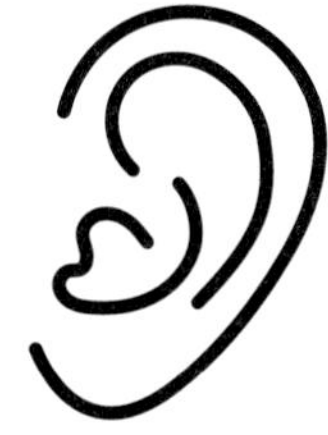

칼귀다 have pixie ears

귀가 잘생겼다/예쁘다 have nice/pretty ears, one's ears are nice/pretty

부처님 귀 같다 have ears like Buddha's, one's ears look like those of Buddha

귀에 점이 있다 have a mole[spot] on one's ear

귀를 뚫었다(상태) have pierced ears, have[get] one's ears pierced

SENTENCES TO USE

그는 얼굴에 비해 귀가 작아요.
His ears are small compared to his face.

그 신부님은 귓불이 커서 부처님 귀 같아요.
The priest's earlobes are so big that they look like Buddha's ears.

그녀는 귀가 칼귀라서 귀걸이를 하기가 어려워요.
She has pixie ears, so it's difficult for her to wear earrings.

나는 오른쪽 귀에 점이 있어요. 사람들은 그걸로 나랑 쌍둥이 여동생을 구별하죠.
I have a mole on my right ear. That's how people tell me apart from my twin sister.

그녀는 귀는 뚫었지만 귀걸이는 거의 하지 않아요.
She has pierced ears but rarely wears earrings.

UNIT 6

'귀' 관용 표현

MP3 012-2

(누가 자기 얘기를 해서) 귀가 가렵다 one's ears are burning

귀가 얇다, 팔랑귀다 take others' words uncritically, be easily influenced by others, be easily swayed by others' words

열심히 귀를 기울이다 be all ears, listen intently[attentively] to

귀가 솔깃하다 become interested in ~, be attracted to ~

귀에 못이 박히다 be sick (and tired) of hearing ~, be fed up with hearing ~, have heard ~ millions of times

(언어에) 귀가 뚫리다
come[begin] to understand 언어

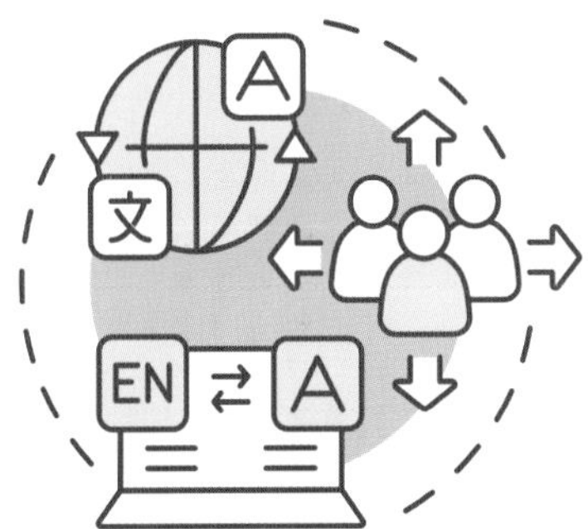

SENTENCES TO USE

누가 내 흉을 보나 봐요. 귀가 가렵네요.
It seems like someone is speaking ill of me. My ears are burning.

그는 귀가 얇아서 생각이 자주 바뀌어요.
He is easily swayed by others' words, and changes his mind often.

아이들은 선생님이 하는 이야기에 열심히 귀를 기울이고 있었어요.
The children were listening intently to the teacher's story.

나는 그 사람이 고생한 얘기는 귀에 못이 박히도록 들었어요.
I'm sick of hearing stories about the hardships he endured.

그는 영어를 공부하고 여러 해 만에 귀가 뚫렸어요.
He came to understand English after many years of studying it.

UNIT 7 입, 입술, 치아

MP3 013

입

MP3 013-1

* 외모 관련 표현은 무례하게 들릴 수 있으므로 사용에 유의해야 함

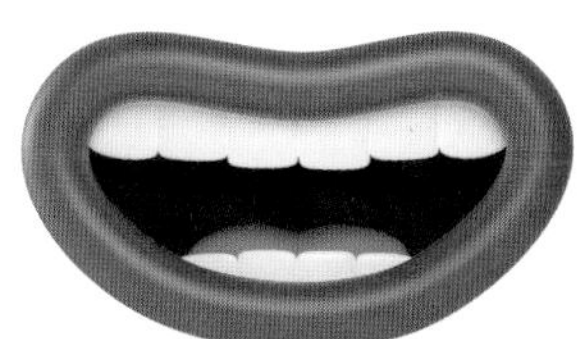

입이 크다
have a big mouth,
one's mouth is big
* have a big mouth는 '입이 싸다'의 의미로도 씀

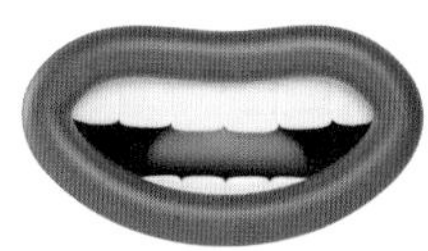

입이 작다
have a small mouth,
one's mouth is small

입이 튀어나왔다
have a protruding mouth,
one's mouth is protruding

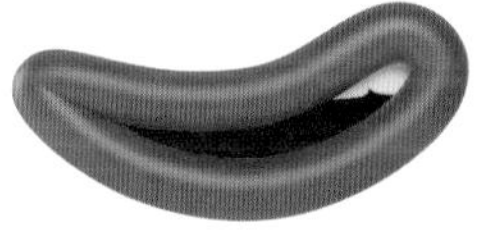

입꼬리가 올라갔다
have upturned mouth corners,
one's mouth corners are upturned

입꼬리가 처졌다
have downturned mouth corners,
one's mouth corners are downturned

SENTENCES TO USE

배우 줄리아 로버츠는 입이 무척 큰데, 그게 그녀의 매력 중 하나죠.
The actress Julia Roberts has a very big mouth, which is part of her charm.

그녀는 입은 작은데 입술은 도톰해요.
She has a small mouth, but her lips are full.

그 코미디언은 입이 튀어나와서 말이 많은 듯한 인상을 풍깁니다.
The comedian has a protruding mouth, which gives the impression that he is talkative.

입꼬리가 올라가 있으면 밝고 긍정적으로 보이죠.
If you have upturned mouth corners, you appear to be a bright and positive person.

나는 입꼬리가 처져서 좀 우울해 보이는 것 같아요.
I think I look a bit unhappy because I have downturned mouth corners.

'입' 관용 표현

MP3 013-2

입바른 소리를 하다 speak plainly[directly, in a straightforward manner]

입만 살다 be all talk and no action, have only got a mouth, don't keep one's word

입에 대다 eat ~, drink ~

~라고 입을 모으다 all say that 주어+동사, say ~ in unison[chorus]

입이 가볍다[싸다] have a big mouth

입이 무겁다 be close-mouthed, be a man of few words, can hold one's tongue

입이 짧다 have a small[poor] appetite, be a picky eater, eat like a bird

입을 떼다 begin to talk[speak]

SENTENCES TO USE

그녀는 입바른 소리를 자주 해서 때로는 사람들을 화나게 해요.
She often speaks too plainly, so sometimes she upsets people.

그는 입만 살아서 아무것도 해내는 게 없어요.
He's all talk and no action, so nothing ever gets done.

그녀는 너무 긴장돼서 어젯밤부터 아무것도 입에 대지 않고 있어요.
She is so nervous that she hasn't eaten anything since last night.

그녀는 입이 무거워서 비밀을 얘기해도 돼요.
She can hold her tongue, so you can tell her a secret.

그는 입이 짧아서 갈 수 있는 식당이 몇 군데밖에 없답니다.
He is a picky eater, so there are only a few restaurants he can go to.

입술

MP3 013-3

* 외모 관련 표현은 무례하게 들릴 수 있으므로 사용에 유의해야 함

입술이 두껍다, 입술이 도톰하다 have full[heavy, thick] lips, one's lips are full[heavy, thick]

입술이 얇다 have thin lips, one's lips are thin

윗입술/아랫입술이 두껍다 have a full[heavy] upper/lower lip, one's upper/lower lip is full[heavy]

윗입술/아랫입술이 얇다 have a thin upper/lower lip, one's upper/lower lip is thin

입술산이 또렷하다 have a (defined) Cupid's bow

입술산이 없다 have a flat upper lip, don't have a Cupid's bow

입술산이 선명하지 않다 don't have a defined Cupid's bow

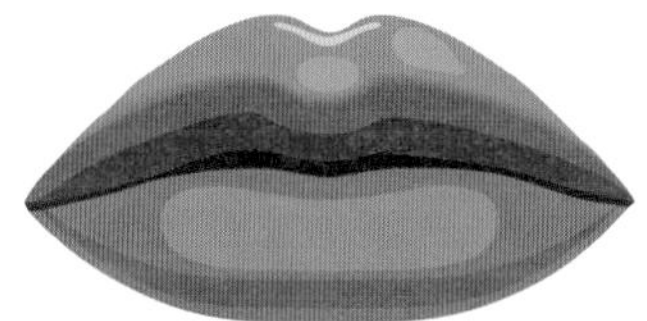

입술이 촉촉하다 have moist lips, one's lips are moist

입술이 부드럽다 have soft[tender] lips, one's lips are soft[tender]

입술이 말랐다(상태) have dry lips, one's lips are dry

입술이 갈라졌다(상태) one's lips are cracked

입술이 트다 one's lips are chapped

입술이 퍼렇다(체온 저하나 산소 부족 등으로) one's lips are blue

SENTENCES TO USE

안젤리나 졸리가 입술이 도톰한 배우의 대명사죠.
Angelina Jolie is the epitome of an actress with thick lips.

입술이 얇았다가 나중에 두꺼운 입술로 나타나는 여배우들이 많아요.
Many actresses initially have thin lips but later appear with full lips.

나는 입술산이 선명하지 않은 게 불만이에요.
I am unhappy with the fact that I don't have a defined Cupid's bow.

그녀는 입술이 늘 말라 있어서 립글로스를 자주 발라요.
Her lips are always dry, so she often applies lip gloss.

나는 겨울이면 입술이 트고 갈라져서 가끔 피도 나요.
In the winter, my lips become chapped, cracked, and sometimes even bleed.

UNIT 7

치아

MP3 013-4

* 외모 관련 표현은 무례하게 들릴 수 있으므로 사용에 유의해야 함

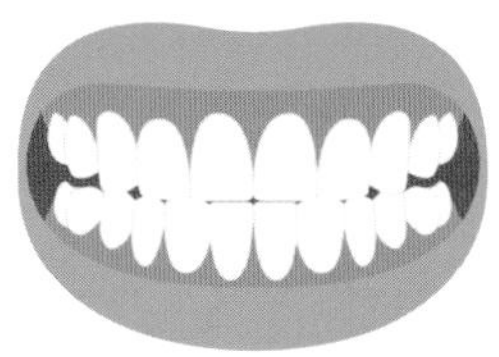

치아가 가지런하다
have straight[even] teeth,
one's teeth are straight[even]

덧니가 있다 have a snaggletooth[double tooth, protruding tooth]

앞니가 나오다
have protruding front teeth,
have an overbite

치아가 하얗다 have white teeth,
one's teeth are white

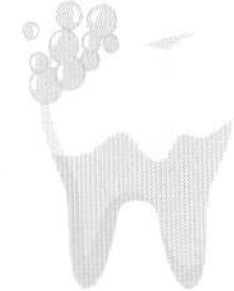

치아가 누렇다 have yellow[yellowish] teeth,
one's teeth are yellow[yellowish]

충치가 있다
have a cavity[decayed tooth]
* cavity는 충치로 인해 생긴 구멍을 가리킴

충치가 없다 have no cavities[decayed teeth]

치아 사이가 벌어져 있다
have a gap between the teeth

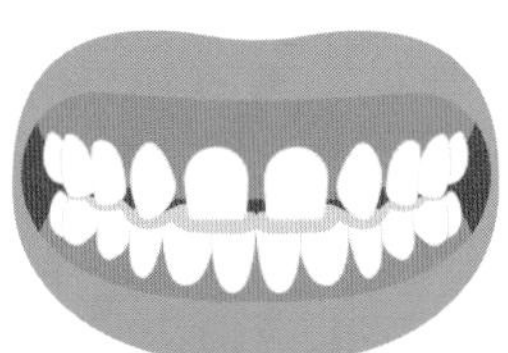

SENTENCES TO USE

그 사람은 치열이 가지런하고 하얘서 웃을 때 보기 좋아요.
His teeth are straight and white, so he looks good when he smiles.

나는 덧니가 있는 사람은 귀여워 보이더라고요.
I think people with a snaggletooth look cute.

그녀는 앞니가 나와서 치아 교정을 했어요.
She had protruding front teeth so she had them fixed.

그는 양치질을 하루에 몇 번씩 하는데도 치아가 누래요.
He has yellow teeth even though he brushes his teeth several times a day.

그 아이는 충치가 많아서 치과 치료를 받고 있어요.
The child has a lot of decayed teeth and is undergoing dental treatment.

치석이 있다 have scale[plaque, tartar] on one's teeth

이가 아프다 have a toothache

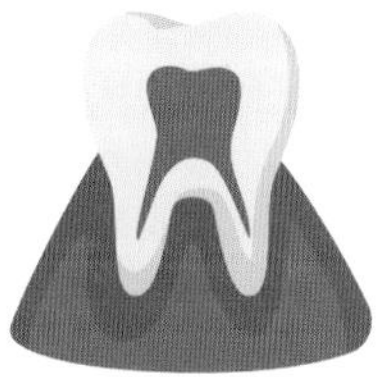

잇몸에 문제가 있다
have a problem with one's gums

금니가 있다 have a gold tooth

치아에 금을 씌우다 have one's tooth capped with gold

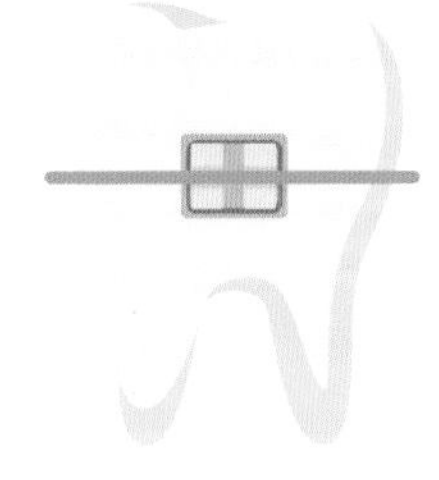

치아 교정을 하고 있다, 교정기를 끼고 있다
have braces on one's teeth

임플란트한 치아가 있다 have a dental implant

치아 임플란트를 받다 get dental implant surgery

SENTENCES TO USE

치석이 있으니 스케일링을 할 때가 된 것 같아요.
I think it's time for scaling because I have plaque on my teeth.

나는 잇몸에 문제가 있어서 양치질할 때 피가 조금씩 나옵니다.
I have a problem with my gums and they bleed a little when I brush my teeth.

나는 충치 치료를 받고 치아에 금을 씌웠어요.
I had my cavities filled and my teeth capped with gold.

그 아이는 치아 교정을 하고 있어요. 보통 3년 정도 걸리죠.
The child has braces on his teeth. It usually takes about three years.

그는 임플란트한 치아가 3개 있어요. 작년에 임플란트 시술을 받았어요.
He has three dental implants. He got dental implant surgery last year.

MORE

치아의 종류 MP3 013-5

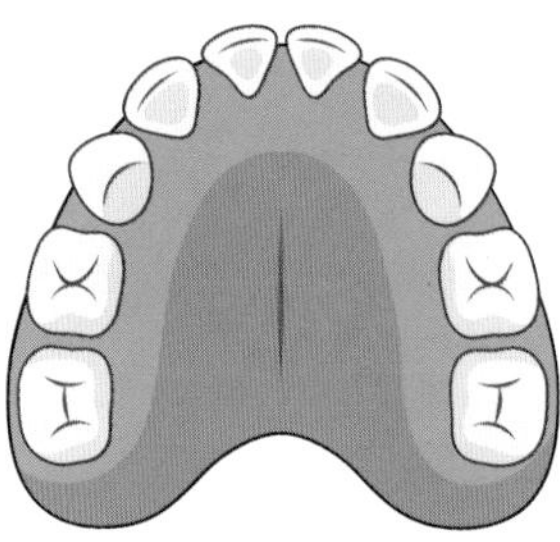

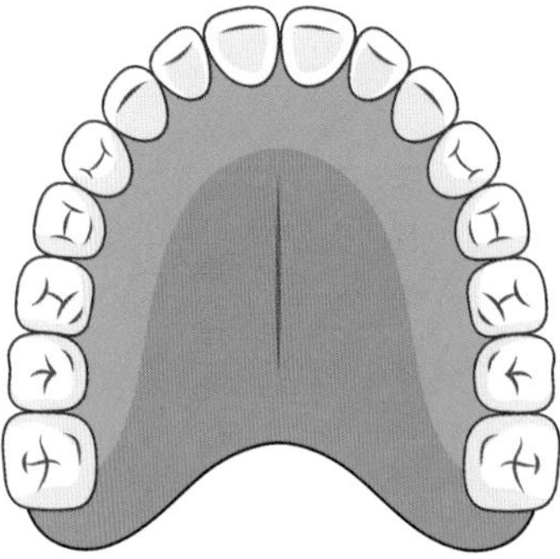

영구치 a permanent tooth

젖니 a baby tooth

윗니 upper teeth

아랫니 lower teeth

앞니(8개) a front tooth, an incisor

송곳니(4개) a canine, a canine tooth

앞어금니(8개) a premolar

* 송곳니와 어금니 사이에 있는 2개의 어금니

어금니(8~12개) a molar

첫째/둘째 어금니 the first/second molar

사랑니 a wisdom tooth

* 맨 끝에 있는 어금니로, 사랑니 4개가 모두 있으면 영구치 수가 32개, 하나도 없으면 28개 등으로 사랑니 수에 따라 영구치 수에 차이가 있음

충치
a decayed tooth, a cavity

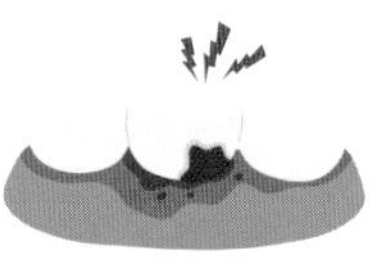

덧니
a snaggletooth, a double tooth, a protruding tooth

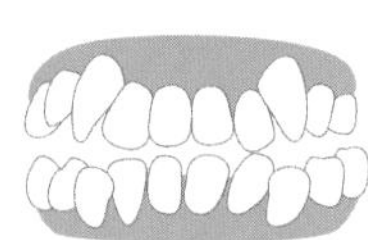

죽은 이
a dead tooth

* 이가 깨지거나, 썩거나, 금이 가거나, 감염되어 신경으로 혈액이 공급되지 않는 상태

UNIT 8 목소리

MP3 014

목소리가 좋다 have a good[pleasant] voice, one's voice is good[pleasant]

목소리가 좋지 않다 have a bad[an unpleasant] voice, don't have a good voice(좀 더 공손한 표현), one's voice is bad[unpleasant]

* unpleasant가 bad보다 부드러운 표현

목소리가 곱다 have a beautiful voice, one's voice is beautiful

목소리가 상냥하다 have a gentle voice, one's voice is gentle

목소리가 부드럽다 have a soft voice, one's voice is soft

목소리가 낮다[저음이다] have a low[deep] voice, one's voice is low[deep]

목소리가 높다[고음이다]
have a high voice, one's voice is high

목소리가 크다 have a loud voice, one's voice is loud

목소리가 작다 have a quiet voice, one's voice is quiet

목소리가 맑다 have a clear voice, one's voice is clear

목소리가 탁하다 have a raspy[hoarse] voice, one's voice is raspy[hoarse]

SENTENCES TO USE

그녀는 목소리가 고와서 성우가 되라는 얘기를 종종 들어요.
Because she has a beautiful voice, she is often told to become a voice actress.

그는 얼굴도 잘생기고 목소리도 부드럽고 저음이라서 인기가 많아요.
He is popular because he has a handsome face and a soft, low voice.

그는 어려 보였는데 목소리는 아주 저음이었어요.
Although he had a youthful appearance, he had a very low voice.

우리 할머니는 청력이 안 좋아서 목소리가 크세요.
My grandmother has a loud voice because she has poor hearing.

그 중년 남성은 담배를 많이 피워서인지 목소리가 탁해요.
The middle-aged man has a raspy voice, perhaps because he smokes a lot.

UNIT 8

목소리가 가늘다[가냘프다] have a thin voice, one's voice is thin

목소리가 굵다 have a deep[thick] voice, one's voice is deep[thick]

목소리가 낭랑하다 have a sonorous voice, one's voice is sonorous

목소리가 남자답다 have a manly voice, one's voice is manly

목소리가 여성스럽다 have a feminine voice, one's voice is feminine

목소리가 날카롭다 have a sharp voice, one's voice is sharp

목이 쉬다 have a hoarse voice[throat], one's voice[throat] is hoarse, have a frog in one's throat

목소리가 갈라지다 one's voice cracks

목소리가 떨리다 one's voice trembles

목소리가 안 나오다, 목이 잠기다 lose one's voice, one's voice is gone(신체적 상태나 감정의 북받침으로 소리가 안 나오는 것을 뜻함)

SENTENCES TO USE

그 아이는 목소리가 작고 가늘어서 뭐라고 하는지 알아듣기가 힘들어요.
The child's voice is quiet and thin, so it's hard to understand what he's saying.

그 여성은 목소리가 높은 데다 날카로워서 오래 듣고 있기 부담스러워요.
The woman's voice is high and sharp, so it's difficult to listen to for a long time.

2시간 동안 강연하고 났더니 목이 쉰 상태예요.
My throat is hoarse after giving a lecture for two hours.

사람들 앞에 서면 전 너무 긴장해서 목소리가 떨려요.
When I stand in front of people, I get so nervous that my voice trembles.

목이 심하게 아파서 오늘은 목소리가 잘 안 나와요.
I have a severe sore throat, so my voice is nearly gone.

UNIT 9 체형, 몸매

키

MP3 015-1

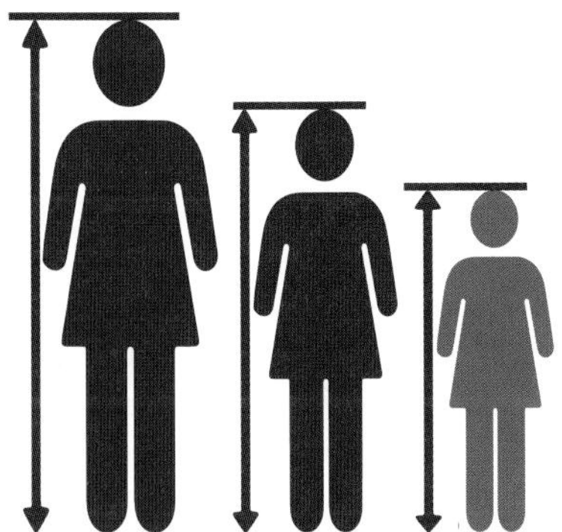

키가 크다 be tall

키가 작다 be short

중간 키다 be of medium height

평균 키다 be of average height

키가 큰 편에 속하다 be on the tall side

키가 작은 편에 속하다 be on the short side

키가 ~센티미터[~피트 ~인치]다
be ~ centimeters[~ feet ~ inches] tall

SENTENCES TO USE

미란다네 식구들은 다 키가 커요.
All of Miranda's family members are tall.

그는 키가 작지만, 그게 그의 콤플렉스는 아니에요.
He's short, but he's not self-conscious about it.

나는 키가 작지도 크지도 않고, 중간 키예요.
I am neither short nor tall. I am of medium height.

그녀는 노르웨이 여성으로서는 평균 키예요.
She is of average height for a Norwegian woman.

우리 어머니는 키가 큰 편에 속하세요.
My mother is on the tall side.

UNIT 9

체형, 몸매

MP3 015-2

* 외모 관련 표현은 무례하게 들릴 수 있으므로 사용에 유의해야 함

보통 체격이다 be of average build

몸집[체격]이 크다, 건장하다
have a big[large] frame,
be of strong[sturdy] build,
be well built

몸집[체격]이 작다 have a small frame, be of slight build

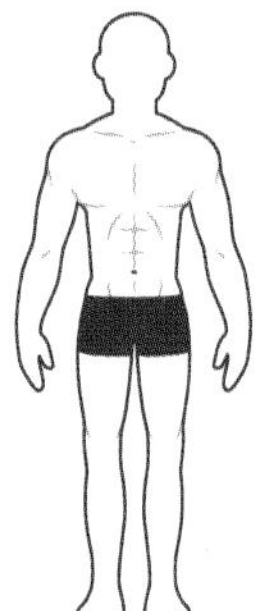
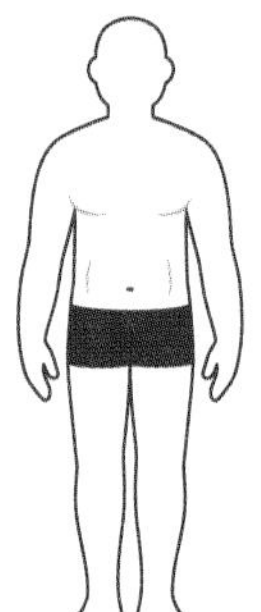
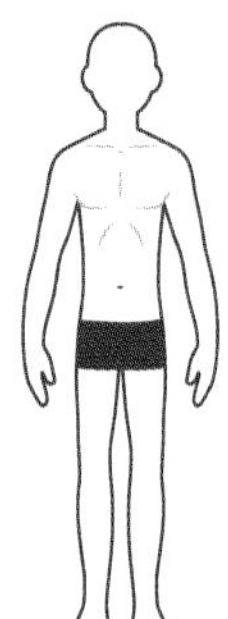

근육질이다 be muscular

(몸이) **운동으로 단련됐다** be fit from exercise

배에 복근이 있다 have abdominal muscles, have abs

배에 식스팩이 있다 have a six-pack

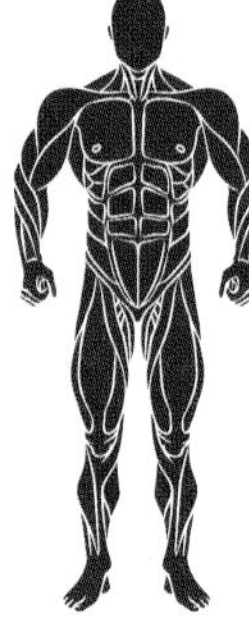
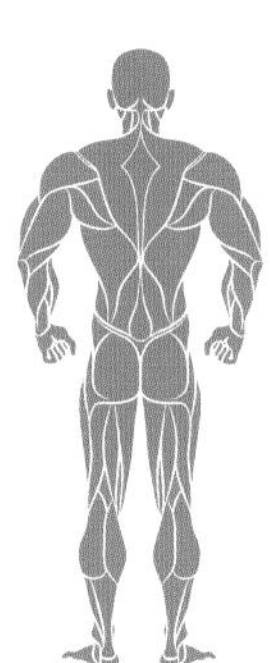

SENTENCES TO USE

그 기자는 몸집이 커서 종종 운동선수로 오해받아요.
The journalist has a big frame and is often mistaken for an athlete.

동남아시아 사람들은 몽골 인종보다 몸집이 작은 편이에요.
Southeast Asians are smaller than Mongolians.

그 남자는 키도 크고 근육질이기도 합니다.
The man is tall and muscular.

그 사람이 몸은 말랐지만 운동으로 단련됐어요.
He is skinny but fit from exercise.

그는 꾸준히 복근 운동을 해서 식스팩이 있어요.
He constantly works out his abs, so he has a six-pack.

* 외모 관련 표현은 무례하게 들릴 수 있으므로 사용에 유의해야 함

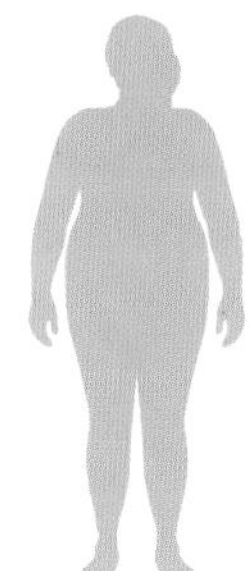

몸무게가 (약) ~킬로그램[파운드]이다
weigh (approximately) ~ kilograms[pounds]

과체중이다 be overweight

뚱뚱하다 be fat (무례한 말이므로 사용에 유의), carry extra weight (완곡한 표현)

비만이다 be obese (격식체, 의학적 표현)

복부 비만이다
have a potbelly, have abdominal[central] obesity

고도비만이다
be severely[extremely] obese
* 의학적 문맥에서는 severely를 쓰는 게 일반적

통통하다 be chubby[plump, stout] * stout는 체격이 건장한 것까지 의미

땅딸막하다 be thickset[stocky]

날씬하다, 호리호리하다 be slim[slender]
* slim은 보기 좋게 날씬한 것,
slender는 여성이 우아한 느낌으로 날씬한 것을 나타냄

마르다 be thin

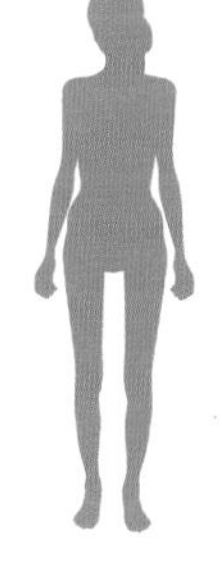

비쩍 마르다
be skinny
* 흔히 보기 싫을 정도로 마른 것을 나타냄

마른 비만이다 be skinny fat

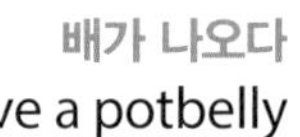

배가 나오다
have a potbelly

배가 납작하다 have a flat stomach

SENTENCES TO USE

나는 키가 160센티미터에 몸무게는 53킬로그램 정도 나가요.
I am 160 centimeters tall and weigh approximately 53 kilograms.

나는 젊었을 때는 말랐었는데, 지금은 과체중이에요.
I was thin when I was young, but now I am overweight.

너는 비만은 아니야. 그냥 통통한 거지.
You are not obese. You're just chubby.

그녀는 날씬하고 목이 길고 가늘었는데, 그는 그 모습에 반했어요.
She was slender with a long, thin neck, and he fell in love with it.

그는 많이 먹는데도 늘 말랐어요.
Event though he eats a lot, he always stays thin.

그는 마른 비만으로, 배가 나왔어요.
He is skinny fat and has a potbelly.

MORE

여성의 체형을 나타내는 표현 

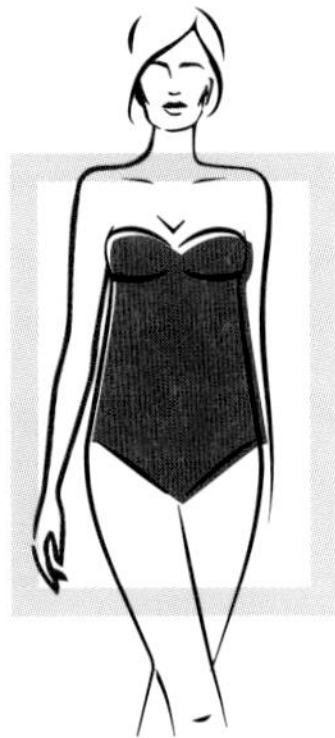

일자형이다 (가슴–허리–골반 폭이 비슷하다)
have a rectangle[straight] body shape

사과형이다 (어깨, 가슴 등 상체가 발달하고 골반이 상체보다 작다)
have an apple body shape

삼각형[서양배형]이다 (가슴과 허리가 좁고 골반이 넓다)
have a triangle[pear] body shape

역삼각형이다 (어깨가 넓고 골반이 좁다)
have an inverted triangle[a top heavy] body shape

모래시계형이다 (어깨와 골반 폭이 비슷하고 허리가 잘록하다)
have an hourglass figure[body shape]

상체

MP3 015-4

* 외모 관련 표현은 무례하게 들릴 수 있으므로 사용에 유의해야 함

목이 길다 have a long neck, one's neck is long

목이 짧다 have a short neck, one's neck is short

목이 굵다 have a thick neck, one's neck is thick

목이 가늘다 have a thin neck, one's neck is thin

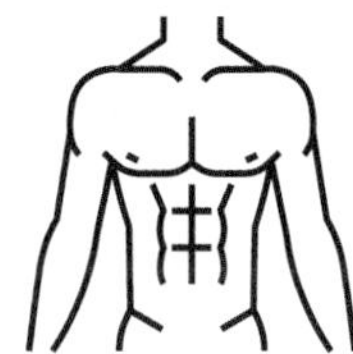

어깨가 넓다 have broad shoulders, one's shoulders are broad

어깨가 좁다 have narrow shoulders, one's shoulders are narrow

어깨가 처졌다 have sloped[sloping] shoulders

직각 어깨다 have square shoulders

어깨가 앞으로 굽었다 have rounded shoulders, one's shoulders are bent forward

가슴 근육이 발달했다 have a broad[wide, big] chest

SENTENCES TO USE

미남 미녀들은 보통 목도 길더군요.
Handsome men and beautiful women usually have long necks.

나는 목이 짧아서 터틀넥은 입기 불편해요.
I have a short neck, so wearing a turtleneck is uncomfortable for me.

그는 키가 크고 어깨가 넓어서 무슨 옷이든 다 잘 어울려요.
He is tall and has broad shoulders, so he looks good in any clothes.

그녀는 어깨가 처져서 가방이 자꾸 흘러내려요.
She has sloped shoulders, so her bag keeps slipping down.

그 남자아이는 어깨가 앞으로 굽어서 키가 안 커 보이네요.
The boy doesn't look tall because he has rounded shoulders.

UNIT 9

* 외모 관련 표현은 무례하게 들릴 수 있으므로 사용에 유의해야 함

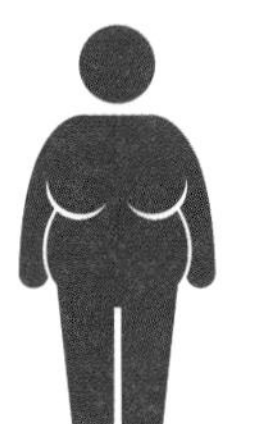
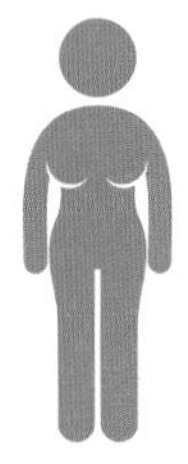

가슴이 크다 have large[big] breasts, one's breasts are large[big]

가슴이 작다 have small breasts, one's breasts are small

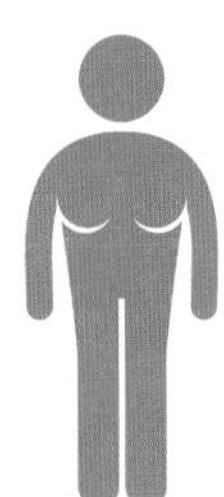

허리가 굵다 have a large[wide] waist, one's waist is large[wide]

* large waist는 허리둘레가 굵은 것, wide waist는 정면에서 봤을 때 가로폭이 넓은 것

허리가 가늘다 have a small[thin, slim] waist, one's waist is small[thin, slim]

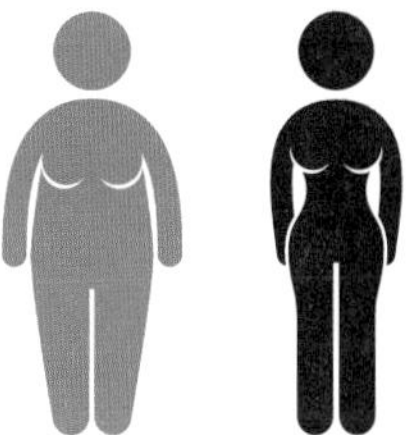

허리가 없다 have no waist, have an undefined waist

나이가 들어 허리가 굽다 one's back is bent with age

배가 나오다(상태) have a potbelly

배가 나오다(변화) develop a potbelly

허리둘레가 ~센티미터[인치]다
have a waist size of ~ centimeters[inches], measure ~ centimeters[inches] around the waist

SENTENCES TO USE

십 대 소녀인 제니는 가슴이 큰 게 콤플렉스예요.
Jenny, a teenage girl, is self-conscious about having large breasts.

비비안 리는 허리가 가는 것으로 유명했어요.
Vivien Leigh was famous for having a small waist.

나는 허리가 없어서 옷 입을 때마다 신경이 쓰여요.
I have an undefined waist, so it bothers me every time I put on clothes.

우리 할머니는 평생 농사를 지으셔서 나이 드신 후 허리가 굽으셨어요.
My grandmother has been farming all her life and her back is bent with age.

그는 40대가 되면서 배가 나왔어요.
He developed a potbelly in his forties.

하체

MP3 015-5

* 외모 관련 표현은 무례하게 들릴 수 있으므로 사용에 유의해야 함

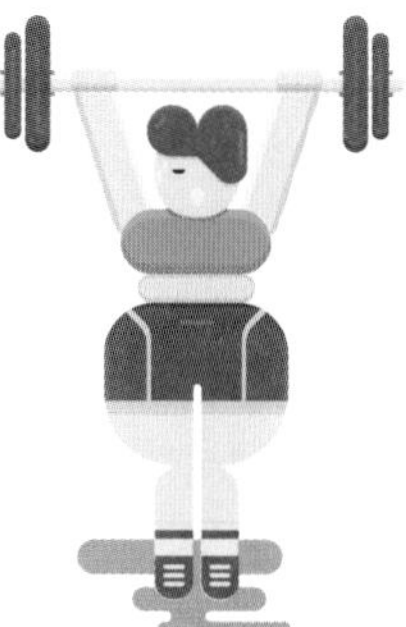

하체 비만이다 be overweight in one's[the] lower body, one's lower body carries excess weight

하체가 말랐다 one's lower body is slim[thin]

엉덩이가 크다 have big[large] buttocks,
have a big[large] butt,
one's buttocks are big[large],
one's butt is big[large]

* butt은 비격식체

엉덩이가 작다
have small buttocks[a small butt],
one's buttocks are small

엉덩이가 힙업되어 있다
have lifted[toned] buttocks, have a lifted[toned] butt,
one's buttocks are lifted[toned], one's butt is lifted[toned]

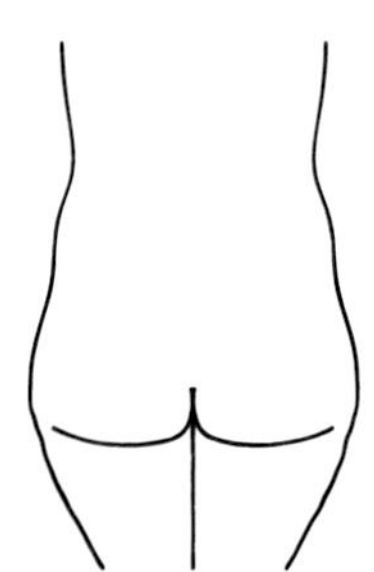

엉덩이가 처졌다
have saggy buttocks, have a saggy butt,
one's buttocks are saggy, one's butt is saggy

엉덩이가 펑퍼짐하다
have a wide butt,
one's buttocks are wide

엉덩이가 납작하다
have a flat butt,
one's buttocks are flat

SENTENCES TO USE

그 소녀는 하체 비만이라서 고민이에요.
The girl is worried because she is overweight in her lower body.

우리 엄마는 복부 비만인데, 하체는 말랐어요.
My mother has a potbelly, but her lower body is slim.

그 여성 연예인은 엉덩이가 큰 걸로 유명하죠.
The female celebrity is famous for having big buttocks.

그녀는 엉덩이가 처져서 매일 힙업 운동을 해요.
She does hip-up exercises every day because she has saggy buttocks.

그는 엉덩이가 납작해서 뒷모습이 볼품없어요.
He has a flat butt and doesn't look good from the back.

UNIT 9

다리

MP3 015-6

* 외모 관련 표현은 무례하게 들릴 수 있으므로 사용에 유의해야 함

다리가 길다 have long legs, be long-legged, one's legs are long

다리가 짧다 have short legs, one's legs are short

다리가 굵다 have thick legs, one's legs are thick

다리가 가늘다 have thin legs, one's legs are thin

다리가 곧다 have straight legs

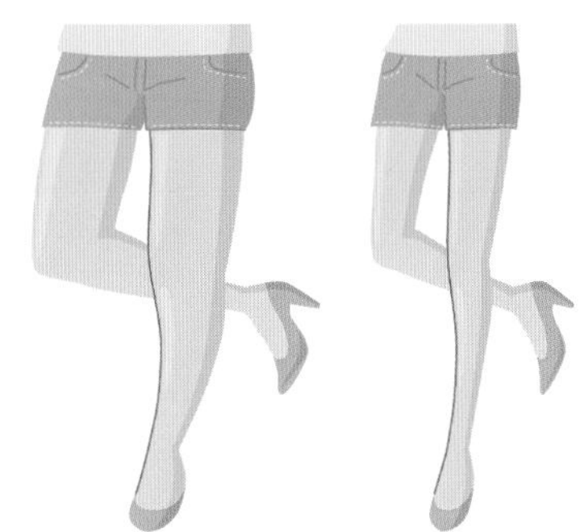

다리가 예쁘다, 각선미가 좋다
have pretty [beautiful, attractive] legs

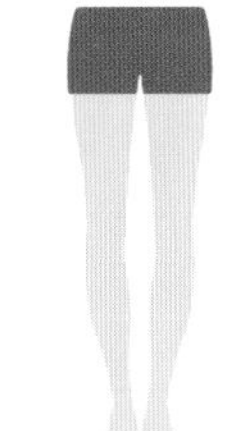

다리가 O자로 휘었다
be bowlegged

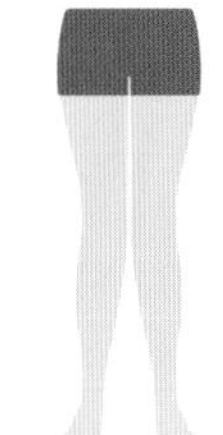

안짱다리다
be pigeon-toed, walk with one's feet turned inward

SENTENCES TO USE

요즘 젊은이들은 대부분 전 세대 사람들보다 다리가 길어요.
Most young people these days have longer legs than people of previous generations.

다리가 짧은 사람들은 같은 거리를 더 많은 걸음으로 걸어가죠.
People who have short legs walk the same distance with more steps.

그 여자아이는 상체는 날씬한데 다리는 굵어요.
The girl has a slim upper body but thick legs.

그녀는 다리가 곧고 예뻐요. 모두가 그녀를 부러워해요.
She has straight, pretty legs. Everyone envies her.

그 여자는 다리가 O자로 휘어서 바지보다는 긴 치마를 입는 걸 선호해요.
The woman is bowlegged, so she prefers to wear long skirts rather than pants.

* 외모 관련 표현은 무례하게 들릴 수 있으므로 사용에 유의해야 함

다리(종아리)가 매끈하다 have smooth legs, one's legs are smooth * 다리 피부가 매끄럽고 털이 없다는 뜻

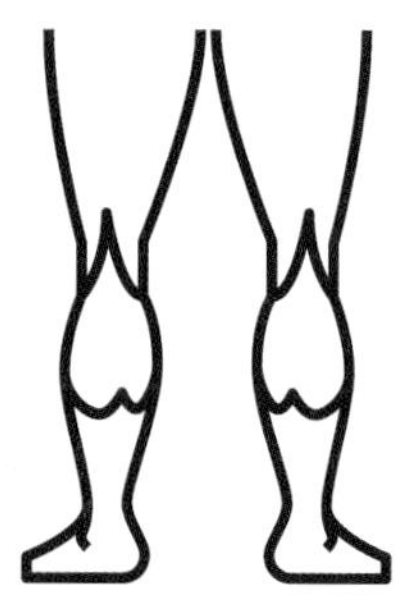

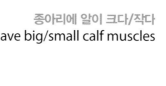

종아리에 알이 크다/작다 have big/small calf muscles

다리에 털이 많다 have hairy legs, have a lot of hair on one's legs

다리에 털이 없다 have no hair on one's legs

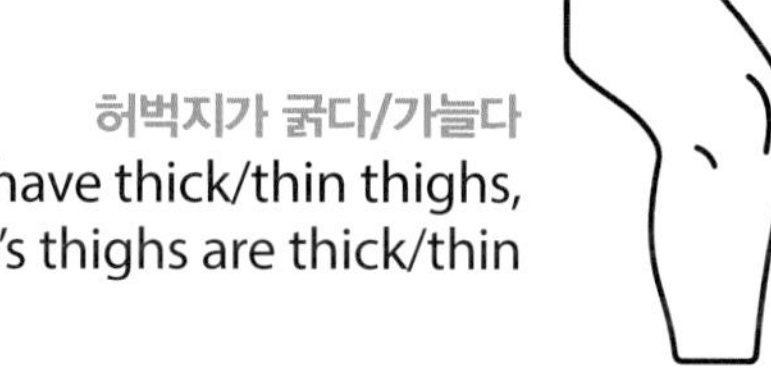

허벅지가 굵다/가늘다 have thick/thin thighs, one's thighs are thick/thin

종아리가 굵다/가늘다 have thick/thin calves, one's calves are thick/thin

허벅지에 근육이 많다/적다 have big/small thigh muscles

SENTENCES TO USE

그녀는 정기적으로 제모를 하기 때문에 다리가 무척 매끈해요.
She has very smooth legs because she shaves them regularly.

우리 언니는 종아리에 알이 커서 치마 입는 걸 싫어해요.
My sister has big calf muscles, so she doesn't like to wear skirts.

그 남자는 다리에 털이 하나도 없어요.
The man has no hair on his legs.

그 사람은 허벅지가 무척 굵은데, 65센티미터쯤 된다고 하네요.
He has very thick thighs, said to be about sixty-five centimeters.

노년에 건강한 삶을 누리려면 허벅지에 근육이 많아야 해요.
To remain healthy in old age, you need to have big thigh muscles.

UNIT 10 손, 손가락

손

MP3 016-1

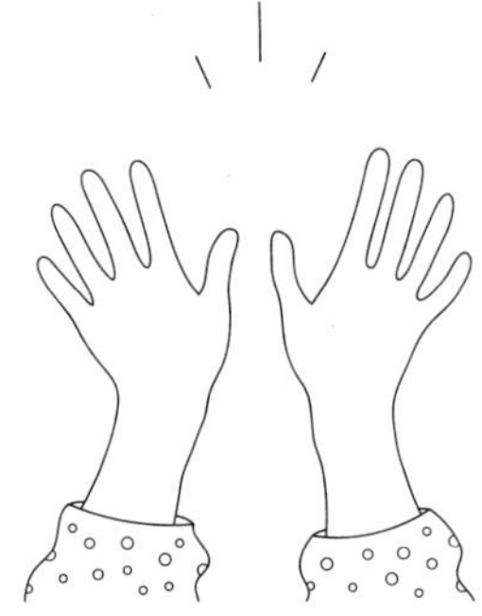

손이 크다 have big[large] hands, one's hands are big[large]

손이 작다 have small hands, one's hands are small

손이 두툼하다 have meaty[thick] hands, one's hands are meaty[thick]

손이 부드럽다[곱다] have soft hands, one's hands are soft

손이 거칠다 have rough hands, one's hands are rough

손이 붓다
one's hands are swollen

손이 크다(관용 표현)
have an open[a free] hand, be open-handed[free-handed], be a big spender

손이 작다(관용 표현)
be close-fisted[tight-fisted, sparing, stingy]

손금이 선명하다 one's palm lines are clear

손금이 좋다/나쁘다 have lucky/ominous lines on one's hand

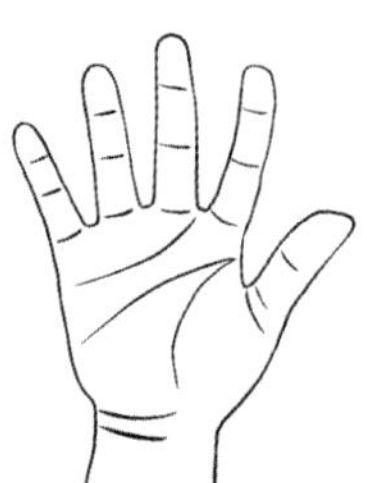

SENTENCES TO USE

그는 손이 커서 한 손으로 공을 쉽게 쥘 수 있었어요.
He had big hands, so he could easily hold the ball in one hand.

그 남자는 몸집에 비해 손이 작아요.
The man has small hands for his body size.

시장의 생선 장수는 손이 두툼했어요.
The fish seller in the market had meaty hands.

그 사람과 악수한 적이 있는데, 손이 부드러웠어요.
I once shook hands with him, and his hands were soft.

그녀는 손이 작아서 파티 음식을 넉넉히 준비하지 않았더군요.
Since she is close-fisted, she did not prepare enough food for the party.

손가락, 손톱

MP3 016-2

손가락이 길다 have long fingers, one's fingers are long

손가락이 짧다 have short fingers, one's fingers are short

손가락이 가늘다 have slim[slender, thin] fingers, one's fingers are slim[slender, thin]

* slender가 가장 긍정적인 의미를 내포

손가락이 굵다 have thick[stubby] fingers, one's fingers are thick[stubby]

* stubby는 짧고 굵은 것을 의미

손톱이 길다 have long fingernails, one's fingernails are long

손톱이 짧다 have short fingernails, one's fingernails are short

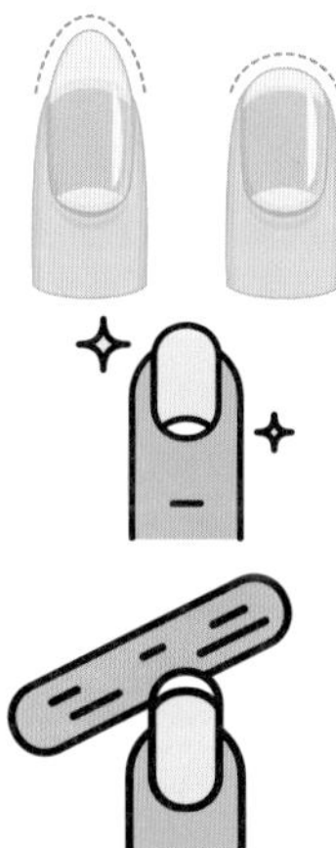

손톱이 깨끗하다 have clean fingernails, one's fingernails are clean

손톱이 잘 손질[관리]돼 있다
have well-manicured fingernails, one's fingernails are well-manicured

손톱 밑에 때가 껴 있다
have dirt[grime] under one's fingernails

손톱에 네일 아트를 하고 있다(상태)
have nail art done on one's fingernails

SENTENCES TO USE

손가락이 길고 손이 크면 피아노 연주에 유리할 수도 있죠.
Having long fingers and large hands may be advantageous for playing the piano.

우리 할머니는 농사일을 많이 하셔서 손가락이 굵으세요.
My grandmother did a lot of farming, so she has thick fingers.

그 영업 사원은 늘 손톱이 잘 손질돼 있어요.
The salesperson's fingernails are always well-manicured.

그 아이는 흙 장난을 해서 손톱 밑에 때가 껴 있었어요.
The child had dirt under his fingernails from playing in the dirt.

그녀는 항상 손톱에 네일 아트를 하고 있어요.
She always has nail art done on her fingernails.

MORE

손과 손가락 세부 명칭

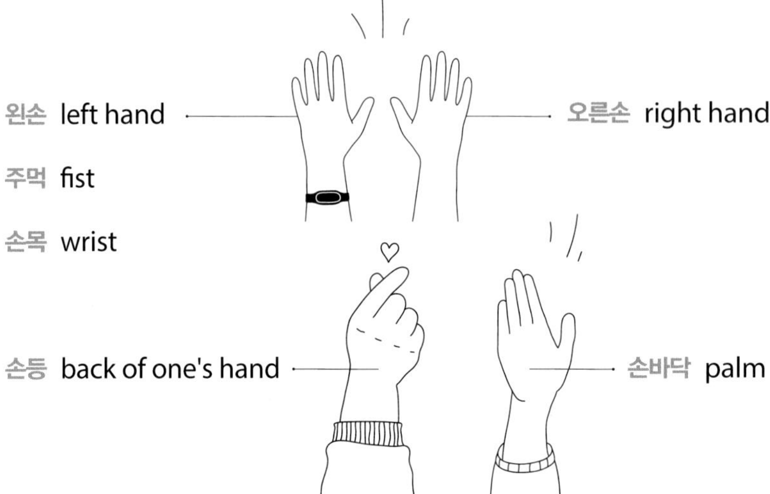

엄지손가락[엄지] thumb, big finger

집게손가락[둘째 손가락, 검지] index finger, forefinger

가운뎃손가락[셋째 손가락, 중지] middle finger

약손가락[넷째 손가락, 약지] ring finger

새끼손가락[소지] little finger

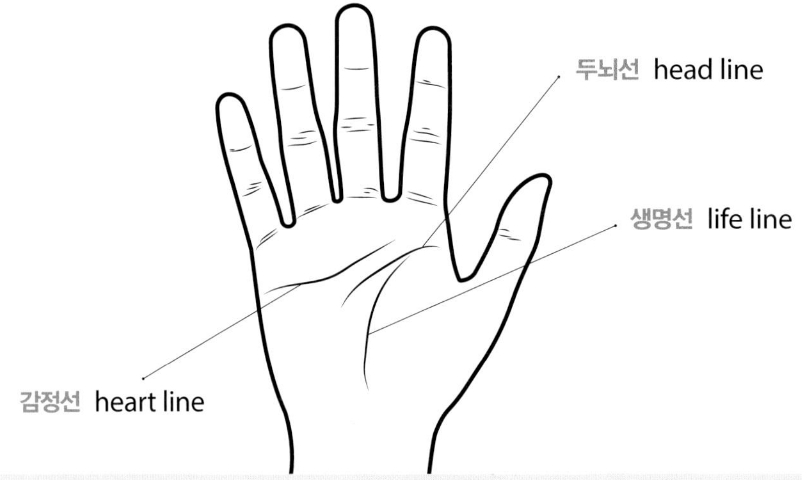

UNIT **11**

발, 발가락

발

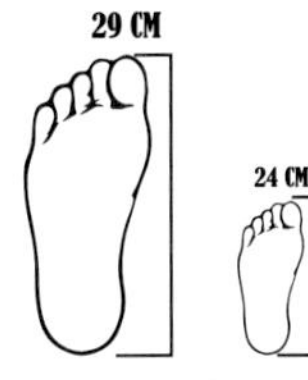

발이 크다/작다
have big/small feet,
one's feet are big/small

발 사이즈가 ~이다
one's shoe size is ~,
wear[take] a size ~ in shoes

평발이다 have flat feet[fallen arches], be flat-footed

발볼이 넓다 have wide feet

칼발이다 have narrow feet

팔자걸음을 걷다
have duck feet(회화체),
walk with one's feet turned outward

발이 깨끗하다 one's feet are clean

발이 더럽다 one's feet are dirty

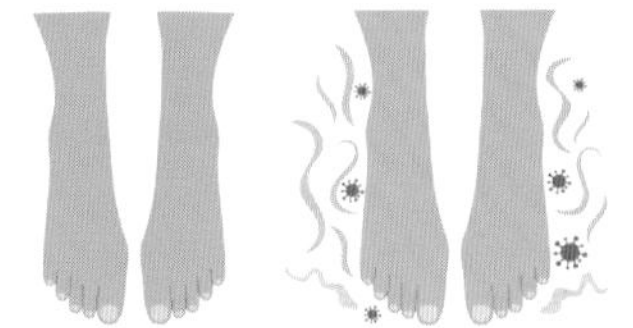

발뒤꿈치에 각질이 있다
have dead skin on one's heels

SENTENCES TO USE

그 모델은 키가 큰데 발은 작아요.
The model is tall, but her feet are small.

그녀는 엄마를 닮아서 평발이에요.
She has flat feet, just like her mother.

나는 발볼이 넓어서 내 치수보다 하나 더 큰 신발을 신어야 해요.
I have wide feet, so I have to wear one size larger.

우리 엄마는 팔자걸음을 걸어요. 걸음걸이를 교정해 보려고 했지만, 실패하셨죠.
My mom walks with her feet turned outward. She tried to fix it, but she failed.

나는 발뒤꿈치에 각질이 있어서 여름에는 여간 신경이 쓰이는 게 아니에요.
I have dead skin on my heels, which bothers me in the summer.

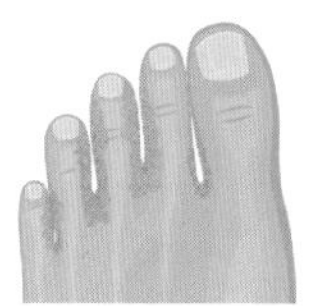

발에 무좀이 있다
have[suffer from] athlete's foot

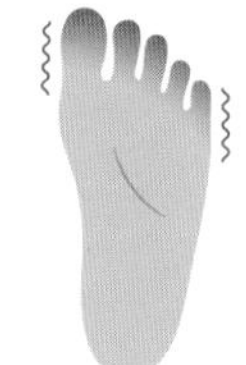

발에 동상이 걸렸다
have[suffer from] frostbite on one's foot

발가락

발가락에 털이 나 있다 have hair on one's toes

발톱이 길다
have long toenails,
one's toenails are long

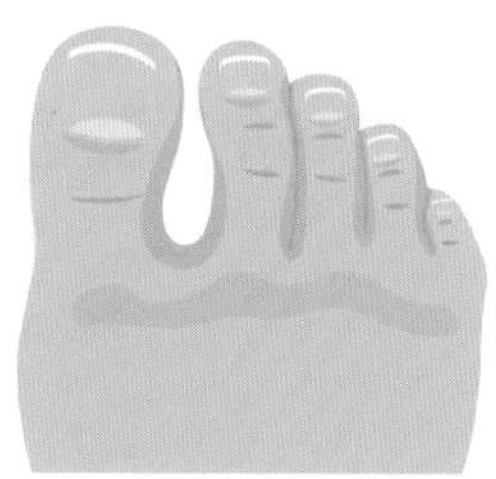

발톱이 짧다
have short toenails,
one's toenails are short

발톱 관리를 받다 have[get] a pedicure

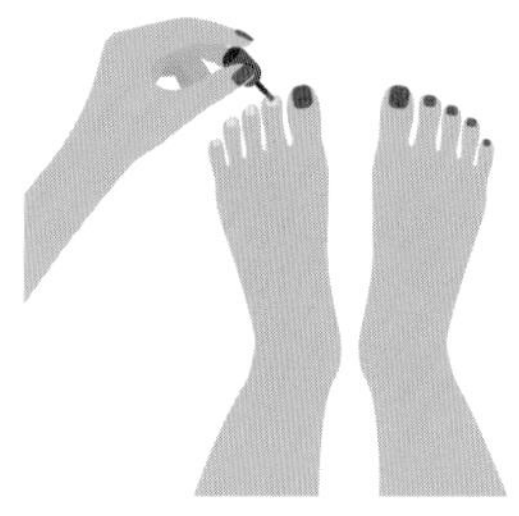

발톱에 (~색) 매니큐어를 칠하다
have one's toenails painted ~(색)

SENTENCES TO USE

그는 발에 무좀이 있어서 연고를 발라요. 하지만 효과가 없어요.
He has athlete's foot, so he applies ointment. But it doesn't help.

설산을 등반한 후로 발에 동상이 걸려서 고생 중입니다.
I am suffering from frostbite on my feet after climbing a snowy mountain.

발가락에 털이 나 있는 게 정상이야. 창피해하지 마.
It's normal to have hair on your toes. Don't be ashamed of it.

발톱이 길어서 자를 때가 됐네요.
My toenails are long, so it's time to clip them.

그 여자분은 발톱에 파란색 매니큐어를 칠하고 있었어요. 여름에 아주 잘 어울리는 것 같아요.
She had her toenails painted blue. I think they look great for summer.

MORE

MP3 019

발과 발가락 세부 명칭

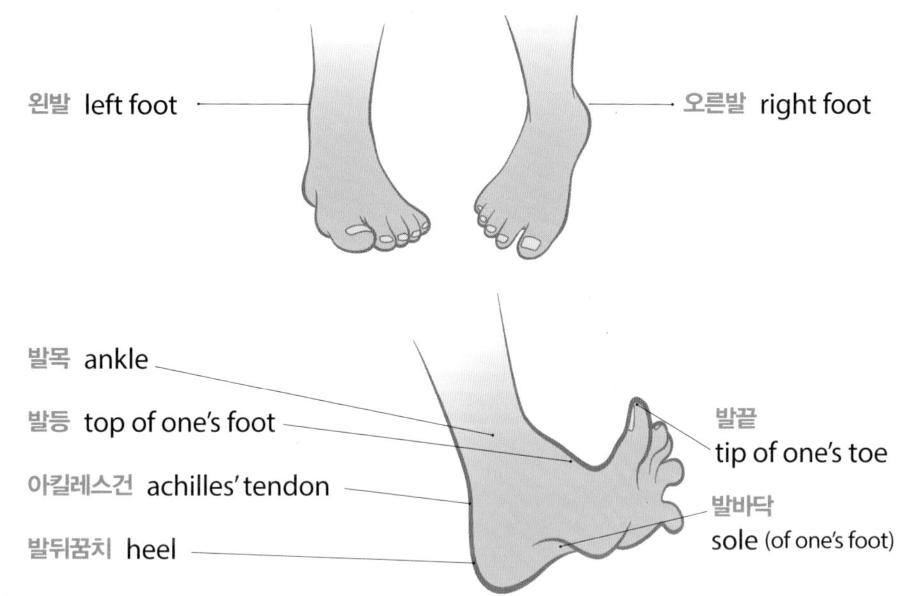
왼발 left foot
오른발 right foot
발목 ankle
발등 top of one's foot
아킬레스건 achilles' tendon
발뒤꿈치 heel
발끝
tip of one's toe
발바닥
sole (of one's foot)

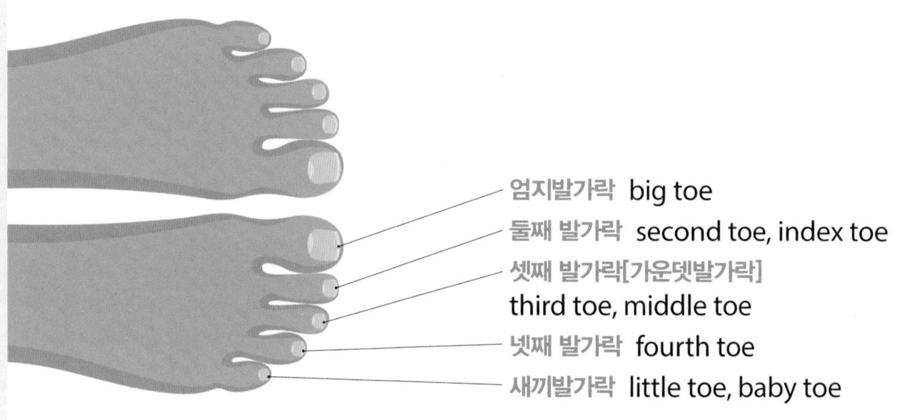
엄지발가락 big toe
둘째 발가락 second toe, index toe
셋째 발가락[가운뎃발가락]
third toe, middle toe
넷째 발가락 fourth toe
새끼발가락 little toe, baby toe

CHAPTER

4

건강과 질병

UNIT 1

생애 주기

나이가 ~살이다 be ~ years old

십 대/이십 대/삼십 대/사십 대 …다
be in one's teens/twenties/thirties/forties ...

젊다 be young

늙었다 be old

갓 태어났다, 갓난아기다 be newborn[just born],
be a newborn (baby)

태어난 지 ~일 됐다 be ~ days old, was[were] born ~ days ago

영유아기(에 있)다, 어린 아기다 be in (one's) infancy[babyhood]
* 젖먹이 시절부터 만 3세 정도까지

유년기(에 있)다 be in (one's) early childhood
* 생후 1년~1년 반부터 만 6세까지

아동기(에 있)다, 어린 시절이다 be in (one's) childhood
* 영아기부터 만 12세까지 포괄

SENTENCES TO USE

그 사람은 62세인데, (나이에 비해) 훨씬 젊어 보여요.
The man is 62 years old, but he looks much younger.

그 사람 부모님은 아마 50대일 거예요.
His parents are probably in their fifties.

그 부부가 병원에 데리고 온 아기는 갓난아기였어요.
The baby the couple brought to the hospital was a newborn.

그 사람 아기가 오늘로 태어난 지 123일이 됐어요. 그러니까 아직 어린 아기라는 거죠.
Her baby is 123 days old today, which means she is still in her infancy.

그 사람 막내딸은 유년기에 백혈병으로 세상을 떠났어요.
His youngest daughter died of leukemia in her early childhood.

청소년기다, 십 대다 be in one's adolescence

사춘기다 be going through puberty, be in[at] puberty

청년이다 be in one's youth, be a young man(남성에게)/woman(여성에게), be young people(주어가 복수일 때)

중년이다 be middle aged, be of middle age, be in the middle of one's life

(여성) 갱년기다 be going through menopause, be in menopause, be menopausal

(남성) 갱년기다 be going through andropause[male menopause], be in andropause[male menopause]

노년이다 be in one's old age

SENTENCES TO USE

우리 딸은 요즘 사춘기라 말을 거의 하지 않아요.
My daughter rarely talks these days because she's going through puberty.

어느새 내가 중년이 되었네요.
I've become middle aged before I knew it.

그녀는 갱년기여서 한겨울인데도 걸핏하면 땀이 나요.
She is going through menopause and sweats frequently, even in the middle of winter.

그 사람 요즘 남성 갱년기여서 자주 기분이 우울해져요.
He is going through andropause these days, so he often feels depressed.

그녀는 자신이 벌써 노년이라는 사실이 믿기지 않았어요.
She couldn't believe she was already in her old age.

UNIT 2

체력

건강하다 be healthy

건강하지 않다 be unhealthy[not healthy], be in poor health

체력이 강하다[좋다] be (physically) strong, have a strong body

체력이 약하다 be (physically) weak, have a weak body

컨디션이 좋다 be in good shape[condition], feel well

컨디션[몸]이 안 좋다 be in bad shape[condition], be out of condition, don't feel well, be unwell

기운이[에너지가, 활기가] 넘치다 be full of energy[life], be in high spirits, be energetic

기운이 없다 have no energy, be out of energy, be in low spirits, feel low

SENTENCES TO USE

그의 할머니는 87세이신데 여전히 건강하세요.
His grandmother is 87 years old and still healthy.

그는 어려서부터 체력이 약했어요.
He has been physically weak since childhood.

오늘 컨디션이 영 안 좋네요. 점심은 건너뛸게요.
I'm not feeling very well today. I will skip lunch.

앨리스는 언제 봐도 에너지가 넘쳐요. 비결이 뭘까요?
Alice is always full of energy. What's her secret?

그녀는 그 수술을 받은 뒤로 몇 달째 기운이 없었어요.
She had no energy for several months after the surgery.

(~로) 몸이 아프다 be sick[ill, unwell] (with ~)

(피로 등으로) 몸이 무겁다 feel heavy

몸이 가뿐하다[가볍다] feel light

나른하다 feel listless[lethargic, drowsy]
* drowsy는 특히 나른하고 졸린 상태를 뜻함

피곤하다 be tired

몹시 지치다, 진이 빠지다, 기진맥진하다
be exhausted[worn out]
* worn out이 좀 더 회화체

몸이 붇다, 살이 찌다
gain weight, put on weight

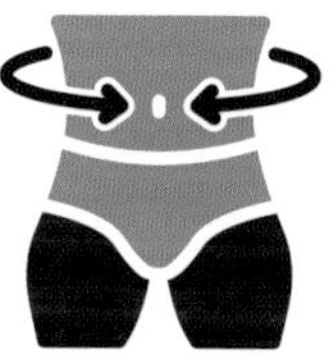

살이 빠지다
lose weight

몸이 마르다 get thinner, become leaner

몸이 유연하다 have a flexible[supple, lithe] body
* supple, lithe는 격식체 느낌

몸이 뻣뻣하다 be stiff

SENTENCES TO USE

오늘 아침에 일어났을 때부터 몸이 계속 무겁네요.
I've been feeling heavy since I woke up this morning.

어젯밤에 잘 잤더니 오늘은 몸이 가벼워요.
I slept well last night and I feel light today.

온종일 어린 조카를 돌봤더니 진이 빠졌어요.
I'm exhausted from taking care of my young nephew all day.

40이 넘으면서 그는 몸이 불었어요.
When he turned 40, he gained weight.

그녀는 몸이 유연해서 요가도 아주 잘해요.
She has a flexible body and is very good at yoga.

UNIT 3

생리 현상

졸리다
be sleepy[drowsy]

하품이 나다
yawn

머리에 기름이 끼어 있다 one's hair is oily[greasy]

머리에 비듬이 있다 have dandruff

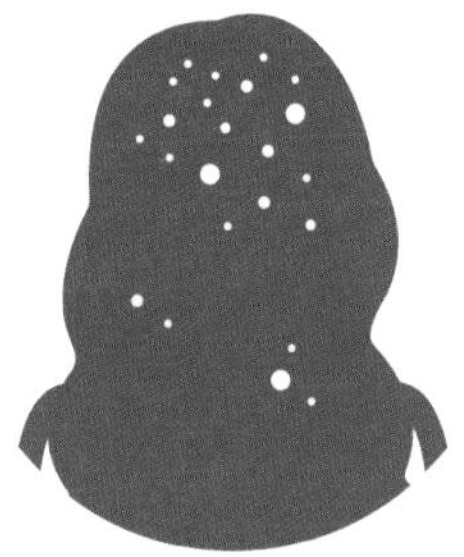

땀이 나다
sweat, perspire (격식체)

얼굴이 붉어지다 blush, flush, one's face turns[gets, becomes] red, get[become] red in the face

눈물이 나다[글썽거리다] have[get] tears in one's eyes

눈곱이 끼다 have sleep in one's eyes

귀지가 끼다 have earwax, have wax in one's ears

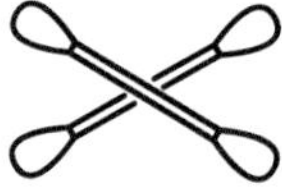

SENTENCES TO USE

저는 편두통이 심할 때는 하품이 계속 납니다.
I keep yawning when I have a severe migraine.

그는 머리를 매일 감지만 늘 머리에 기름이 끼어 있어요.
His hair is always greasy even though he washes it every day.

나는 머리에 비듬이 있어서 요즘은 검은색 옷을 입지 않아요.
I avoid wearing black clothes these days because I have dandruff.

나는 갱년기라서 얼굴이 자주 붉어져요.
My face often turns red because I'm going through menopause.

우리 고양이 눈에 눈곱이 끼어 있어서 떼어 주었어요.
My cat had sleep in her eyes, so I wiped it from her eyes.

콧물이 나다 have[get] a runny nose

코딱지가 끼어 있다 have a booger in one's nose

* booger는 속어지만 일상에서 흔히 쓰임

코를 골다 snore

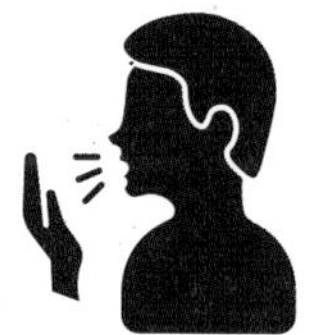

침을 흘리다
drool, dribble

입 냄새가 나다
have bad[foul] breath

재채기가 나다 sneeze

기침이 나다 cough, have a cough

목에 가래가 끓다, 가래가 끼어 있다
have some phlegm (stuck) in one's throat

트림하다
burp, belch

SENTENCES TO USE

나는 찬바람을 쐬면 콧물이 나요.
I get a runny nose when I'm exposed to cold wind.

그는 입 냄새가 나는데, 그것이 큰 고민이에요.
He has bad breath, which is a significant problem for him.

나는 매운 음식 냄새를 맡으면 재채기가 나요.
Smelling spicy food makes me sneeze.

그 남자가 말하는데 목에 가래가 끼었더라고요.
The man had some phlegm stuck in his throat as he spoke.

남들과 식사하는 중에 트림하는 건 무례한 거죠.
It is rude to burp while eating with others.

UNIT 3

(~에) 사레가 들리다 choke on ~,
~ go down the wrong pipe

딸꾹질이 나다 have[get] (the) hiccups, hiccup

배가 부르다 be full

배가 고프다 be hungry

배에 가스가 차다
have gas, be gassy

방귀가 나오다
pass gas, break wind, fart (속어)

소변이 마렵다 need to go to the bathroom,
need to do[make, go] number one,
need to pee[urinate]

* number one: 소변

대변이 마렵다 need to go to the bathroom,
need to do[make, go] number two,
need to have a bowel movement (의학적/공적 표현)

* number two: 대변

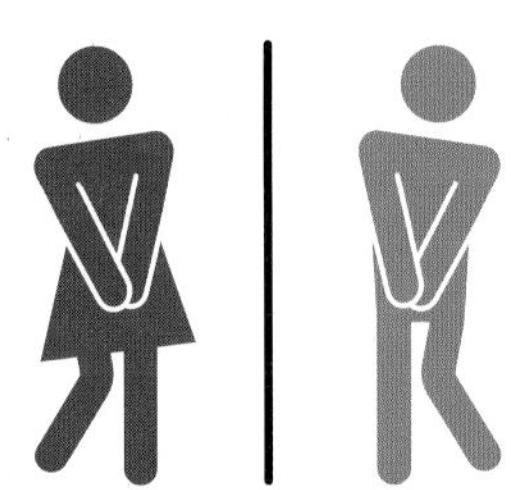

SENTENCES TO USE

그는 물을 마시다가 사레가 들렸어요.
He choked on water while drinking it.

미사 중에 딸꾹질이 났는데 한동안 멈추지를 않더라고요.
I had hiccups during Mass and they didn't stop for a while.

나는 돼지고기를 먹을 때마다 배에 가스가 차고 설사할 때도 많아요.
Every time I eat pork, I have gas and often have diarrhea.

무엇 때문인지 오늘은 방귀가 자주 나오네요.
For some reason, I've been passing gas a lot today.

커피를 마셨더니 금방 소변이 마려웠어요.
After drinking coffee, I immediately needed to go to the bathroom.

UNIT

4 통증과 증상

통증

MP3 023-1

(신체 부위)가 아프다 have[experience, suffer from] a pain in ~, one's ~ ache(s)[hurt(s)]

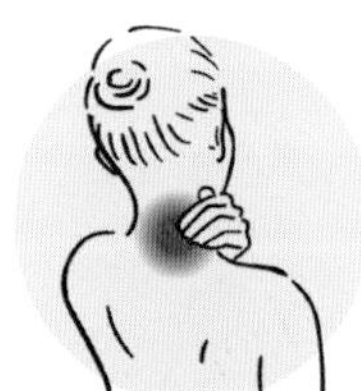

뒷목이 아프다(목 근육) have[experience, suffer from] a pain in one's neck, one's neck aches[hurts]

목이 아프다(목구멍) have a sore throat

어깨가 아프다 have[experience, suffer from] a pain in one's shoulders, one's shoulders ache[hurt]

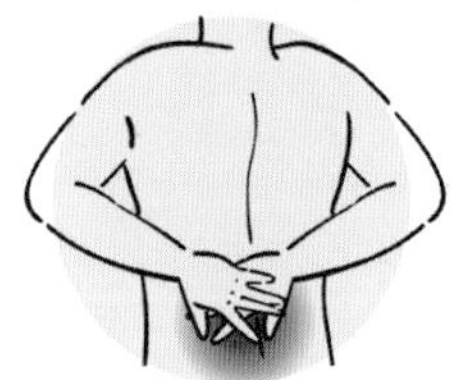

허리가 아프다 have[experience, suffer from] a pain in one's back, one's back aches[hurts], have a backache

다리가 아프다 have[experience, suffer from] a pain in one's legs, one's legs ache[hurt]

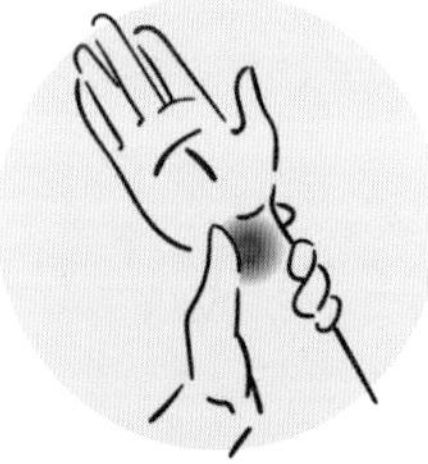

손목이 아프다
have[experience, suffer from] a pain in one's wrist, one's wrist aches[hurts]

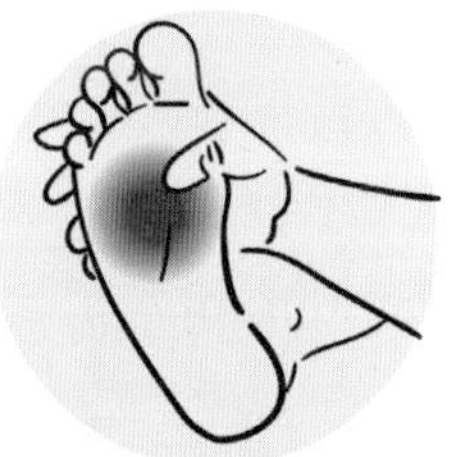

발바닥이 아프다
have[experience, suffer from] a pain in the soles of one's feet, the soles of one's feet ache[hurt]

SENTENCES TO USE

그녀는 감기로 며칠째 목이 아파요.
She has had a sore throat for several days because of a cold.

나는 매일 컴퓨터로 여러 시간 작업을 해서 자주 어깨가 아파요.
I work on the computer for many hours every day, so my shoulders often ache.

그들은 밭에서 몇 시간 동안 일해서 허리가 아파요.
Their backs ache from working in the fields for hours.

그는 오래 서 있었더니 지금 다리가 아파요.
He's been standing for a long time and now his legs hurt.

5시간 가까이 걸었더니 발바닥이 아팠어요.
After walking for nearly five hours, the soles of my feet were aching.

UNIT 4

~ 통증이 있다 have[experience, suffer from] (a) -ache

머리가 아프다, 두통이 있다
have[experience, suffer from] a headache

편두통이 있다, 편두통을 앓다
have[experience, suffer from] (a) migraine

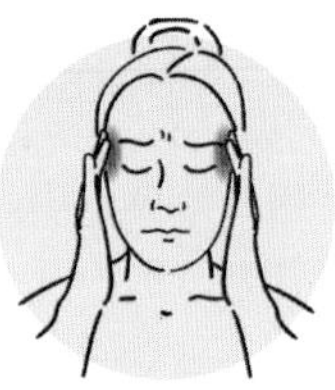

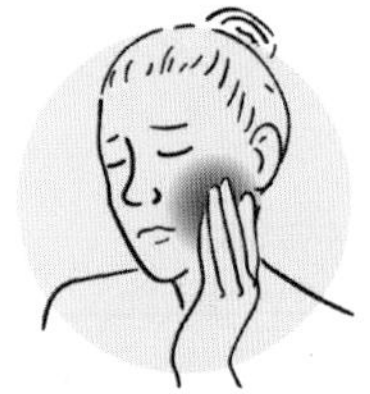

이가 아프다, 치통이 있다
have[experience, suffer from] (a) toothache
* 미국 영어에서는 a를 붙이고, 영국 영어에서는 안 붙이는 게 일반적

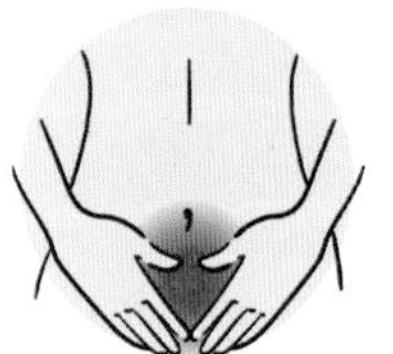

배가 아프다, 복통이 있다
have[experience, suffer from] (a) stomachache
* 미국 영어에서는 a를 붙이고, 영국 영어에서는 안 붙이는 게 일반적

생리통이 있다 have[experience, suffer from] menstrual pain[period pain, (menstrual) cramps]

근육통이 있다
have[experience, suffer from] muscle[muscular] pain, have sore muscles

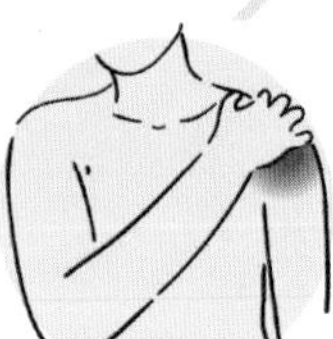

SENTENCES TO USE

그녀는 십 대 초반부터 편두통을 앓아 왔어요.
She has suffered from migraines since her early teens.

우리 아들은 어젯밤부터 이가 아픈데, 어떤 약도 안 듣는 것 같아요.
My son has had a toothache since last night, and no medicine seems to work.

그녀는 생리통이 심해서 꼭 진통제를 먹어야 해요.
She has severe menstrual pain and needs to take a painkiller.

그는 건설 현장에서 일해서 늘 근육통이 있어요.
He works on construction sites and always experiences muscle pain.

다양한 통증

MP3 023-2

~가 아프다, 쑤시다
~ hurt,
~ ache (지속적이고 강한 통증이 느껴지는 것),
~ be sore (주로 근육이 아픈 것)

~가 욱신거리다, 지끈거리다
~ throb, ~ ache

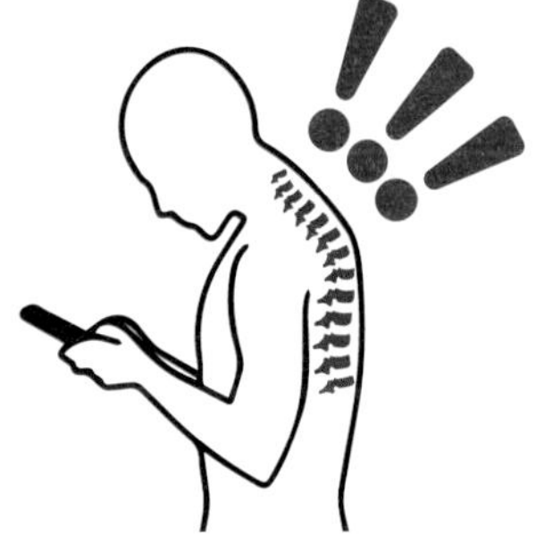

~가 뻐근하다
~ feel stiff,
feel stiff in ~,
have (a) stiff ~

~가 화끈거리다
~ burn

(피부, 목, 눈 등)이 따갑다, 쓰라리다, 따끔거리다
~ sting (주어가 따갑게 만든다는 뜻으로도 쓰임),
~ smart (주로 영국에서 쓰임), ~ prickle

~가 찌릿하다
feel[have] a twinge in one's ~

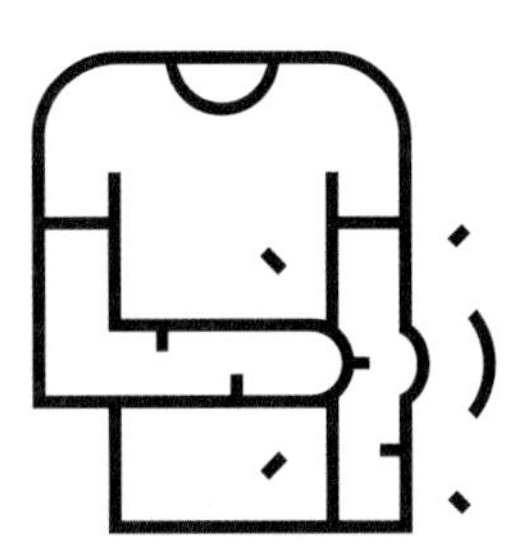

~가 가렵다
~ itch,
have an itch on ~,
~ get[become] itchy (가려움이 시작되는 느낌)

SENTENCES TO USE

어제 새 구두를 신고 걸었더니 발이 아팠어요.
My feet hurt from walking in new shoes yesterday.

그 사람에게서 온 문자 메시지를 읽으니 머리가 지끈거렸어요.
Reading the text message from that person made my head throb.

갱년기 때문인지 가끔 얼굴이 화끈거려요.
Maybe because of menopause, my face sometimes burns.

찬물을 대면 화상 부위가 따가워요.
My burn stings when I put cold water on it.

겨울이면 날씨가 건조해서 내 피부도 건조해지고 가려워집니다.
In winter, the weather is dry, so my skin becomes dry and itchy.

After walking for nearly five hours, **the soles of my feet were aching.**

증상

MP3 023-3

어지럽다, 현기증이 나다
be[feel] dizzy[light-headed]

숨이 차다 be out of breath, be[feel] breathless

호흡이 곤란하다, 숨 쉬기가 힘들다
have trouble breathing, it's hard to breathe

심장이 두근거리다 one's heart is pounding

가슴이 답답하다 feel heavy[stuffy, tight] in one's[the] chest

가슴[심장]에 통증이 있다
have[feel, suffer from] chest pain,
have[feel, suffer from] pain in one's[the] chest

* have와 suffer from은 지속성과 심각성을 띠지만, feel은 단순히 통증을 지각한 것을 강조

얼굴[안색]이 창백하다 look pale, have a pale complexion

열이 나다[있다] have a fever

고열이 나다 have a high fever

미열이 있다 have a slight[mild] fever

SENTENCES TO USE

쭈그리고 앉아 있다 일어나면 현기증이 나요.
I feel dizzy when I stand up from squatting.

그 약을 먹고 나니 심장이 막 두근거려요. 부작용인가요?
My heart is pounding after taking the medicine. Is it a side effect?

그 남자는 가슴에 통증을 느껴서 911을 불렀어요.
The man felt chest pain and called 911.

응급실에 방금 들어온 환자는 안색이 무척 창백해요.
The patient who just entered the emergency room looks very pale.

코로나19를 앓았을 때 그녀는 섭씨 40도 가까이 고열이 났어요.
When she had COVID-19, she had a high fever of nearly 40 degrees Celsius.

UNIT 4

오한이 나다, 한기가 들다 have[feel, get] a chill[chills], feel[be] chilly

손/발이 차다 have cold hands/feet, one's hands/feet are cold

손이 떨리다 one's hands tremble[shake]

* tremble은 미세하게 떠는 것, shake는 눈에 띌 정도로 떠는 것을 의미

손/발이 저리다 one's hands/feet are numb

식은땀이 나다, 식은땀을 흘리다 break out in a cold sweat

혈압이 떨어지다/오르다 one's blood pressure drops/rises[goes up]

(눈이나 얼굴이) 붓다 be swollen

구역질이 나다, 토할 것 같다 feel sick, feel like throwing up, feel nauseous (의학적 느낌)

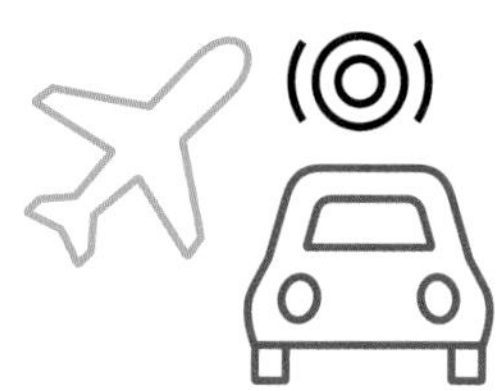

(차)멀미가 나다 get[feel] carsick, have[get] carsickness[motion sickness]

* motion sickness는 차멀미를 비롯해 뱃멀미, 비행기 멀미 등 모든 탈것으로 인한 멀미를 나타냄

SENTENCES TO USE

나는 몸이 아프면 먼저 오한이 나고 그다음에 열이 심하게 오릅니다.
When I get sick, first I have a chill and then a bad fever.

그녀는 늘 손발이 차가워요. 의사들은 혈액 순환이 잘 안 돼서 그렇다고 해요.
Her hands and feet are always cold. Doctors say it's because of poor circulation.

그는 악몽을 꾸며 식은땀을 흘렸어요.
He had a nightmare and broke out in a cold sweat.

그녀는 그 이야기를 들으니 혈압이 오르는 것 같았어요.
She felt her blood pressure rise when she heard that story.

택시를 탔더니 멀미가 나서 토할 것 같았어요.
I got carsick when I took a taxi and felt like throwing up.

식욕이 없다 have no appetite

소화가 안 되다 can't digest,
have[suffer from] indigestion,
have trouble[difficulty] digesting

목마르다, 갈증이 나다 be[feel] thirsty

소변이 잘 나오지 않다
have trouble[difficulty] urinating

소변을 너무 자주 보다
urinate too frequently

소변 색이 뿌옇다 have cloudy[hazy] urine,
one's urine is cloudy[hazy]

혈뇨를 보다 have blood in one's urine[pee],
have[get] hematuria (hematuria: 혈뇨)

소변에 거품이 많다 have a lot of foam in one's urine,
have foamy urine, one's urine is foamy

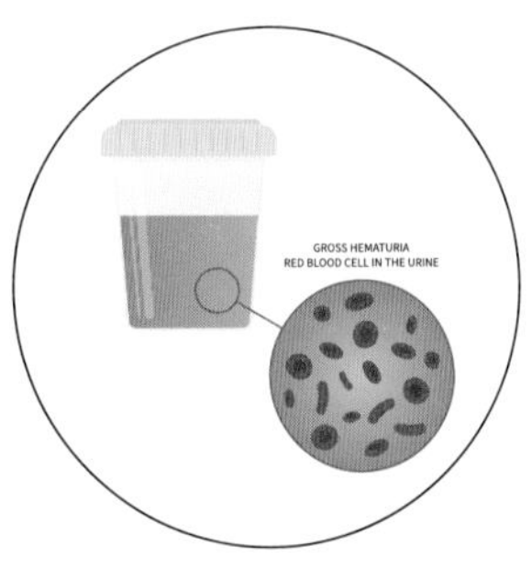

SENTENCES TO USE

그녀는 여름이면 식욕이 없어서 살이 빠지는 편이에요.
She has no appetite in summer and tends to lose weight.

나는 편두통이 있을 때는 속이 메스껍고 소화가 안 돼서 아무것도 먹을 수가 없어요.
When I have a migraine, I feel sick and have indigestion so I can't eat anything.

얼마 전부터 소변 색이 뿌예서 좀 걱정이에요.
I'm a little worried because my urine has been cloudy for a while now.

그는 혈뇨를 봐서 병원에 갔어요.
He went to the hospital because he had blood in his urine.

소변에 거품이 많으면 단백질이 많이 들어 있다는 뜻일 수도 있어요.
A lot of foam in the urine could indicate a high level of protein.

장이 안 좋다, 장에 문제가 있다 have bowel trouble

변비다, 대변을 잘 못 보다 be constipated,
have[suffer from] constipation,
have trouble[difficulty] defecating

설사하다 have diarrhea

혈변을 보다 have bloody stool

피부 발진이 나다 have[suffer from] a skin rash

피부가 가렵다 one's skin itches,
one's skin is itchy

잠이 오지 않다, 불면증이 있다 can't sleep(회화체),
have[suffer from] insomnia(insomnia: 불면증),
be an insomniac(insomniac: 불면증 환자)

갑자기 체중이 줄다 lose weight suddenly

만성 피로가 있다, 만성 피로에 시달리다
have[suffer from] chronic fatigue,
be chronically fatigued

SENTENCES TO USE

혈변을 봤다면 최대한 빨리 병원에 가는 게 좋아요.
If you have bloody stool, you should go to the hospital as soon as possible.

그는 얼마 전부터 온몸에 피부 발진이 나서 고생 중이에요.
He has been suffering from a skin rash all over his body for some time now.

그녀는 5년 넘게 불면증으로 고생하고 있어요.
She has been suffering from insomnia for more than five years.

갑자기 체중이 줄어서 좀 걱정이에요.
I'm a little worried because I have lost weight suddenly.

요즘 많은 사람들이 만성 피로에 시달리고 있어요.
These days, many people suffer from chronic fatigue.

UNIT 5

질병

MP3 024

~(병)이 있다, ~(병)에 걸리다
have ~, suffer from ~

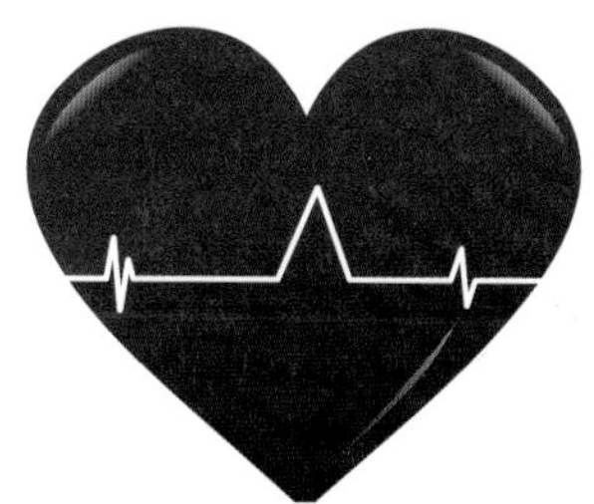

지병[고질병]이 있다, 지병[고질병]으로 고생이다
have[suffer from] a chronic disease[illness]

지병[고질병]인 ~가 있다, 지병[고질병]인 ~로 고생이다
have[suffer from] chronic ~, suffer chronically from ~, be a chronic sufferer of ~

감기에 걸리다
have[get, catch] a cold

독감에 걸리다
have[get] the flu, come down with the flu

코로나19에 걸리다
have[get] COVID-19, be[get] infected with COVID-19

폐렴에 걸리다
have[get, catch, suffer from] pneumonia

성인병[생활습관병]이 있다
have[suffer from] a lifestyle disease

암에 걸리다
have[get, suffer from] cancer

정신 질환이 있다
have[suffer from] a mental illness[disease]

SENTENCES TO USE

나이 60이 넘으면, 보통 지병 한두 가지는 있지요.
When you are over 60, you usually have one or two chronic diseases.

나는 고질병인 편두통으로 고생합니다. 정말 지긋지긋해요.
I suffer from chronic migraines. I'm so tired of dealing with them.

한여름인데 그는 감기에 걸렸어요.
It's midsummer, and he has a cold.

나는 지난여름에 코로나19에 걸렸어요. 예상과 달리 증상이 심하지 않았어요.
I got COVID-19 last summer. Unlike what I had expected, it was mild.

잘사는 나라일수록 더 많은 사람들이 생활습관병을 앓아요.
The more prosperous the country, the more people suffer from lifestyle diseases.

UNIT 5

고혈압이다, 혈압이 높다
have[suffer from] high blood pressure

당뇨병이다
have[suffer from] diabetes,
be diabetic

(공복) 혈당이 높다
one's (fasting) blood sugar level is high

고지혈증이다
have[suffer from] (a) high (blood) cholesterol (level) * level을 붙일 때는 관사 a 사용,
one's (blood) cholesterol level is high

심장병[심장질환]이 있다 have[suffer from] heart disease

배탈이 나다, 소화불량이다
have[suffer from] indigestion

위장병[위병]이 있다
have[suffer from] a stomach disease[disorder]

장질환이 있다
have[suffer from] a bowel disease

과민대장증후군이다
have[suffer from] irritable bowel syndrome (IBS)

변비가 있다
be constipated, have[suffer from] constipation

SENTENCES TO USE

그녀는 아버지를 닮아서 고혈압이 있어요.
She has high blood pressure just like her father.

우리 엄마는 70대 중반부터 당뇨병을 앓고 계세요.
My mother has been suffering from diabetes since her mid-70s.

우리 엄마는 40대 때부터 심장병을 앓고 있어요.
My mother has had heart disease since she was in her 40s.

나는 과민대장증후군이라 스트레스를 받으면 설사를 해요.
I have irritable bowel syndrome, so I have diarrhea when I get stressed out.

그녀는 어렸을 때부터 변비였어요.
She has had constipation since she was a child.

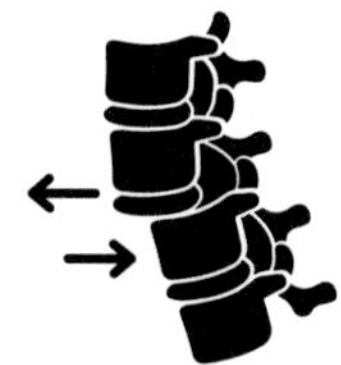

허리 디스크다[추간판 탈출증이다]
have[suffer from] a slipped disc[a herniated disc]
* herniated disc가 더 의학적이고 정확한 표현

관절염이 있다 have[suffer from] arthritis

비염이 있다 have[suffer from] rhinitis

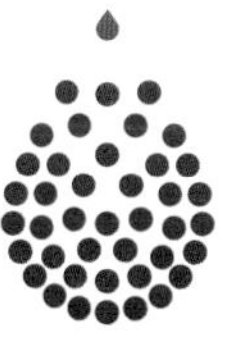

빈혈이다 have[suffer from] anemia, be anemic

비만이다 be overweight, be obese
* overweight는 BMI(체질량) 지수 25~29.9 사이, obese는 30 이상을 의미

우울증이다 have[suffer from] depression[depressive disorder]

불면증이다 have[suffer from] insomnia, be an insomniac

수면장애가 있다 have[suffer from] a sleep disorder

~에 문제가 있다 have trouble with ~

~을 다치다 injure ~, hurt ~,
have an injury on ~(더 격식을 갖춘 표현)

~로 치료를 받다 receive treatment for ~,
be treated for ~

~에 수술을 받다
have an operation for 질병·상처[on 신체 부위],
undergo surgery for 질병·상처[on 신체 부위]

SENTENCES TO USE

많은 사람이 비염이 있는데, 이게 삶의 질에 크게 영향을 끼칠 수가 있어요.
Many people have rhinitis and it can significantly impact their quality of life.

우울증을 앓는 사람들 수가 해마다 늘고 있습니다.
The number of people suffering from depression is increasing every year.

그는 계단에서 넘어져서 얼굴을 다쳤어요.
He fell down the stairs and injured his face.

그녀는 당뇨로 10년 넘게 치료를 받고 있어요.
She has been receiving treatment for diabetes for over 10 years.

그녀의 어머니는 작년에 척추관 협착증으로 수술을 받으셨어요.
Her mother underwent surgery for spinal stenosis last year.

각종 질병

* 동사 have를 쓰면 중립적인 의미를, suffer from을 쓰면 그 병을 앓아서 힘들다는 의미를 내포함
* suffer from이 아니라 suffer를 쓰는 경우가 있으니 유의

성인병[생활습관병]을 앓다 have[suffer from] a lifestyle disease

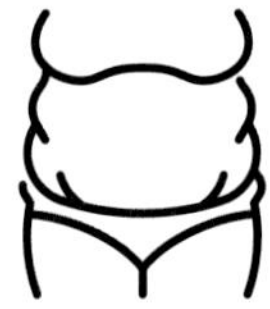

유전병을 앓다 have[suffer from] a genetic disease

고혈압이다 have[suffer from] high blood pressure

당뇨병이다 have[suffer from] diabetes, be diabetic

고지혈증을 앓다 have[suffer from] hyperlipidemia, have[suffer from] (a) high (blood) cholesterol (level) * level을 붙일 때는 관사 a를 사용

심장질환을 앓다 have[suffer from] heart disease

심혈관질환을 앓다 have[suffer from] cardiovascular disease

심장판막증을 앓다 have[suffer from] heart valve disease

부정맥을 앓다 have[suffer from] an arrhythmia

협심증을 앓다 have[suffer from] angina

심근경색을 일으키다 have[suffer (from)] a myocardial infarction

심부전(증)을 앓다 have[suffer from] cardiac insufficiency[heart failure]

심장마비를 일으키다 have[suffer] (a) cardiac arrest[a heart attack]

폐렴을 앓다 have[suffer from] pneumonia

결핵을 앓다 have[suffer from] tuberculosis

뇌경색을 일으키다 have[suffer from] a cerebral infarction

뇌출혈을 일으키다 have[suffer] a cerebral[brain] hemorrhage

뇌졸중을 일으키다 have a stroke

갑상선 질환을 앓다 have[suffer from] thyroid disease

위장병을 앓다 have[suffer from] a stomach disease[disorder]

위염을 앓다 have[suffer from] gastritis

MP3 025

위궤양을 앓다 have[suffer from] a stomach ulcer

간염을 앓다 have[suffer from] hepatitis

간경화를 앓다 have[suffer from] (liver) cirrhosis

신장질환을 앓다 have[suffer from kidney disease

신부전(증)을 앓다 have[suffer from] kidney insufficiency[failure]

* kidney insufficiency는 신장 기능이 떨어진 것을, kidney failure는 신장 기능이 거의 상실된 것을 의미

장염을 앓다 have[suffer from] enteritis

알레르기성 비염을 앓다 have[suffer from] allergic rhinitis

허리 디스크를 앓다 have[suffer from] a slipped disc[a herniated disc]

목 디스크를 앓다 have[suffer from] a herniated cervical disc

관절염을 앓다 have[suffer from] arthritis

신경통을 앓다 have[suffer from] neuralgia

골다공증이다 have[suffer from] osteoporosis

담석증을 앓다 have[suffer from] gallstones

신장결석이 있다 have[suffer from] kidney stones

요로결석이 있다 have[suffer from] urinary stones

우울증을 앓다 have[suffer from] depression[depressive disorder]

조울증을 앓다 have[suffer from] bipolar disorder [manic-depressive disorder]

불안장애를 앓다 have[suffer from] anxiety disorder

공황장애를 앓다 have[suffer from] panic disorder

조현병을 앓다 have[suffer from] schizophrenia

치매를 앓다 have[suffer from] dementia

MORE

양성 종양이다 have[suffer from] a benign tumor

악성 종양이다 have[suffer from] a malignant tumor

뇌종양이다 have[suffer from] a brain tumor

뇌암에 걸리다 have[suffer from] brain cancer * 뇌암: 악성 뇌종양

후두암에 걸리다 have[suffer from] laryngeal cancer

두경부암에 걸리다 have[suffer from] head and neck cancer

구강암에 걸리다 have[suffer from] oral cancer

식도암에 걸리다 have[suffer from] esophageal cancer

갑상선암에 걸리다 have[suffer from] thyroid cancer

폐암에 걸리다 have[suffer from] lung cancer

유방암에 걸리다 have[suffer from] breast cancer

위암에 걸리다 have[suffer from] stomach cancer[gastric cancer]

간암에 걸리다 have[suffer from] liver cancer

췌장암에 걸리다 have[suffer from] pancreatic cancer

신장암에 걸리다 have[suffer from] kidney cancer

자궁암에 걸리다 have[suffer from] uterine cancer

난소암에 걸리다 have[suffer from] ovarian cancer

자궁경부암에 걸리다 have[suffer from] cervical cancer

전립선암에 걸리다 have[suffer from] prostate cancer

대장암에 걸리다 have[suffer from] colorectal cancer

직장암에 걸리다 have[suffer from] rectal cancer

백혈병[혈액암]에 걸리다 have[suffer from] leukemia[blood cancer]

피부암에 걸리다 have[suffer from] skin cancer

UNIT 6

두뇌 상태

머리가 좋다, 똑똑하다
be smart[intelligent, bright],
have brains

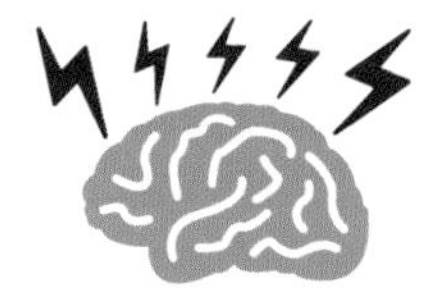

머리가 잘 돌아가다, 두뇌 회전이 빠르다
be quick-witted,
have quick wits[quick perception]

~하는 센스가 있다 have a good sense of ~

눈치가 빠르다 be good at reading the room,
be good at reading people, be tactful

머리가 나쁘다 be not smart, be slow of understanding,
be slow at learning, be stupid, have no brains

* have no brains는 모욕적인 느낌을 주니 사용에 주의.
not smart와 slow of understanding이 덜 공격적인 느낌

이해가 느리다, 머리가 둔하다 be slow-witted
[dim-witted], have slow wits

~하는 센스가 없다 have a poor sense of ~

눈치가 없다 be bad at reading the room,
be bad at reading people, be tactless

* tactless는 눈치 없이 상대의 기분을 상하게 하는 말을 하는 것

SENTENCES TO USE

매튜는 머리도 좋고 근면 성실해요. 믿어도 돼요.
Matthew is smart and diligent. You can trust him.

그는 진짜 두뇌 회전이 빨라서 늘 재미있는 이야기를 생각해 낸답니다.
He is really quick-witted, so he always thinks of funny things to say.

그녀는 패션 센스가 있어서 옷을 잘 입어요.
She has a good sense of fashion, so she dresses well.

그 사람은 머리가 나쁘고 눈치가 없어서 함께 일하려면 답답해요.
He is slow of understanding and bad at reading the room, so it's frustrating to work with him.

그녀는 눈치가 없어서 실수로 사람들을 모욕하는 경우가 잦아요.
She is tactless, so she often insults people by mistake.

UNIT 6

머리가 맑다
have a clear head,
one's head is clear

머리가 멍하다, 집중이 잘 안 되다
be in a daze, one's brain is[feels] foggy, suffer from brain fog
* brain fog(뇌 흐림): 과로, 수면 부족, 스트레스 등으로 생기는 집중력 부족 현상

머리가 무겁다 one's head feels heavy

머리가 안 돌아가다
one's head[brain] isn't working, one's head[brain] is slow, feel stupid

기억력이 좋다 have (a) good[long] memory

깜박깜박하다, 건망증이 심하다
forget things, have an awful memory, have a memory[mind] like a sieve

딴 데 정신이 팔려 있다, 넋이 나가 있다 be absent-minded

정신이 없다, 제정신이 아니다
be beside oneself, be out of one's mind, be not clear-headed

SENTENCES TO USE

어젯밤에 푹 잤더니 오늘은 머리가 맑아요.
I slept well last night, so my head is clear today.

어제 잠을 1시간밖에 못 잤더니 머리가 무거워요.
My head feels heavy because I only got an hour of sleep last night.

졸려서 그런가 지금 머리가 안 돌아가네요.
Maybe because I'm sleepy, my brain isn't working.

저는 최근 들어서 건망증이 심해요. 설마, 치매는 아니겠죠?
I've been forgetting things lately. Surely, it's not dementia, right?

충격적인 소식을 들어서 내가 지금 정신이 없네요.
Hearing the shocking news, I'm beside myself right now.

UNIT 7

장애

MP3 027

장애 일반

MP3 027-1

장애가 있다, 장애인이다 be a person with a disability(더 존중하는 느낌의 표현), have a disability

장애의 정도가 심하다, 중증 장애인이다
be a person with a severe disability, have a severe disability

장애의 정도가 심하지 않다, 경증 장애인이다
be a person with a moderate[mild] disability, have a moderate[mild] disability

신체 장애가 있다 be a person with a physical disability, have a physical disability

정신 장애가 있다 be a person with a mental disability, have a mental disability

지적 장애가 있다 be a person with an intellectual disability, have an intellectual disability

선천적인 장애인이다 be a person with a congenital disability, have a disability since birth

후천적인 장애인이다, 후천적으로 장애를 입다 be a person with an acquired disability, have an acquired disability

SENTENCES TO USE

2020년 기준, 장애가 있는 사람이 한국 전체 인구의 5.1%였습니다.
As of 2020, people with disabilities make up 5.1% of the total population of South Korea.

그의 어머님은 신체 장애가 있지만 늘 낙천적이세요.
His mother has a physical disability. However, she is always optimistic.

그 교수 부부의 딸은 지적 장애가 있어요.
The professor couple's daughter is a person with an intellectual disability.

누구나 후천적인 장애인이 될 수 있습니다.
Anyone can have an acquired disability.

신체적 장애

MP3 027-2

* 118~119쪽의 cannot은 모두 be unable to로 바꿔 쓸 수 있으며, be unable to가 cannot보다 더 온건한 표현

지체(肢體) 장애가 있다 have a physical disability, be a person with a physical disability

오른손/왼손/양손을 못 쓰다 cannot use one's right hand/left hand/hands, lose the use of one's right hand/left hand/hands (사건의 결과를 강조)

걷지 못하다 cannot walk

(오른쪽/왼쪽) 다리를 절다 limp (on the right/left leg)

소아마비를 앓다 have[suffer from] polio

* suffer from은 지금도 고난이 지속된다는 의미를 내포

소아마비로 불구가 되다 be affected[disabled] by polio

* be crippled by polio는 구식이고 공격적인 느낌으로, 쓰지 않는 게 좋음

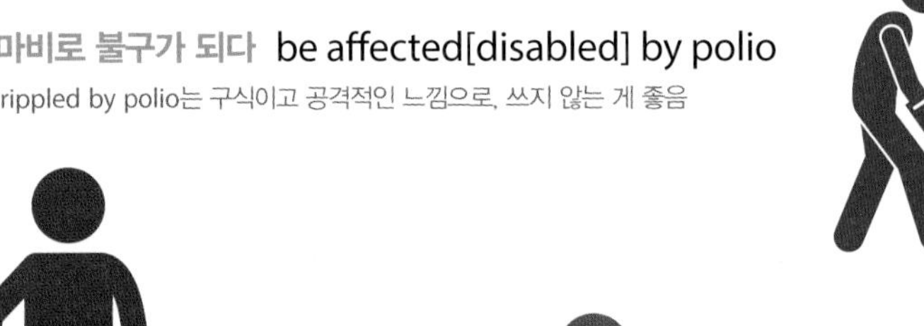

SENTENCES TO USE

그 노인은 뇌졸중으로 왼손을 못 쓰고 왼쪽 다리를 절어요.
The old man can't use his left hand and limps on his left leg due to a stroke.

그 여성은 어렸을 때 소아마비를 앓아서 한쪽 다리를 절었어요.
The woman had polio as a child, which caused her to limp on one leg.

뇌성마비를 앓다 have[suffer from] cerebral palsy

뇌병변 장애가 있다 have a brain lesion

앞을 보지 못하다 be blind, cannot see

시각 장애가 있다
have a visual disability[impairment],
be a person with a visual disability

* 이 표현들은 앞을 전혀 보지 못하는 것부터 어느 정도 볼 수 있는 것까지 포괄

듣지 못하다 be deaf, cannot hear

청각 장애가 있다
have a hearing disability[impairment],
be a person with a hearing disability

* 이 표현들은 소리를 전혀 듣지 못하는 것부터 어느 정도 들을 수 있는 것까지 포괄

말을 못하다 cannot speak, be mute

언어 장애가 있다 have a speech impediment[disorder],
be a person with a speech impediment[disorder]

음성이나 언어로 소통하지 못하다 cannot communicate verbally, be non-verbal

호흡기 장애가 있다 have a respiratory disorder,
be a person with a respiratory disorder

SENTENCES TO USE

그 남자는 뇌병변 장애가 있어서 보행이 불가능합니다.
The man has a brain lesion and is unable to walk.

그는 시각 장애가 있어서 안내견과 함께 외출해요.
He has a visual disability, so he goes out with a guide dog.

청각 장애가 있는 사람들은 대개 말하는 데 어려움을 겪어요.
People with hearing impairments usually have difficulty speaking.

그 여성은 언어 장애가 있어서 의사소통이 자유롭지 못해요.
The woman has a speech impediment and cannot communicate freely.

호흡기 장애가 있어서 그녀는 격렬한 스포츠를 하는 게 힘들어요.
Having a respiratory disorder, she finds it challenging to play intense sports.

UNIT 7

정신적 장애

MP3 027-3

정신 장애가 있다 have a mental disability,
be a person with a mental disability

발달 장애가 있다 have a developmental disability,
be a person with a developmental disability

지적 장애가 있다 have an intellectual disability,
be a person with an intellectual disability

지능지수가 70 이하다
have an IQ of 70 or less, one's IQ is 70 or less

학습 장애가 있다
have a learning disability, have learning difficulties,
be a person with a learning disability[learning difficulties]

난독증이 있다
have dyslexia, be dyslexic

자폐증이/자폐스펙트럼 장애가 있다
have autism/autism-spectrum disorder,
be a person with autism/autism-spectrum disorder

주의가 산만하다
be distracted, lack concentration

SENTENCES TO USE

그녀의 아들은 지적 장애가 있어서 특수 학교에 다녀요.
Her son has an intellectual disability and goes to a special school.

지능지수가 70 이하면 지적 장애가 있는 것으로 판단합니다.
If a person has an IQ of 70 or less, he or she is judged to have an intellectual disability.

톰 크루즈는 난독증이 있었으나 이겨내고 세계적인 배우가 되었죠.
Tom Cruise had dyslexia, but he overcame it and became a world-class actor.

그 과학자는 자폐스펙트럼 장애가 있었어요.
The scientist had autism-spectrum disorder.

우리 딸은 어려서부터 너무 주의가 산만했어요.
My daughter has been so distracted since she was a child.

우울증이[우울장애가] 있다
have[suffer from]
depression[depressive disorder]

불안장애가 있다
have[suffer from]
anxiety disorder

공황장애가 있다
have[suffer from]
panic disorder

분노를 조절하지 못하다 can't control one's anger

분노조절장애가 있다 have[suffer from] intermittent explosive disorder

강박장애가 있다
have[suffer from]
obsessive-compulsive disorder (OCD)

~에 대해 강박적이다[강박증이 있다]
be obsessive about ~

망상이 있다 have delusions

과대망상이 있다 have[suffer from] delusions of grandeur [grandiose delusion, megalomania]

피해망상이 있다 have[suffer from] paranoia[a persecution complex]

환각/환청/환시/섬망이 있다 have a hallucination/ an auditory hallucination/a visual hallucination/delirium

SENTENCES TO USE

가끔 우울하다고 해서 우울증인 건 아니에요.
Just because you feel depressed sometimes doesn't mean you have depression.

요즘, 많은 사람들이 우울장애와 불안장애를 앓아요.
These days, many people suffer from depressive disorder and anxiety disorder.

그 영화는 유명인이 되고 싶은 과대망상을 앓는 남자의 이야기예요.
The movie is about a man who suffers from delusions of grandeur and wants to be a celebrity.

제이크는 피해망상이 있는 것 같아요. 모든 상황에서 자기가 피해자라고 생각하더라고요.
Jake seems to have paranoia. He thinks he is the victim in every situation.

MORE

정신 장애의 종류

- 신경발달장애 neurodevelopmental disorder
  - 지적장애 intellectual disability
  - 의사소통장애 communication disorder
  - 자폐스펙트럼 장애 autism spectrum disorder (ASD)
  - 주의력결핍 과잉행동장애 attention-deficit hyperactivity disorder (ADHD)
  - 운동장애 motor disorder
- 학습장애 learning disability
- 성격장애[인격장애] personality disorder
  - 편집성 성격장애[인격장애] paranoid personality disorder
  - 조현성 성격장애[인격장애] schizoid personality disorder
  - 조현형 성격장애[인격장애] schizotypal personality disorder
  - 반사회성 성격장애[인격장애] antisocial personality disorder
  - 경계선[경계성] 성격장애[인격장애] borderline personality disorder
  - 연극성 성격장애[인격장애] histrionic personality disorder
  - 자기애성 성격장애[인격장애] narcissistic personality disorder
  - 회피성 성격장애[인격장애] avoidant personality disorder
  - 의존성 성격장애[인격장애] dependent personality disorder
  - 강박성 성격장애[인격장애] obsessive-compulsive personality disorder
- 우울장애[우울증] depressive disorder, depression
  - 주요우울장애 major depressive disorder
  - 산후우울증 post-partum depression
  - 갱년기 우울증 involutional depression * 요즘은 잘 쓰이지 않음

- 불안장애 anxiety disorder
  - 범불안장애 generalized anxiety disorder
  - 분리불안장애 separation anxiety disorder
  - 선택적 함구증 selective mutism
  - 사회불안장애[사회공포증] social anxiety disorder, social phobia, sociophobia
  - 공황장애 panic disorder
  - ~ 공포증 ~ phobia
  - 광장공포증 agoraphobia
  - 질병불안장애 illness anxiety disorder

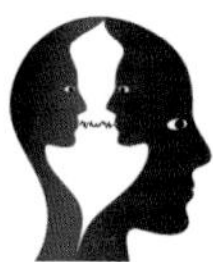

- 양극성 장애[조울증] bipolar disorder, manic-depressive disorder

MP3 028

- 조현병 schizophrenia
- 망상장애 delusional disorder
  과대망상 delusions of grandeur, grandiose delusion, megalomania
  피해망상 paranoia, a persecution complex
- 강박장애 obsessive-compulsive disorder
  수집광 hoarding disorder
- 외상후 스트레스장애 post-traumatic stress disorder (PTSD)
- 해리장애 dissociative disorder
  해리성 기억상실 dissociative amnesia
  해리성 정체성장애 dissociative identity disorder

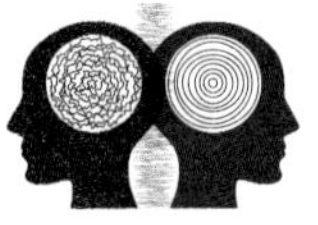

- 식이[섭식]장애 eating disorder
  신경성 식욕부진증, 거식증 anorexia
  신경성 폭식증 bulimia
  폭식장애 binge-eating disorder

- 배설장애 elimination disorder
- 수면장애 sleep disorder
  불면증 insomnia
  과다수면장애 hypersomnolence disorder
  기면증 narcolepsy
  하지불안증후군 restless legs syndrome

- 각성장애 wake disorder
- 품행장애 conduct disorder
- 간헐적 폭발장애[분노조절장애] intermittent explosive disorder
- 병적 방화 pyromania
- 병적 도벽 kleptomania
- 중독성 장애 addictive disorder
  알코올 의존증[중독] alcohol addiction
  카페인 중독 caffeine addiction

- 변태성욕장애 paraphilic disorder
- 성기능 부전 sexual dysfunctions
- 성별 불쾌감 gender dysphoria
  * 자기가 다른 성(性)으로 잘못 태어났다고 느끼는 상태

PART 2

사물

CHAPTER

1

사물의 외형

UNIT 1 사물의 형태

크다 be big[large]

* large는 '넓다'라는 의미도 됨

작다 be small

길다 be long

짧다 be short

(폭이) 넓다 be wide[broad]

* 폭이 넓음을 나타낼 때는 wide를 가장 흔히 씀. broad는 신체 일부에 대해 말할 때 더 자주 쓰며, 전원(田園)을 묘사하는 격식체나 문어체에서 씀.

(폭이) 좁다 be narrow

동그랗다, 둥글다 be round

원형이다 be circular, be a circle

타원형이다 be oval, be an oval

삼각형이다 be triangular, be a triangle

SENTENCES TO USE

시베리아 횡단열차는 세계에서 가장 긴 철도예요.
The Trans-Siberian Railway is the longest railway in the world.

이 골목은 좁아서 차가 지나가기 힘들어요.
This alley is so narrow that it's hard for cars to pass.

우주의 항성들과 행성들은 모두 둥급니다.
The stars and planets in space are all round.

미국 대통령의 집무실은 타원형이에요. 그래서 '오벌 오피스'라고 부르죠.
The office of the President of the U.S. is oval. That's why it is called the "Oval Office."

겨울 밤하늘의 그 세 별을 이으면 삼각형이 돼요.
If you connect those three stars in the winter night sky, they form a triangle.

* 앞의 표현은 명사, 뒤의 표현은 형용사

정사각형이다
be a square,
be square

직사각형이다
be a rectangle,
be rectangular

오각형이다
be a pentagon,
be pentagonal

육각형이다
be a hexagon,
be hexagonal

마름모꼴이다
be a rhombus, be rhombic

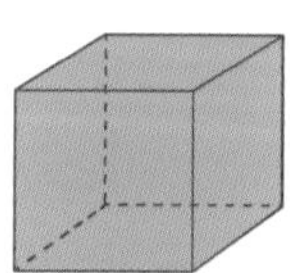

정육면체다
be a cube, be cubic

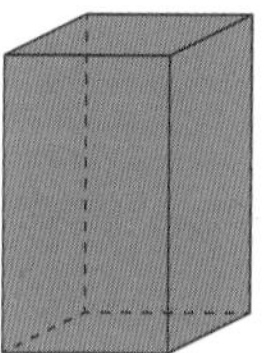

직육면체다
be a cuboid, be cuboid

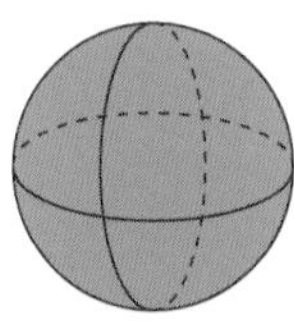

구형이다
be a sphere, be spherical

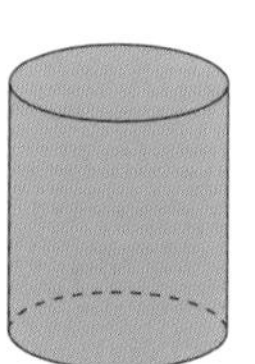

원통형이다
be a cylinder,
be cylindrical

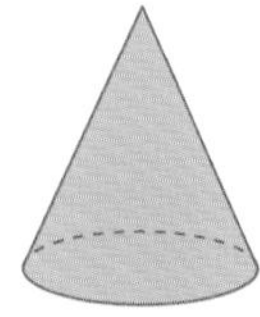

원뿔형이다
be a cone, be conical

SENTENCES TO USE

내 방은 정사각형이고 남쪽으로 창이 나 있어요.
My room is square and has a window to the south.

커뮤니티 센터에 있는 수영장은 직사각형이에요.
The swimming pool at the community center is rectangular.

미국 국방부 건물은 오각형이어서 '펜타곤'이라고 불러요.
The building of the U.S. Department of Defense is called the "Pentagon" because it is pentagonal.

배송 상자는 직육면체라서 공간을 효율적으로 사용할 수 있어요.
The shipping box is a cuboid, ensuring efficient use of space.

감자칩의 형태를 보존하기 위해 디자인된 용기는 원통형이에요.
The container designed to preserve the shape of the potato chips is cylindrical.

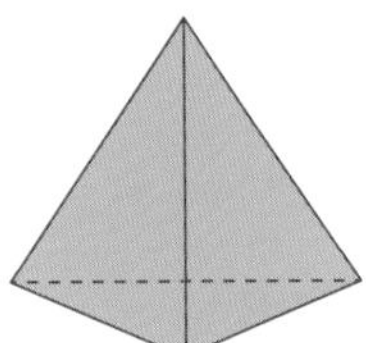

삼각뿔이다 be a triangular pyramid

사면체다 be a tetrahedron

* 삼각뿔과 사면체는 결국 같은 것

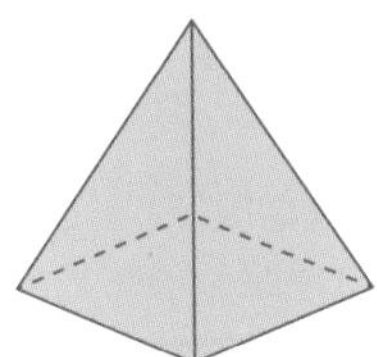

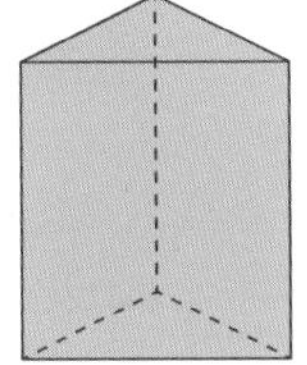

사각뿔이다
be a square pyramid
[quadrangular pyramid]

삼각기둥이다
be a triangular prism

오면체다
be a pentahedron

* 사각뿔과 삼각기둥이 오면체

뾰족하다 be pointed

납작하다, 평평하다 be flat

불룩하다 be bulging

* 안에 뭔가가 들어 있어 불룩하다는 뜻

뭉툭하다 be blunt

각이 지다 be angled

SENTENCES TO USE

오면체 중 하나가 삼각기둥입니다.
One of the pentahedrons is the triangular prism.

그 대성당의 첨탑 끝은 뾰족하고, 십자가가 세워져 있어요.
The tip of the cathedral's spire is pointed, and a cross is erected on it.

먼 옛날, 사람들은 지구가 평평하다고 생각했지요.
Long ago, people thought the Earth was flat.

그 남자의 바지 뒷주머니는 불룩했어요.
The back pocket of the man's trousers was bulging.

그 식탁 모서리는 각이 져서, 부딪쳤더니 아팠어요.
The corner of the table was angled, and it hurt when I bumped into it.

UNIT 2 색깔

MP3 030

겁다, 까맣다 be black

새까맣다 be pitch-black[jet-black, coal-black]

거무스름하다 be blackish[dark]

희다, 하얗다 be white

새하얗다 be pure white[snow white, (as) white as snow]

붉다, 빨갛다 be red

불그스름하다 be reddish

진홍색[주홍색]이다 be crimson [scarlet, cardinal]

암적색이다 be dark[deep] red

SENTENCES TO USE

그 새는 깃털 색이 새까맣습니다.
The bird's feathers are pitch-black.

그녀의 집에 있는 가구들은 모두 흰색이에요. 그것이 방들을 더 넓어 보이게 하죠.
All the furniture in her house is white. That makes the rooms look more spacious.

세탁해서 다림질한 셔츠가 새하얗습니다.
The washed and ironed shirt is pure white.

그 아이는 차가운 겨울바람을 맞아 볼이 불그스름했어요.
The child's cheeks were reddish from the cold winter wind.

추기경이 입는 일상 사제복은 진홍색이에요.
The cardinal's cassock is crimson.

UNIT 2

주황색이다, 오렌지색이다 be orange

산호색이다 be coral (color)

살구색이다 be apricot color

분홍색이다 be pink

진분홍색이다 be deep pink

연분홍색이다 be light[powder] pink

노랗다, 노란색이다 be yellow

연노랑이다 be light yellow

누렇다, 누리끼리하다 be yellowish

겨자색이다 be mustard color

SENTENCES TO USE

네덜란드 축구 국가 대표팀의 유니폼은 주황색이에요.
The uniform of the Dutch national soccer team is orange.

그녀가 오늘 입은 티셔츠는 산호색인데, 너무 잘 어울리네요.
The T-shirt she is wearing today is coral, and it looks so good on her.

벚꽃의 꽃잎은 연분홍색이에요.
Cherry blossom petals are light pink.

유채꽃이 활짝 피어서 들판이 노랬어요.
The field was yellow with rape flowers in full bloom.

그 여성은 파티에서 남색과 겨자색으로 된 드레스를 입고 있었어요.
The woman was wearing a navy and mustard-colored dress at the party.

녹색이다, 초록색이다 be green

밝은 초록색이다, 연녹색이다 be light green

연두색이다 be yellow green

올리브그린 색이다 be olive[dark yellowish-green]

옥색이다 be jade[jade green, aqua green, emerald-colored]

청록색이다 be blue-green[bluish-green]

파랗다, 푸르다, 파란색이다 be blue

푸르스름하다 be bluish

하늘색이다 be sky-blue

남색이다 be navy[navy-blue], be indigo-blue

* 명사일 때는 navy blue, indigo blue처럼 하이픈을 쓰지 않음. indigo blue가 navy blue보다 더 짙으며 살짝 자줏빛이 도는 색

검푸르다 be dark blue

SENTENCES TO USE

한여름의 논은 초록색으로 빛났어요.
The rice fields in midsummer were glowing green.

오늘 산 스웨터는 내가 제일 좋아하는 올리브그린 색이에요.
The sweater I bought today is olive, my favorite color.

그 마을 앞바다는 바닷물이 옥색이었죠. 정말 멋진 풍경이었어요.
The sea water off the village was jade. It was a stunning view.

우주에서 바라보는 지구는 푸른색입니다.
The Earth seen from space is blue.

넘실대는 겨울 바다는 검푸른 색이었어요.
The rolling winter sea was dark blue.

보라색이다 be violet[purple]

연보라색이다 be light violet[light purple, pale violet, lavender]

회색이다 be gray

진회색이다 be dark[charcoal] gray

갈색이다, 밤색이다 be brown

흐린 갈색이다 be tan
* 주로 피부색이나 가죽 색깔을 표현

밝은/짙은 갈색이다 be light/dark brown

은색이다 be silver

금색이다 be gold

SENTENCES TO USE

그 K팝 그룹을 상징하는 색은 보라색이에요. 대부분의 굿즈가 보라색이죠.
The color that symbolizes the K-pop group is purple. Most of the merchandise is purple.

그 소녀가 쓰고 있던 털모자는 연보라색이었어요.
The fur hat the girl was wearing was light violet.

우리 고양이는 회색인데, 발은 흰색이에요.
My cat is gray, but her paws are white.

그 사람 머리는 원래 짙은 갈색인데 지금은 파란색으로 염색했어요.
His hair was originally dark brown, but now it's dyed blue.

그 뮤지컬의 주인공이 쓰고 있던 가면은 은색이었어요.
The mask the main character of the musical was wearing was silver.

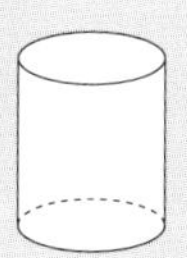

BE A CYLINDER, BE CYLINDRICAL

POTATO
CHIPS

The container
designed to
preserve the
shape of the
potato chips
is
cylindrical.

CHAPTER

2

사물의 성질

UNIT 1

사물의 상태와 성질

상태와 성질 전반

MP3 031-1

좋다 be good[nice]

나쁘다 be bad

새롭다, 새것이다 be new[fresh]

오래되다, 구식이다 be old[outdated]

* outdated는 특히 기술, 패션, 생각 등을 설명할 때 씀

예쁘다, 아름답다 be pretty[beautiful]

세련되다 be refined[sophisticated, polished]

* refined는 특히 매너가 좋은 것, sophisticated는 교양 있고 박식한 것, polished는 자신감 있고 품위 있는 것을 나타냄

깨끗하다 be clean[neat and clean]

깔끔하다, 말끔하다 be neat[tidy, neat and tidy, clean and tidy]

더럽다, 지저분하다 be dirty[messy, unclean]

* messy는 정리가 안 되어 지저분한 것, unclean은 위생상 더러운 것

어수선하다, 너저분하다 be untidy[messy]

추하다, 흉측하다 be ugly[hideous]

SENTENCES TO USE

소금을 너무 많이 섭취하는 건 건강에 나쁘죠.
Consuming too much salt is bad for your health.

그 회의실에 있는 탁자와 의자들은 새거예요.
The tables and chairs in the conference room are new.

가을의 그 도시는 엄청나게 아름다워요.
The city in autumn is incredibly beautiful.

그 남자는 외모도 복장도 몸가짐도 말투도 모두 세련됐어요.
The man is refined in his appearance, dress, demeanor, and speech.

그 화가의 작업실은 들를 때마다 언제나 깔끔하더라고요.
The artist's studio is always tidy whenever I stop by.

쓸모 있다 be useful[of use]

쓸모없다 be useless[of no use, good-for-nothing, no good]

* good-for-nothing, no good은 회화체, 비격식체

(심신이) 편하다 be comfortable

(이용하기에) 편리하다 be convenient

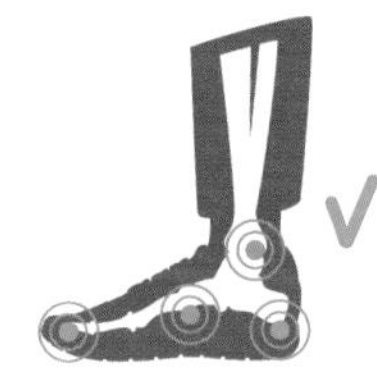

불편하다
be uncomfortable(심신이 편하지 않음),
be inconvenient(이용하기에 편리하지 않음)

내구성이 있다, 오래가다 be lasting[durable], last a long time(캐주얼한 느낌), wear well(옷이나 신발 등이 오래가는 것)

효율적이다, 능률적이다 be efficient

비효율적이다, 능률적이지 못하다 be inefficient

효과적이다 work, be effective

효과가 없다 don't work, be ineffective

SENTENCES TO USE

생일 선물로 립스틱을 받았는데, 화장을 안 하는 나에게는 쓸모가 없네요.
I got a lipstick as a birthday gift, but it's useless to me as I don't wear makeup.

새로 산 소파가 무척 편해서 나는 소파에서 잠을 자주 자요.
The new sofa I bought is so comfortable that I often sleep on it.

그 도서관 앱은 사용하기 무척 편리하고 도움이 돼요.
The library app is very convenient and helpful.

그 팀의 업무 방식은 비효율적이어서 마감 기한을 맞추지 못해요.
The team's way of working is inefficient, and it leads to missed deadlines.

그 어깨 마사지기가 제게는 효과가 없었어요. 진짜 필요한 건 병원에 가는 거예요.
The shoulder massager didn't work for me. What I really need is to go to a hospital.

UNIT 1

촉감

MP3 031-2

매끈하다, 매끄럽다 be smooth

보드랍다 be soft

말랑말랑하다 be soft

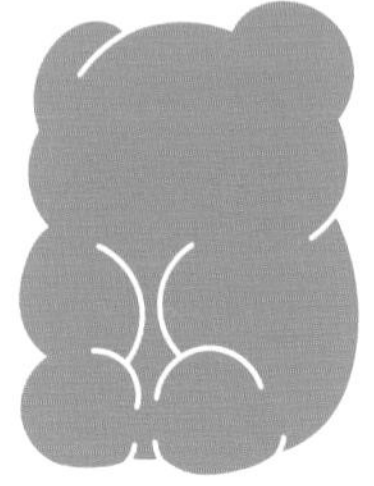

폭신[푹신]하다
be fluffy[cushiony]

* fluffy는 수건이나 봉제 인형이 폭신한 느낌이고, cushiony는 쿠션이나 방석처럼 부드럽고 편안한 느낌

탄력이 있다
be elastic[springy]

* elastic은 늘어났다 다시 돌아오는 성질, springy는 매트리스처럼 튕기는 느낌

뻣뻣하다 be stiff

딱딱하다, 단단하다
be hard[firm, solid]

* firm은 약간의 유연성은 있지만 전반적으로 딱딱한 것, solid는 완전히 단단하고 안정성을 지닌 것

(표면이) 평평하지 않다, 울퉁불퉁하다 be uneven[bumpy]

(형체가) 고르지 않다 be uneven

(표면이) 거칠다 be rough

날카롭다 be sharp[pointed]

* sharp는 날이 잘 들어 날카로운 것, pointed는 끝이 뾰족하여 날카로운 것

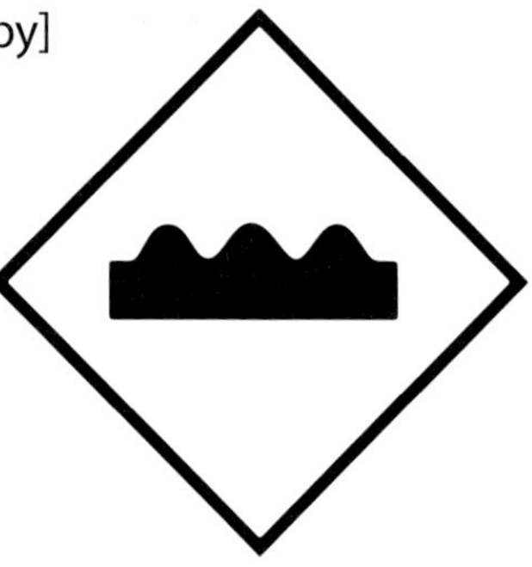

SENTENCES TO USE

그 아이는 말 그대로 피부가 비단결처럼 매끄러워요.
The child's skin is as smooth as silk.

우리 고양이 털은 무척 부드러워요. 쓰다듬으면 마음이 편안해져요.
My cat's fur is very soft. It relaxes me when I pet it.

겨울 담요가 말랑말랑하고 따뜻해요.
The winter blanket is soft and warm.

그 도로는 포장되어 있지 않아 울퉁불퉁했어요.
The road was bumpy because it was unpaved.

그는 치열이 고르지 않았는데, 그게 나름대로 귀여웠어요.
His teeth were uneven, but they were cute in their own way.

온도, 습도

MP3 031-3

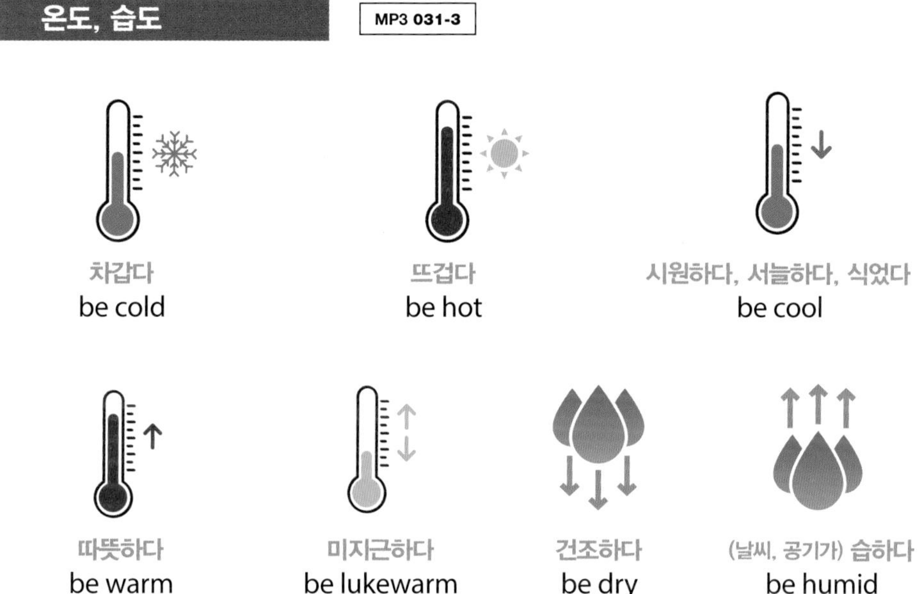

축축하다, 눅눅하다 be damp

후텁지근하다 be muggy

SENTENCES TO USE

그 아이는 사탕을 만져서 손이 끈적끈적했어요.
The child's hands were sticky because he touched the candy.

보일러를 틀지 않아서 마룻바닥이 차갑네요.
The floor is cold because the boiler is not turned on.

국이 식어서 미지근해요. 데우지 그래요?
The soup has cooled down and is now lukewarm. Why don't you heat it up?

방이 너무 건조해서 가습기를 틀어야겠어요.
The room is so dry that I need to turn on the humidifier.

그 섬은 여름에 무척 습해요. 숨쉬기가 힘들 정도입니다.
The island is very humid in the summer. It's hard to breathe.

UNIT 2

콘텐츠의 성질

새롭다 be new[fresh, novel]

* fresh는 새롭고 신선함, novel은 새롭고 기발함을 의미

참신하다 be original[fresh, novel]

* original은 독창성을 강조

흥미롭다, 재미있다 be interesting

* 흥미를 유발하며 재미있는 느낌

웃기다, 재미있다 be funny[entertaining, amusing]

* 웃음이나 미소를 지어내게 재미있는 느낌

눈을 뗄 수 없을 정도로 흥미롭다 be compelling[fascinating]

(흥미로워서) 자극이 되다 be stimulating[exciting]

인기 있다 be popular

유행[트렌드]에 뒤처지다 fall behind the trend(s), be outdated (구식이라 더 이상 쓸모가 없다는 의미 내포)

극히 평범하다, 틀에 박히다 be conventional

상투적이다, 진부하다 be hackneyed[cliché, stale, banal]

* cliché는 clichéd로 쓸 수 있음

SENTENCES TO USE

그 신인 감독의 영화는 연출 기법이 무척 참신했어요.
The new director's film had a very novel directing technique.

그 배우의 새 TV 시리즈가 무척 재미있어서 많은 나라에서 인기가 있어요.
The actor's new TV series is so interesting that it is popular in many countries.

그 작가는 트렌드에 뒤처지지 않기 위해서 여러 가지로 노력하고 있어요.
The writer is trying in many ways not to fall behind the trends.

그 팀장이 내놓는 아이디어는 대부분 지극히 평범해요.
Most of the ideas the team leader comes up with are conventional.

인물들이 너무 진부해서 그 소설은 많이 안 팔렸어요.
The characters in the novel were very cliché, so it didn't sell a lot of copies.

재미없다 be uninteresting

따분하다 be boring

합리적이다, 사리에 맞다 be rational [reasonable, logical, sensible]

불합리하다, 사리에 맞지 않다 be irrational [unreasonable, illogical]

상식적이다, 상식에 맞다
be sensible[common sense], make sense

비상식적이다
do not fit[do not conform to] common sense

선정적이다
be sensational

역겹다
be disgusting[nauseating]
* nauseating은 구역질 날 정도로 역겨운 것을 의미

혐오스럽다
be disgusting [detestable, hateful]

SENTENCES TO USE

오늘 들은 오디오북은 따분해서 듣다가 중간에 잠이 들고 말았어요.
The audiobook I listened to today was boring, so I fell asleep in the middle.

그 작품에서 그려지는 신분 제도는 불합리해 보여요.
The status system depicted in that work seems to be unreasonable.

그 장면에서 그 인물의 행동은 상식에 맞지 않았어요.
The character's behavior in the scene did not conform to common sense.

그 유튜브 채널에 올라오는 영상들은 꽤 선정적이에요.
The videos uploaded to the YouTube channel are quite sensational.

늘 돈을 최우선시하는 그녀의 모습은 보기에 조금 혐오스러워요.
It's kind of disgusting to see her always putting money first.

다채롭다 be various[varied, diverse]
* 범위가 다양하다는 걸 강조할 때는 diverse

유익하다
be useful[helpful, beneficial, instructive, informative]
* helpful은 도움 제공, beneficial은 이로운 결과를 가져다 줌, instructive는 교육적이고 교훈적임, informative는 정보 제공 측면에서 유익함

오락적 가치가 크다 have lots of entertainment value, be full of entertainment value

논쟁의 여지가 있다
be controversial

대중적이다
be popular

정보성이 강하다
be highly informative

교육적이다
be educational

무료다
be free (of charge)

SENTENCES TO USE

그 OTT 서비스에서 제공하는 미디어 콘텐츠는 다채롭습니다.
The media content provided by the OTT service is diverse.

그 프로그램은 십 대 청소년뿐 아니라 성인들에게도 유익합니다.
The program is beneficial not only to teenagers but also to adults.

그 영화가 다루는 주제는 논쟁의 여지가 많습니다.
The topic the movie deals with is very controversial.

그 채널에서 방영되는 프로그램들은 대체로 정보성이 강해요.
The programs on that channel are generally highly informative.

오늘 여기서 상영하는 영화는 무료예요. 흔치 않은 기회죠.
The movie that's playing here today is free. It's a rare opportunity.

사실에/실화에 기초하다 be based on facts/a true story

유치하다 be childish[infantile, juvenile]

* infantile은 격식체로 미숙한 행동을 암시,
juvenile은 젊은이들의 미숙함을 암시

풍자적이다
be satirical

빈정대다 be sarcastic

난해하다
be difficult[hard, convoluted]

추상적이다 be abstract

경험적이다, 경험에 근거를 두다
be empirical[experiential]

구체적이다
be concrete[specific]

형이상학적이다 be metaphysical

형이하학적이다 be physical

SENTENCES TO USE

영화 〈킹스 스피치〉는 실화에 기초했습니다.
The movie *The King's Speech* is based on a true story.

그 소설가의 작품들은 대부분 풍자적이에요.
Most of the novelist's works are satirical.

그 시인의 시들은 너무 난해해서 이해하기가 힘들어요.
The poet's poems are too difficult to understand.

초보자 대상 강의는 추상적이기보다는 경험적이거나 구체적인 게 좋습니다.
Lectures for beginners should be empirical or specific rather than abstract.

그가 하는 이야기들은 대부분 너무 형이상학적이라서 이해하기가 어려워요.
Most of the stories he tells are too metaphysical to understand.

UNIT 3

수량 표현

MP3 033

~가 많다(셀 수 있는 것) have a lot of[many] ~, there are a lot of[many] ~

* 긍정문에는 many보다 a lot of를 씀

~가 많다(셀 수 없는 것) have a lot of ~, there is a lot of ~

* 긍정문에는 much는 거의 쓰지 않음

~가 조금 있다(셀 수 있는 것) have some[a few] ~, there are some[a few] ~

~가 조금 있다(셀 수 없는 것) have some[a little] ~, there is some[a little] ~

~가 별로 없다 don't have many/much ~

~가 거의 없다 have few/little ~

SENTENCES TO USE

주말이라 놀이공원에 사람들이 많았어요.
Since it was the weekend, there were a lot of people at the amusement park.

그 도시는 눈이 많이 내려요.
They have a lot of snow in the city.

집에 빵과 우유, 달걀이 조금 있으니 며칠은 버틸 수 있어요.
I have some bread, milk, and eggs at home, so I can last for a few days.

지금 시간이 별로 없으니 회의는 짧게 합시다.
We don't have much time now, so let's keep the meeting short.

그는 친구가 거의 없지만 주말에 할 일을 찾는 데 아무 문제가 없습니다.
He has few friends, but he has no problem finding things to do on the weekend.

MORE

MP3 034

수를 읽는 방법 (연도, 날짜, 시간, 전화번호 등)

1) 연도

- 두 자리씩 나누어서 읽거나, 우리말로 '이천이십삼년'이라고 읽는 것처럼 읽는다.

1970년 nineteen seventy

2002년 two thousand (and) two

2024년 twenty twenty-four (일반적이고 회화체)
two thousand twenty-four (공식적인 느낌)

2525년 twenty-five twenty-five

2) 날짜

- '월-일' 순서로 읽고, 일은 서수로 읽는다.

5월 12일 May twelfth

10월 23일 October twenty-third

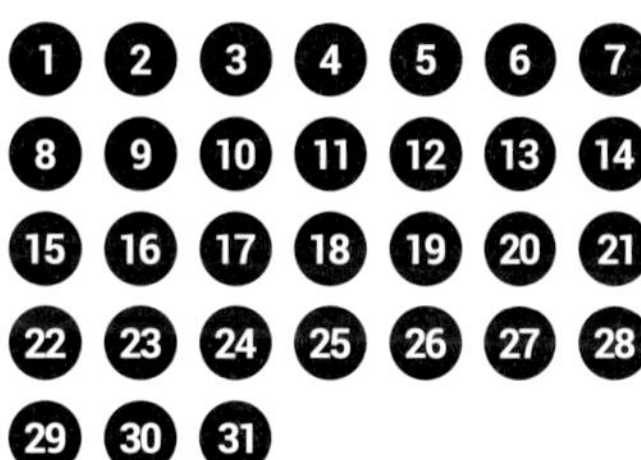

1일 first	2일 second	3일 third
4일 fourth	5일 fifth	6일 sixth
7일 seventh	8일 eighth	9일 ninth
10일 tenth	11일 eleventh	12일 twelfth
13일 thirteenth	14일 fourteenth	15일 fifteenth
16일 sixteenth	17일 seventeenth	18일 eighteenth
19일 nineteenth	20일 twentieth	21일 twenty-first
22일 twenty-second	23일 twenty-third	24일 twenty-fourth
25일 twenty-fifth	26일 twenty-sixth	27일 twenty-seventh
28일 twenty-eighth	29일 twenty-ninth	30일 thirtieth
31일 thirty-first		

3) 시간

- '시'와 '분'을 따로 기수로 읽는다.

  1시 8분 one o eight

  11시 24분 eleven twenty-four

- 오전이면 a.m.을, 오후면 p.m.을 뒤에 붙이면 더 정확해진다.

  오전 7시 30분 seven thirty a.m.

  오후 5시 17분 five seventeen p.m.

- to를 써서 '~분 전'을 나타낼 수 있다.

  5시 5분 전 five to five

  12시 10분 전 ten to twelve

- past를 써서 '~분 후'를 나타낼 수 있다.

  10시 5분 five past ten (10시를 지나 5분이므로 10시 5분)

  12시 10분 ten past twelve

4) 가격

- 액수가 2를 넘을 때는 dollar, cent, euro, pound 등 화폐 단위 뒤에 -s를 붙인다.

  5달러 99센트 five dollars ninety-nine cents

  * 단위를 생략하고 five, ninety-nine으로 읽기도 한다.

  25유로 twenty-five euros

  120파운드 one hundred and twenty pounds

5) 전화번호

- 숫자를 따로따로 하나씩 읽고 0은 'zero'나 '오'로 읽는다.
- 단위에 따라 끊어 읽는다.

+012-345-6789

  82–02–987–6543 eighty two, zero[o]-two, nine-eight-seven, six-five-four-three

  010–8765–4321 zero[o]-one-zero[o], eight-seven-six-five, four-three-two-one

6) 아파트 호수, 호텔 객실 번호

- 세 자리 번호는 숫자를 순서대로 각각 읽는다.

  902호 room nine o two
  315호 room three one five

- 네 자리 번호는 두 자리씩 묶어서 읽는다.

  1004호 room ten o four
  1710호 room seventeen ten

7) 항공편 번호

- 세 자리 숫자는 각각 따로 읽고, 네 자리 숫자는 각각 따로 읽거나 두 자리씩 묶어서 읽는다.

  AZ498 A Z four nine eight
  FL1228 F L one two two eight / F L twelve twenty-eight

PART 3

의식주

CHAPTER 1

의복

UNIT 1

옷의 상태

(옷이) 새것이다 be new

(옷이) 깨끗하다 be clean
* '깨끗하게 세탁돼 있다'는 의미도 포함

(옷이) 다려져 있다 be ironed

(옷이) 낡았다
be worn

(옷이) 더럽다
be dirty

(옷이) 구겨졌다 be wrinkled[creased]

~에 뭐가 묻었다 there's something on ~

~에 머리카락이 한 가닥 붙어 있다
there is a strand of hair stuck[attached] to ~,
a strand of hair is stuck[attached] to ~
* 여러 가닥 붙어 있을 때는 there are some strands of hair stuck[attached] to ~,
some strands of hair are stuck[attached] to ~

SENTENCES TO USE

내 속옷과 수건을 어제 세탁해서 깨끗합니다.
I washed my underwear and towels yesterday, so they are clean.

그가 오늘 입을 하늘색 셔츠가 다려져 있어요.
The sky blue shirt he's going to wear today is ironed.

이건 내가 아주 좋아하는 스웨터인데, 낡았어요.
This is my favorite sweater, but it is worn.

트렌치코트를 입고 앉았더니, 코트 아랫부분이 구겨졌어요.
I was sitting in a trench coat, and the bottom was wrinkled.

너 코트에 머리카락 붙어 있다. 내가 떼어 줄게.
There is a strand of hair stuck to your coat. I'll take it off.

(옷감이) 얇다
be thin

(옷감이) 두껍다
be thick

...에 ~ 얼룩이 져 있다
there is a ~ stain on ...

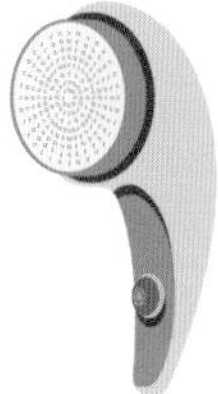

~에 보푸라기가 일다
there is lint on ~,
~ be linted, ~ pill, ~ get linty

(옷이) 색이 바래다 fade, be faded

(옷이) 찢어지다
be torn

(옷을) 수선해야 하다
need[have] to be mended

~에 구멍이 나다
there's a hole in ~

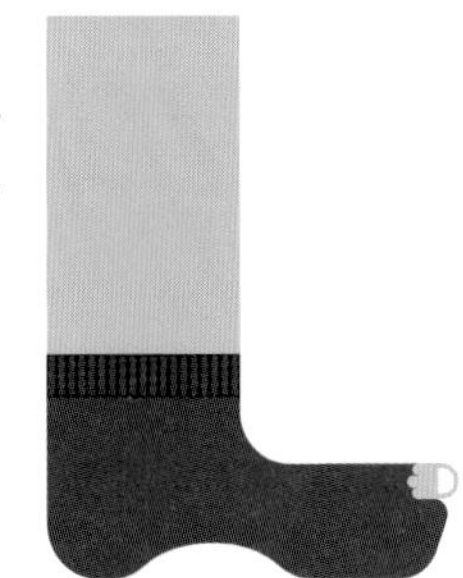

SENTENCES TO USE

티셔츠 앞면에 커피 얼룩이 져 있어요.
There is a coffee stain on the front of the T-shirt.

이 스웨터는 두 번 입었는데 벌써 보푸라기가 일기 시작했어요.
I've worn this sweater twice, and it's already starting to pill.

수영장 물의 염소 때문인가 내 보라색 수영복이 색이 바랬어요.
My purple swimsuit faded, possibly due to chlorine in the swimming pool.

트레이닝복 바지에 구멍이 났어요. 그것도 모르고 뛰러 나간 거 있죠.
There's a hole in my jogging pants. I went for a run without realizing it.

이 재킷은 찢어져서 수선해야 해요.
This jacket is torn and needs to be mended.

UNIT 2

옷차림

(옷)을 입고 있다(상태)
wear ~

(신발, 목도리, 장갑, 모자, 마스크 등)을
신고/두르고/끼고/쓰고 있다(상태)
wear ~

긴 소매/반소매/민소매 셔츠를 입고 있다(상태)
wear a long-sleeved/short-sleeved/sleeveless shirt

긴 바지/칠부바지를 입고 있다(상태)
wear long pants/capris[capri pants]

청바지를 입고 있다(상태)
wear jeans

반바지를 입고 있다(상태)
wear shorts

긴/짧은 치마를 입고 있다(상태)
wear a long/short skirt

SENTENCES TO USE

저는 겨울에 목도리 두르고 장갑을 끼지 않고는 외출하지 못해요.
I can't go out in winter without wearing a scarf and gloves.

코로나19가 잠잠해졌지만 그녀는 여전히 마스크를 쓰고 다녀요.
Although COVID-19 has subsided, she still wears a mask.

그는 팔에 화상 자국이 있어서 여름에도 긴소매 셔츠를 입습니다.
He has burn marks on his arm, so he wears a long-sleeved shirt even in summer.

그 사람은 공식 프레젠테이션 자리에서 청바지에 검정 스웨터를 입은 모습으로 유명했어요.
He was famous for wearing jeans and a black sweater at official presentations.

날이 너무 더워서 아이들은 모두 반바지에 샌들을 신고 있었어요.
The children were all wearing shorts and sandals because it was so hot.

(옷)이 A에게 잘 어울리다 ~ look good on A, A looks good in ~, ~ suit A well

(옷)이 A에게 안 어울리다 ~ don't look good on A, A doesn't look good in ~, ~ don't suit A well

(옷)이 A에게 (사이즈가) (딱) 맞다 ~ fit A (perfectly)

(옷)이 A에게 (사이즈가) 잘 맞지 않다 ~ don't fit A well

(옷이) ~에게 크다 be big for ~

(옷이) ~에게 작다 be small for ~

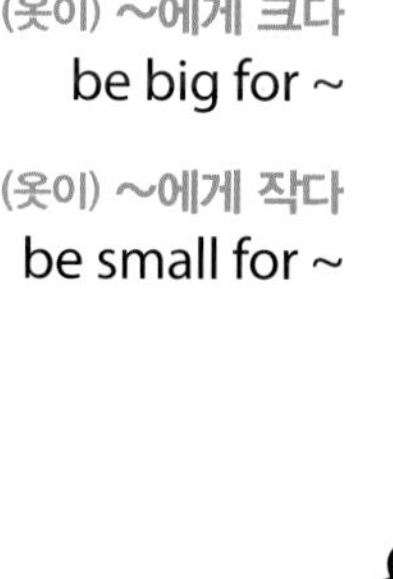

(옷이) 헐렁하다 be loose

(옷이) 꽉 끼다 be tight

옷이 (몸 부위)가 헐렁하다 be loose in ~

옷이 (몸 부위)가 꽉 끼다 be tight in ~

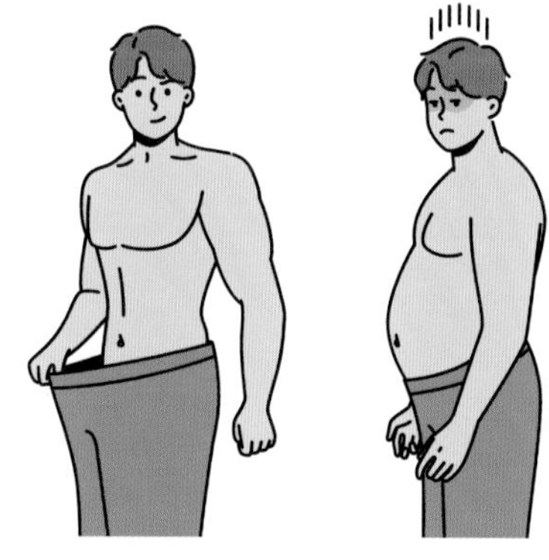

SENTENCES TO USE

그녀에게는 밝은색 옷이 잘 어울려요.
She looks good in bright clothes. / Bright clothes look good on her.

체형 때문인지 그는 정장이 안 어울리더라고요.
Perhaps because of his body type, suits don't suit him well.

그 재킷은 그녀에게 딱 맞아요. 수선할 필요가 없어요.
The jacket fits her perfectly. It doesn't need to be mended.

살이 빠져서 예전에 잘 맞던 바지가 헐렁해요.
I've lost weight, so the pants that used to fit me are loose.

살이 쪄서 그 스웨터가 어깨 부분이 이제 꽉 끼어요.
The sweater is tight in the shoulders now since I have gained weight.

(옷)이 (~에게) 어깨가 크다 be big in the shoulders for ~, be big for one's shoulders

(옷)이 (~에게) 어깨가 작다 be small in the shoulders for ~, be small for one's shoulders

소매가 길다 sleeves are long, have long sleeves

소매가 짧다 sleeves are short, have short sleeves

(옷이) 허리가 크다
be big in one's[the] waist

(옷이) 허리가 작다
be small in one's[the] waist

바지가 ~에게 길다
pants[trousers] are long for[on] ~

바지가 ~에게 짧다
pants[trousers] are short for[on] ~

SENTENCES TO USE

그 재킷은 아이에게 어깨가 조금 컸어요.
The jacket was a little big in the shoulders for the child.

그녀는 팔이 좀 짧아서 그 셔츠 소매가 그녀에게는 좀 길어요.
She has rather short arms, so the sleeves of the shirt are a bit long for her.

그 치마는 허리가 너무 커서 저한테 안 맞아요.
The skirt is too big in the waist so it doesn't fit me.

그는 키가 작아서 기성복 바지는 다 그에게 너무 길어요.
He is short, so all the off-the-rack trousers are too long for him.

옷차림이 단정하다 be neatly dressed

잘 차려입다 be well dressed, dress well[nicely]

(항상) 옷을 잘 입다 be a good dresser, always dress well, be always well-dressed

스타일이 좋다 have (a) good style

옷차림이 수수하다 be modestly dressed, dress plainly

옷차림이 화려하다 be dressed in fancy[flashy] clothes

옷차림이 고급스럽다 be dressed luxuriously

꾸안꾸 스타일이다 be effortlessly fashionable[chic]

명품을 입고 있다 wear luxury brand clothes

(옷이) 명품이다 be a luxury brand

옷차림이 초라하다 be poorly[shabbily] dressed

옷차림이 튀다[눈에 띄다] stand out in one's attire[clothing, dress]

옷차림이 특이하다 dress[be dressed] strangely [in a strange way], be unusual in one's dress

SENTENCES TO USE

그 여성은 언제나 옷차림이 단정해요. 한 번도 흐트러진 모습을 본 적이 없어요.
The woman is always neatly dressed, and I've never seen her unkempt.

중요한 모임이어서 다들 잘 차려입었습니다.
It's an important meeting, so everyone is well dressed.

올리비아는 스타일이 좋고 항상 옷을 잘 입어요.
Olivia has good style and always dresses well.

그 남자는 명품을 입고 있는데, 그 옆에서 내 옷차림은 초라하게 느껴지네요.
He's wearing luxury brand clothes, while I feel poorly dressed next to him.

그 싱어송라이터는 늘 옷차림이 특이해요.
The singer-songwriter always dresses in a strange way.

옷 종류

상의

코트 coat

* 보온이나 패션용으로 셔츠 위에 입는 웃옷의 총칭

외투 overcoat

* 보통 무릎 아래까지 오는 긴 코트

패딩 padded jacket[coat], puffer jacket[coat]

양복 suit

재킷 jacket

트렌치코트 trench coat

파카 parka

* 모자 달린 방한복, 방수 및 방풍 천으로 된 모자 달린 스포츠 재킷

아노락 anorak

* 모자가 달린 가볍고 짧은 재킷으로, 앞에 지퍼나 단추가 없음

바람막이 windbreaker(미국), windcheater(영국)

원피스 dress

오버올즈 overalls * 일명 '멜빵바지'

티셔츠 T-shirt

맨투맨 티셔츠 sweatshirt

후드 티셔츠 hoodie

셔츠 shirt

와이셔츠 dress shirt

블라우스 blouse

긴팔 ~ long-sleeved ~

반팔 ~ short-sleeved ~

민소매 ~ sleeveless ~

카디건 cardigan

스웨터 sweater(미국), pullover(미국), jumper(영국)

터틀넥 turtleneck

조끼 vest, waistcoat(영국)

* 영국에서 vest는 셔츠 안에 입는 속옷을 의미함

망토 cape, cloak

우비 raincoat

하의

바지 pants, trousers(주로 영국)

청바지 jeans

면바지 chinos

양복 바지 suit pants

반바지 shorts

나팔바지 bell-bottoms

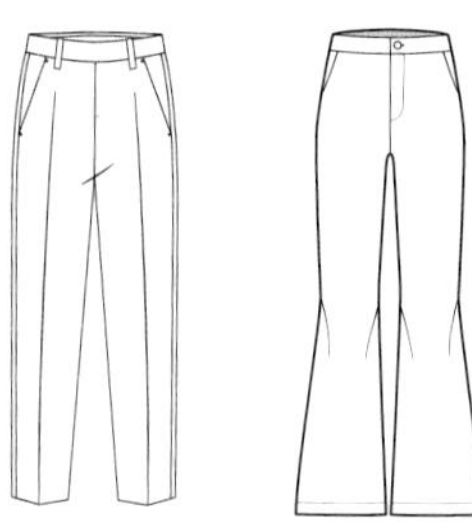

치마 skirt

긴 치마 long skirt, maxi skirt

중간 길이 치마 midi skirt

미니스커트 mini skirt

플레어스커트 flared skirt

A라인 스커트 A-line skirt

H라인 스커트 pencil skirt

주름치마 pleated skirt

랩스커트 wrap skirt

기타

잠옷 pajamas, sleepwear(집합적 의미), nightgown (여성용 원피스형 잠옷), nightdress(nightgown의 영국식 표현)

운동복, 트레이닝복 sweatsuit, tracksuit, jogging suit

운동복 바지 sweatpants, jogging pants

수영복 swimsuit, bathing suit(구식)

MORE

속옷

속옷 underwear

팬티 underpants(일반적인 의미로, 일상 회화에서는 잘 쓰지 않음)

남성용 팬티 briefs

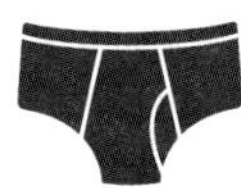

남성용 사각 팬티 boxer shorts, boxers

여성용 팬티 panties

브래지어 bra, brassiere

러닝셔츠 undershirt

신발

운동화 running shoes, athletic shoes(미국), sneakers(미국), trainers(영국), training shoes(영국)

슬립온 slip-ons

* 끈을 매지 않고 신고 벗을 수 있는 운동화

단화, 로퍼 loafers

옥스퍼드화 oxfords

* 끈으로 묶게 되어 있는 남성 가죽 구두

하이힐 high heels, heels, pumps

웨지힐 wedge heels

* 통굽 구두

슬링백 slingbacks

* 발뒤꿈치 쪽이 끈으로 되어 있는 구두

오픈토 open-toe shoes

* 발가락 쪽이 트인 구두

모카신 moccasins

* 부드러운 가죽으로 만든 납작한 신발

UNIT 3 옷감

옷감 일반

MP3 038-1

두껍다, 도톰하다, 두툼하다 be thick, have a thick texture

얇다 be thin, have a thin texture

부드럽다 be soft

까슬하다, 까끌하다 be rough

(속이) 비치다 be see-through[transparent, sheer]

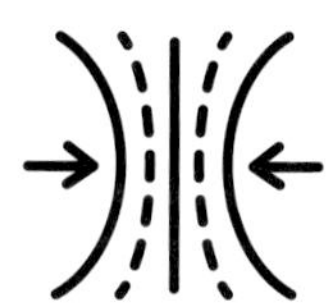

신축성이 있다
be stretchy,
have stretch

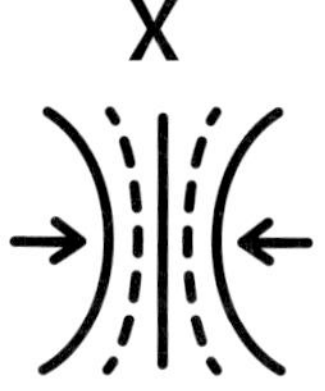

신축성이 없다
be non-elastic,
have no stretch

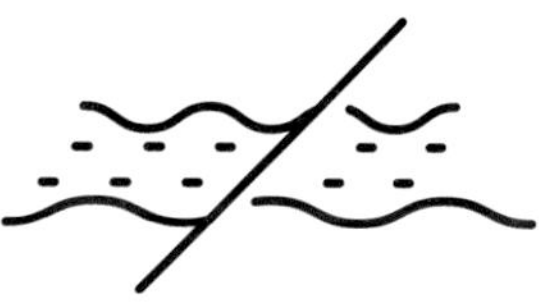

구김이 안 가다
be wrinkle-free
[wrinkle-resistant]

옷감이 색이 빠지다[이염되다]
the fabric bleeds

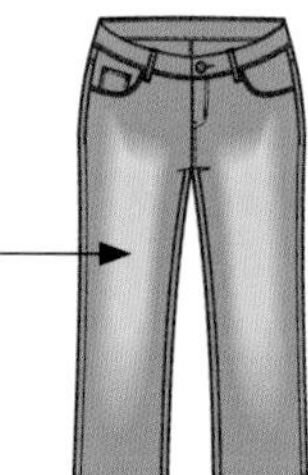

SENTENCES TO USE

이 후드티는 도톰해서 쌀쌀한 날에 입기 좋아요.
This hoodie is thick, so it's good to wear on chilly days.

그 재킷은 얇아서 요즘 입기에는 너무 추워요.
The jacket is thin, so it's too cold to wear these days.

그 셔츠는 옷감이 훤히 비쳐서 속에 뭔가를 입어야 해요.
The shirt is see-through, so you have to wear something underneath.

이 스웨터는 신축성이 있어서 입고 벗기 편해요.
This sweater is stretchy, so it's easy to put on and take off.

이 블라우스의 소재는 구김이 안 갑니다. 다림질이 필요 없어요.
The material of this blouse is wrinkle-free. It doesn't need to be ironed.

드라이클리닝을 해야 하다
need to[must] be dry-cleaned

손세탁이 가능하다
can be hand washed, be hand washable
(주로 제품 설명서에 쓰임)

손세탁이 불가능하다
cannot be hand washed

세탁 후 줄어들 수 있다 may shrink after washing

열에 강하다, 열에 쉽게 손상되지 않다 be heat-resistant[heatproof]

보풀이 나다/보풀이 나지 않다 pill[lint]/do not pill[lint]

다림질이 가능하다/불가능하다 can be ironed/cannot be ironed

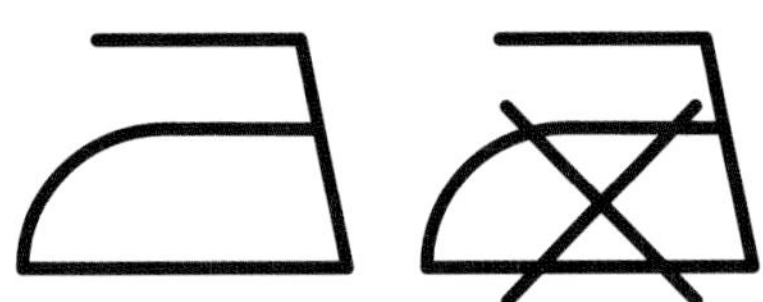

SENTENCES TO USE

이 제품은 반드시 드라이클리닝을 해야 합니다.
This product needs to be dry-cleaned.

이 블라우스는 손세탁이 가능한가요?
Can this blouse be hand washed?

이 스웨터는 소재가 울이어서 세탁 후 줄어들 수 있습니다.
This sweater may shrink after washing because it is made of wool.

이 카디건은 보풀이 잘 나지 않아요. 오래 입으실 수 있어요.
This cardigan doesn't pill easily. You can wear it for a long time.

그 니트 원피스는 다림질이 가능합니다.
The knit dress can be ironed.

옷감 소재

MP3 038-2

천연섬유로 만들었다, 소재가 천연섬유다
be made of a natural fiber

합성섬유로 만들었다, 소재가 합성섬유다
be made of a synthetic fiber

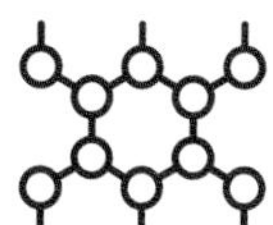

소재가 면이다/면혼방이다
be made of cotton/a cotton blend

소재가 모다/모혼방이다
be made of wool/a wool blend

소재가 마다
be made of hemp

소재가 가죽/합성가죽이다
be made of leather/synthetic leather

소재가 기능성 섬유다
be made of a performance fabric[fiber]

소재가 A ~퍼센트, B ~퍼센트다
be (made of) ~ percent A and ~ percent B

SENTENCES TO USE

내 옷들은 대부분 소재가 천연섬유예요.
Most of my clothes are made of natural fibers.

지난주에 새로 산 코트는 모혼방이에요.
The new coat I bought last week is made of a wool blend.

이 원피스는 소재가 마라서 통기성이 좋고 시원해요.
This dress is made of hemp, so it is breathable and cool.

그 소파 커버는 기능성 섬유로 만들어졌어요.
The sofa's cover is made of a performance fabric.

이 티셔츠는 소재가 면 60퍼센트에 폴리에스테르 40퍼센트네요.
This T-shirt is made of 60% cotton and 40% polyester.

MORE

옷감 종류 MP3 038-3

천연섬유 natural fiber

면 cotton

모 wool

마 hemp

실크 silk

데님 denim

면혼방 a cotton blend

모혼방 a wool blend

마혼방 a hemp blend

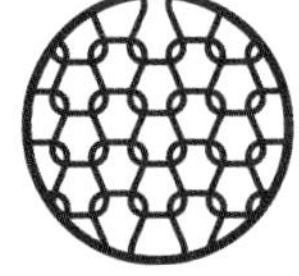

합성섬유 synthetic fiber

나일론 nylon

폴리에스테르 polyester

폴리우레탄 polyurethane

아크릴 acryl

가죽 leather

인조가죽 artificial leather, synthetic leather, leatherette, imitation leather, faux leather

모피 fur

인조모피 fake fur, faux fur

기능성 섬유 performance fabric[fiber]

폴라플리스 polar fleece

스판덱스 spandex, lycra (상표명)

옷의 무늬

MP3 038-4

무늬가 없다 have no pattern, there is no pattern on ~

프린트가 있다 there is a print on ~

줄무늬다
be striped,
have a striped pattern

체크무늬[격자무늬]다
be checkered,
have a checkered pattern

물방울무늬다
have a polka-dot pattern

꽃무늬다 have a flower pattern

헤링본 무늬다
have a herringbone pattern

물결무늬다 have a wavy pattern

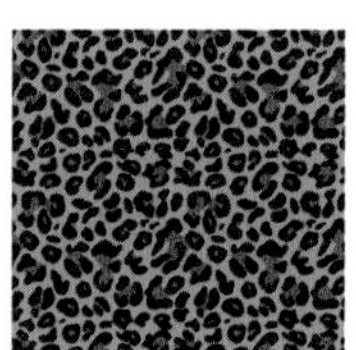

호피 무늬다
have a leopard (skin) pattern

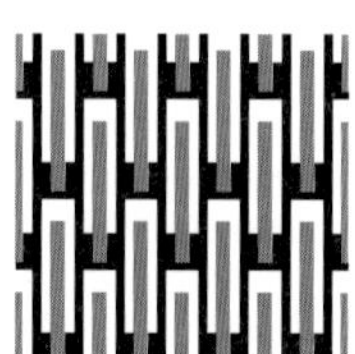

기하학적 무늬다
have a geometric pattern

SENTENCES TO USE

오늘 그가 입고 있는 티셔츠에는 아무 무늬도 없어요.
The T-shirt he is wearing today has no pattern on it.

오늘 새로 산 앞치마는 줄무늬예요.
The new apron I bought today has a striped pattern.

그날 그녀가 입고 있던 원피스는 물방울무늬였어요.
The dress she was wearing that day had a polka-dot pattern.

그 남자의 재킷은 헤링본 무늬였던 것으로 기억해요.
I remember the man's jacket had a herringbone pattern.

그녀의 옷 중 많은 수가 호피 무늬예요. 그녀가 특히 좋아하는 무늬거든요.
Many of her clothes have a leopard pattern. It's her favorite pattern.

CHAPTER

2

음식

UNIT 1

음식의 맛

맛있다 taste good, be tasty, be delicious(무척 맛있을 때)

별로 맛이 없다 don't taste very good

~ 맛이 난다 taste like ~

별 특별한 맛이 없다 have no special[particular] taste, don't have any special[particular] taste

아무 맛이 없다 be tasteless

맛이 풍부하다 be rich in flavor
* 음식의 맛이 다양함을 뜻함

맛이 진하다 taste rich
* 깊고 풍부한 맛으로, 농후한 맛과 약간의 기름진 풍미를 포함

맛이 깊다 have a deep flavor[taste]

맛이 강하다 taste strong, have a strong taste[flavor]

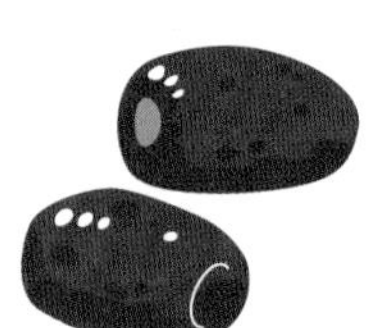

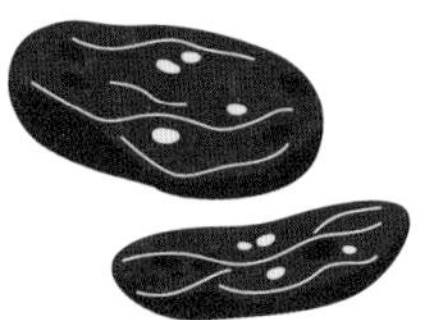

SENTENCES TO USE

크림 파스타를 처음 만들어 봤는데, 맛있었어요.
I made cream pasta for the first time, and it tasted good.

저한테 민트초코 아이스크림은 치약 맛이 나요.
For me, mint chocolate ice cream tastes like toothpaste.

전복은 별 특별한 맛이 없는데 왜 많이들 좋아하는지 모르겠어요.
Abalone doesn't have any special taste, so I don't know why many people like it.

우리 엄마가 만드는 비프 스튜는 맛이 진해요. 호밀빵과 잘 어울려요.
The beef stew my mom makes tastes rich. It goes well with rye bread.

어떤 사람들은 이 특정 향신료가 들어간 요리는 못 먹어요. 맛이 강해서요.
Some people can't eat dishes with this specific spice because it has a strong taste.

맛이 자극적이다 taste[be] pungent, have a pungent taste[flavor]

맛이 자극적이지 않다, 밍밍하다 taste bland[plain]

싱겁다 be not salty enough, be not well salted

진하다 be thick(국, 수프 등), be strong(커피, 술)

짜다, 짭짤하다 taste[be] salty

달다 taste[be] sweet, taste[be] sugary

시다 taste[be] sour

* 레몬 같은 과일의 시고 시큼한 맛

(맛이) 쓰다 taste[be] bitter

* 커피나 초콜릿의 쓴맛

맵다, 매콤하다 taste[be] spicy, taste[be] hot

얼큰하다 taste[be] spicy and hearty, have a spicy kick

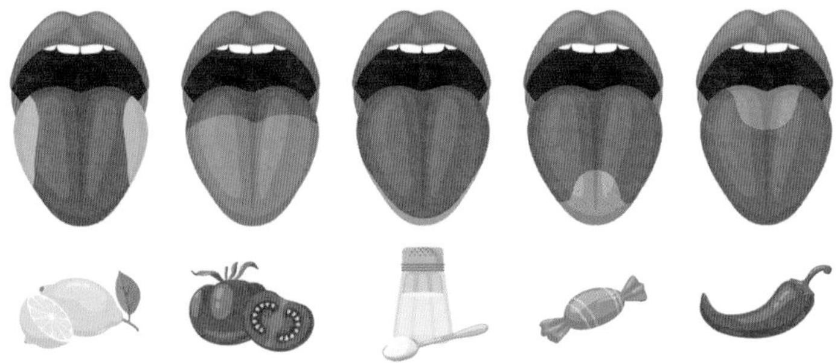

SENTENCES TO USE

이 식당 음식들은 맛이 자극적이에요.
The food at this restaurant has a pungent taste.

이 음식은 당뇨 환자식이라 좀 밍밍해요.
This food tastes bland because it is for diabetics.

우리 할머니가 만드는 음식은 다 좀 짜요.
All the food my grandmother makes is a little salty.

커피를 처음 마셨을 때는 쓰기만 했어요.
When I first drank coffee, it just tasted bitter.

그 식당의 카레는 맛있는데 좀 매워요.
That restaurant's curry is delicious, but it's a little spicy.

떫다 taste[be] astringent

고소하다
taste[be] nutty
* nutty는 특히 견과류의 고소한 맛과 향을 지닌 것을 가리킴

감칠맛이 나다, 풍미 있다,
(음식) 냄새가 좋다
be savory

담백하다 taste[be] light, taste[be] clean,
have a light[clean] taste

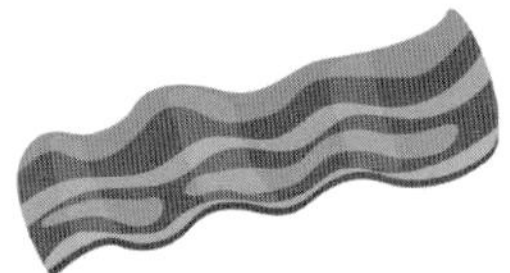

기름지다, 느끼하다
be oily[greasy, fatty]
* oily와 greasy는 기름을 많이 사용한 것,
fatty는 음식 자체에 지방이 많은 것

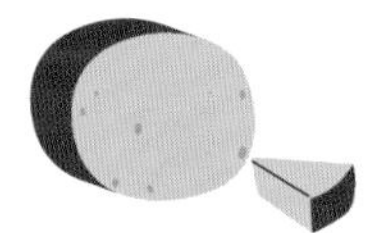

훈제한 맛이다
taste smoked, have a smoked flavor[taste]

(상큼하게) 톡 쏘다
taste[be] (refreshingly) tangy,
have a (refreshingly) tangy taste

SENTENCES TO USE

갓 짜낸 참기름 냄새가 너무 좋네요.
The smell of freshly squeezed sesame oil is very savory.

그 사람이 만든 꼬리곰탕은 맛이 담백했어요.
The oxtail soup he made had a light taste.

새우튀김이 너무 기름져서 하나밖에 못 먹겠어요.
The fried shrimps are so oily that I can only eat one.

이 연어는 훈제한 맛이 나네요.
This salmon tastes smoked.

레모네이드는 달면서도 상큼하게 톡 쏘는 맛이에요.
Lemonade has a sweet yet refreshingly tangy taste.

2 식감

MP3 040

부드럽다 be soft

딱딱하다 be hard, be stale (빵 등이 오래되어 딱딱해진 상태)

껍질이 딱딱하다 be crusty

바삭바삭하다, 아삭하다
be crispy[crisp, crunchy]

쫄깃쫄깃하다
be chewy

면이 쫄깃쫄깃하다
be chewy[al dante] (al dente는 특히 파스타에 사용), have a chewy texture

(고기가) 연하다 be tender

(고기가) 질기다 be tough

잘 바스러지다
be crumbly
* 과자나 파이 등이 부스러지는 것

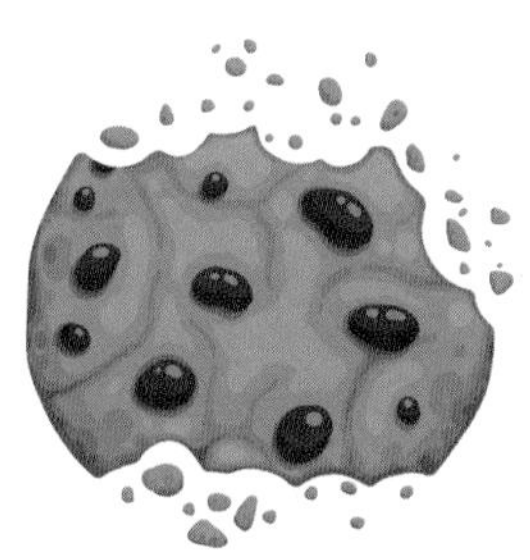

SENTENCES TO USE

이 빵은 겉껍질은 딱딱하지만 안은 부드러워요.
This bread is crusty on the outside but soft on the inside.

오징어와 채소 튀김이 바삭바삭하고 맛이 좋았어요.
The fried squid and vegetables were crispy and delicious.

그 식당의 국수는 면발이 쫄깃쫄깃했어요.
The noodles at that restaurant were chewy.

오늘 우리가 구운 고기는 연해서 먹기가 편했어요.
The meat we grilled today was tender and easy to eat.

고기가 질겨서 의치를 낀 우리 할머니는 드시지를 못했어요.
The meat was so tough that my grandmother, who has dentures, couldn't eat it.

UNIT 2

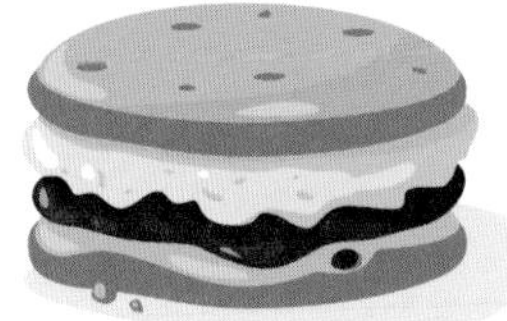

쫀득하다, 꾸덕하다
be gooey

촉촉하다 be moist

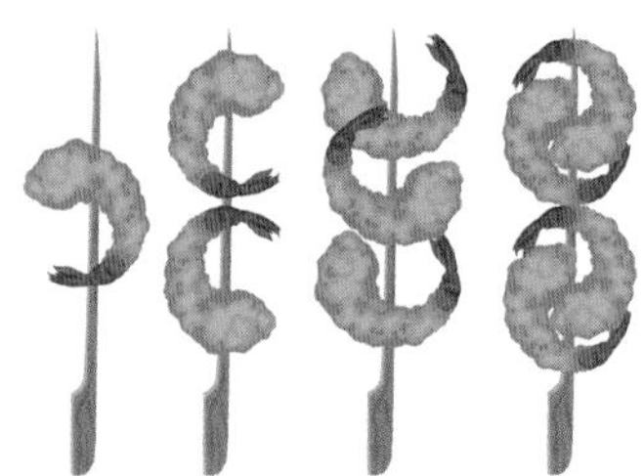

겉바속촉이다
be crispy on the outside and tender on the inside

눅눅하다
be soggy
* 시리얼 등이 우유 등에 너무 오래 담긴 상태의 식감,
또는 시간이 지나서 바삭한 식감이 사라진 상태

면이 퍼지다[불다]
be soggy[mushy and soggy]
* mushy and soggy는 너무 익어서 부드러워진 상태

과즙/육즙이 풍부하다
be juicy

육질이 탄력 있다
be firm

(너무 익어서) 흐물흐물하다 be mushy

SENTENCES TO USE

이 초코 브라우니는 꾸덕하고 맛있어 보여요.
This chocolate brownie looks gooey and delicious.

이 파이, 겉바속촉인걸.
This pie is crispy on the outside and tender on the inside.

구운 김이 며칠 새에 눅눅해져 버렸어요.
The roasted laver became soggy within a few days.

끓인 지 시간이 좀 돼서, 라면이 불었어요.
It's been a while since I made it, and the ramen has become soggy.

이번에 산 복숭아는 과즙이 매우 풍부하네요.
The peaches I bought this time are very juicy.

UNIT 3

식재료와 음식의 상태

MP3 041

식재료의 상태

MP3 041-1

신선하다, 싱싱하다
be fresh

신선[싱싱]하지 않다, 오래됐다
be stale
* 주로 빵, 케이크 등이 오래된 것이나 고기나 달걀 등이 썩어 가는 것을 나타냄

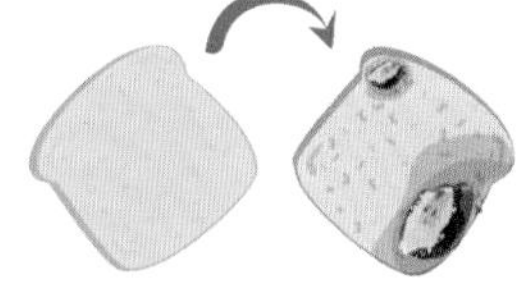

질이 좋다 be of good quality

고품질이다 be of high quality

질이 안 좋다, 저품질이다 be of bad[poor, low] quality

품질 등급이 높다/낮다 be of a high/low grade
* 특정 표준을 강조할 때 사용

(과일, 채소 등이) 익다/덜 익다
be ripe/unripe[not ripe]

지나치게 익다
be overripe

상하다
have gone bad,
be spoiled

SENTENCES TO USE

그 가게의 채소들은 항상 신선해요. 나는 거기 단골이에요.
The vegetables in the store are always fresh. I'm a regular customer there.

그 양계장 달걀은 품질이 좋아요.
The eggs from that poultry farm are of good quality.

텃밭에 있는 토마토가 익어서 오늘 몇 개 따서 먹었어요.
The tomatoes in the garden were ripe so I picked and ate some of them today.

그 바나나는 덜 익어서 껍질이 초록색이에요.
The banana is not ripe, so the peel is green.

그 샌드위치는 상했어요. 버려야 해요.
That sandwich has gone bad. You should throw it away.

UNIT 3

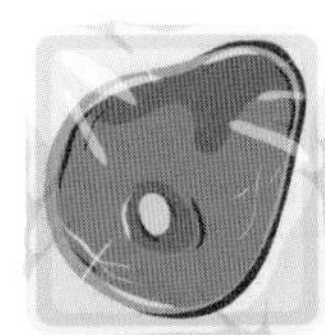

냉동되어 있다, 얼어 있다
be frozen

통조림돼 있다
be canned

(음식이) 병조림돼 있다 be (packed) in a jar
* 피클 등 저장식품을 병에 담아 두는 경우

(술이나 음료가) 병에 담겨 있다 be bottled
* 술이나 음료를 만들어 병에 담아 두는 경우

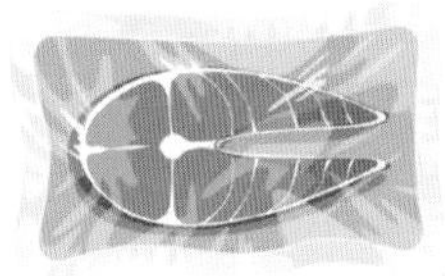

진공 포장되어 있다
be vacuum-packed

냉장 보관해야 하다 must be (kept) refrigerated, must be kept in the fridge

냉동 보관해야 하다 must be kept frozen

유기농이다(화학 비료를 쓰지 않았다) be organic

가공되지 않다 be unprocessed[not processed]

국내산이다 be domestic, be domestically produced

수입산이다 be imported

SENTENCES TO USE

닭이 냉동돼 있어서 요리하기 전에 해동해야 해요.
The chicken is frozen and needs to be thawed before cooking.

엄마가 만든 피클이 병조림돼 있어요.
The pickles my mother made are packed in jars.

이 케이크는 꼭 냉장 보관하셔야 해요.
This cake must be refrigerated.

이 양배추는 유기농이라 조금 비싸요.
This cabbage is a little expensive because it is organic.

돼지고기는 국내산이고 쇠고기는 수입산입니다.
The pork is domestic and the beef is imported.

음식의 상태 (맛 제외)

MP3 041-2

잘 조리되다, 잘 익다
be well-cooked

덜 조리되다, 덜 익다
be undercooked

너무 오래 조리되다, 너무 익다 be overcooked

타다 be burnt

따뜻하다/미지근하다
be warm/lukewarm

뜨겁다/차갑다
be hot/cold

푸짐하다
be plentiful[abundant]

음식의 양이 많다/적다 the food portions are large/small

되다, 되직하다, 빡빡하다 be thick

묽다 be thin

SENTENCES TO USE

내놓기 전에 고기가 잘 익었는지 확인하세요.
Please make sure the meat is well-cooked before serving.

면이 좀 덜 익었네요.
The noodles are a little undercooked.

당근이 너무 익은 것 같아요.
I think the carrots are overcooked.

빵이 탔네. 안 먹는 게 좋을 것 같아요.
The bread is burnt. I think it would be better not to eat it.

비프스튜가 아직 따뜻해요. 어서 드세요.
The beef stew is still warm. Go ahead and eat some.

소스가 너무 빡빡해요. 물을 더 넣어야겠어요.
The sauce is too thick. I need to add more water.

CHAPTER

3

주거

UNIT 1

건물의 종류

단독 주택
a house, a detached house,
a standalone house

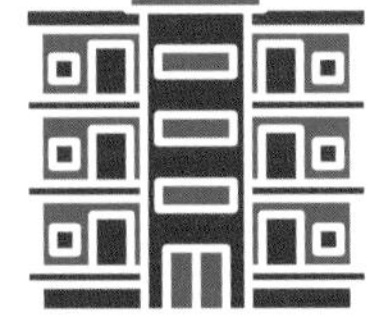

아파트, 공동주택
an apartment,
a flat(영국)

* 아파트 건물을 가리킬 때는 an apartment building으로 표현

고층 아파트 a high-rise apartment building

아파트 단지가 크다 the apartment complex is large[big]

빌라
a townhouse, a row house,
a terraced house(영국)

* town[row, terraced] house는 같은 형태의 집들이 연결돼 있는 것으로, 우리나라의 빌라와는 조금 차이가 있고, 우리나라에도 서양의 town house 같은 형태의 가옥이 있다.

고급 빌라 a luxury townhouse

대저택
a mansion

원룸 a studio (apartment)

전원주택, 시골의 저택 a country house

SENTENCES TO USE

내가 유년 시절을 보낸 집은 아파트가 아니라 단독 주택이었어요.
The place where I spent my childhood was a house, not an apartment.
* 물리적인 '건물'로서의 집은 house, '누군가의 집'은 home이나 place로 표현

이 지역 주택 대부분이 공동주택이에요.
Most of the houses in this area are apartment buildings.

이 도시의 아파트 단지들은 규모가 큽니다.
The apartment complexes in this city are large.

그의 집은 재학 중인 대학교 근처에 있는 원룸이에요.
His place is a studio apartment near his university.

그녀의 집은 허드슨 밸리에 있는 예쁜 전원주택입니다.
Her place is a lovely country house in the Hudson Valley.

낮은/높은 건물 a low/tall building

작은/큰 건물 a small/big building

5층(짜리) 건물 a five-story building
* 숫자 자리에 다른 숫자를 넣어 층수 표현

고층 빌딩 a high-rise building

상가 건물 a commercial building

주상복합 건물
a residential-commercial complex[building],
a multipurpose building

~색 건물 a ~ building
* ~ 자리에 색깔 형용사를 넣어 건물의 색을 표현

빨간 벽돌 건물
a red brick building

유리로 된 건물 a glass building, a building made of glass

노출 콘크리트 건물 an exposed concrete building

SENTENCES TO USE

그 병원은 12층 건물의 2층에 있어요.
The clinic is on the second floor of a 12-story building.

그들의 집은 새로 지은 주상복합 건물에 있어요.
Their home is in a new residential-commercial complex.

우리 집은 빨간 벽돌 건물입니다. 찾기 쉬워요.
My house is a red brick building. It's easy to spot.

그 시청사는 유리로 된 건물이에요. 주변 건물들에 대조되어 눈에 확 띄어요.
The city hall is a glass building, which stands out against the surrounding buildings.

그 출판사 건물은 노출 콘크리트 건물이에요.
The publishing house building is an exposed concrete building.

UNIT 2 건물의 특성

건물 일반

MP3 043-1

(건물이) 동/서/남/북향이다 face east/west/south/north

(집이나 사무실, 상점이) ~층이다[~층에 있다] be on the ~th floor

* 1층/2층/3층은 1st/2nd/3rd floor

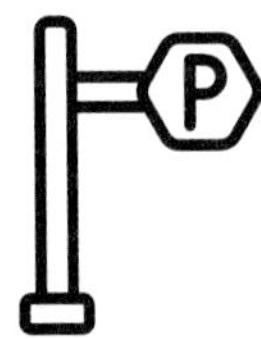

주차장이 있다
have a parking lot, provide parking

지하 주차장이 있다
have an underground [a basement] parking lot

지상 주차장이 있다
have a ground-level parking lot

옥상이 있다 have a rooftop

엘리베이터가 있다 have an elevator

에스컬레이터가 있다 have an escalator

계단만 있다 only have stairs[stair access]
there are only stairs in ~

SENTENCES TO USE

우리 집은 남동향이라 오전에 햇빛이 들어와요.
Our house faces southeast, so it gets sunlight in the morning.

그녀의 집은 아파트 4층이에요.
Her house is on the 4th floor of an apartment building.

우리 아파트는 지하 주차장만 있어요.
Our apartment only has an underground parking lot.

그 사람들 집은 옥상이 있어서 옥상에서 종종 바비큐를 해 먹어요.
Their house has a rooftop, and they often have barbecues there.

그 건물은 엘리베이터가 없어서 어르신들이 오르내리기 불편해요.
The building doesn't have an elevator, so it's hard for the elderly to go up and down.

옥상에 헬리콥터 이착륙대가 있다
have a helicopter (landing) pad on the rooftop,
there is a helicopter (landing) pad on the rooftop of ~

옥외 광고탑이 있다 have an outdoor advertising tower

벽에 간판이 걸려 있다 signs[signboards] are hanging on the wall of ~,
there are signs[signboards] hanging on the wall of ~

벽에 플래카드가 걸려 있다 a placard is hanging on the wall of ~

(건물이) 낡았다 be old

(건물이) 건설[공사] 중이다
be under construction

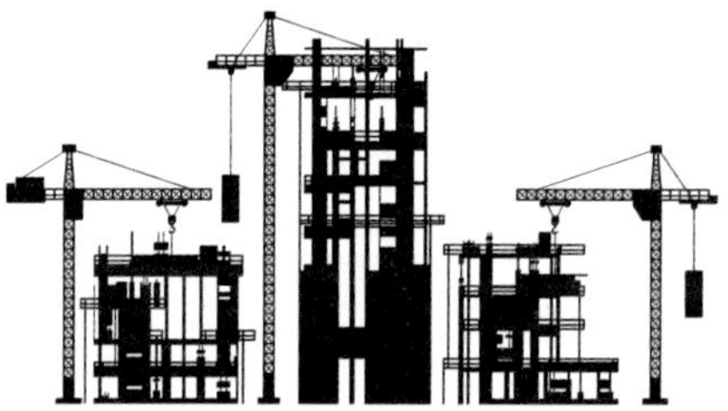

(건물 벽의) 페인트칠이 벗겨져 있다
the paint has peeled off (벗겨진 상태 강조), the paint is peeling off (벗겨지고 있는 과정 강조)

벽에 금이 가 있다
there is a crack in the wall of ~

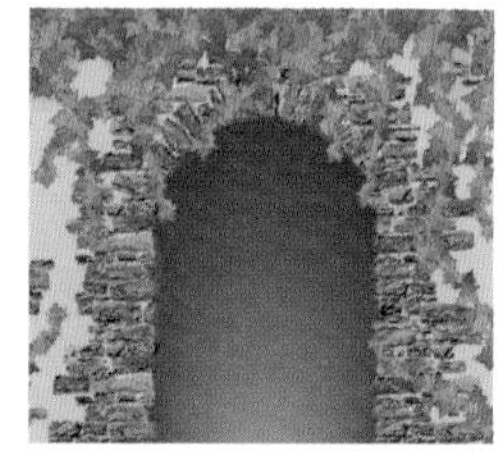

벽이 담쟁이덩굴로 덮여 있다
the walls are covered with ivy

SENTENCES TO USE

그 병원 옥상에는 헬리콥터 이착륙대가 있습니다.
There is a helicopter landing pad on the rooftop of the hospital.

그 상가 건물 벽에는 간판이 많이 걸려 있어요.
There are many signs hanging on the walls of the commercial building.

그 박물관은 2년째 공사 중입니다.
The museum has been under construction for two years.

우리 아파트 건물 외벽에 금이 몇 군데 가 있어요.
There are several cracks in the exterior walls of our apartment building.

그 교회 벽은 담쟁이덩굴로 덮여 있습니다.
The walls of the church are covered with ivy.

마당이 있다 have a yard

앞마당/뒷마당이 있다 have a front yard/backyard

정원이 있다 have a garden, there is a garden (at ~)

정원에 나무가 많다 there are a lot of[many] trees in the garden

정원에 꽃이 많다 there are a lot of[many] flowers in the garden

텃밭이 있다 have a vegetable garden, there is a vegetable garden at ~

마당이 잔디밭이다 one's yard is a lawn

(주택에) 지하실이 있다 have a basement[cellar]

* basement는 지하층을 가리키고, cellar는 지하 저장고로, 사람이 사는 공간은 아님

(주택에) 차고가 있다 have a garage

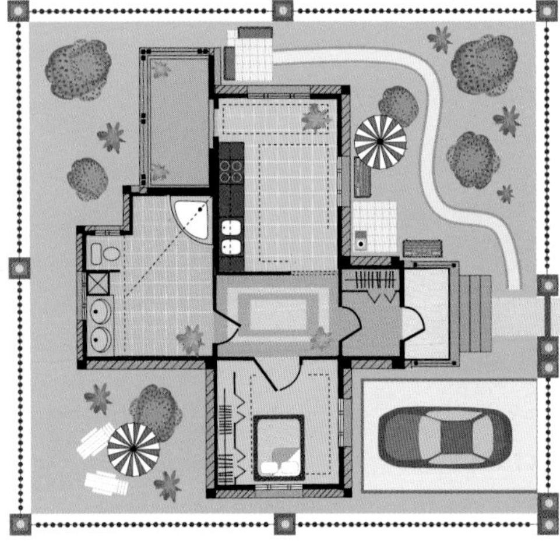

SENTENCES TO USE

내가 어렸을 때 살던 집은 앞마당과 뒷마당이 있었어요.
The house I lived in as a child had a front yard and a backyard.

그녀의 정원에는 나무와 꽃이 많아요. 참 아름답죠.
There are many trees and flowers in her garden. It's so beautiful.

우리 집에는 텃밭이 있어서 나는 장을 거의 안 봐요.
My house has a vegetable garden, so I hardly go grocery shopping.

그때 내가 살던 집에는 지하 저장고가 있어서 거기에 와인을 저장할 수 있었어요.
The house where I lived at the time had a cellar, so I could store wine there.

그의 집에는 차고가 있어서 주차를 걱정할 필요가 없어요.
His house has a garage, so he doesn't have to worry about parking.

집 내부

MP3 043-2

~평방미터다/평방피트다 be ~ square meters/square feet

* 미국에서는 square feet가 주로 쓰임

방이 ~개다 have ~ room(s)

베란다가 있다/없다 have a balcony/have no balcony

방이/거실이/주방이/욕실이 넓다 have a large room/living room/kitchen/bathroom

방이/거실이/주방이/욕실이 좁다 have a narrow room/living room/kitchen/bathroom

천장이 높다/낮다 have a high/low ceiling

창이 ~쪽으로 나 있다 the window faces ~, have a window facing ~

(집에) 가구와 가전제품이 갖춰져 있다 be furnished

(집이) 풀옵션이다 be fully furnished

가구와 가전제품이 갖춰진 원룸이다/아파트다
be a furnished studio (apartment)/
be a furnished apartment

풀옵션 원룸이다/아파트다
be a fully furnished studio (apartment)/
be a fully furnished apartment

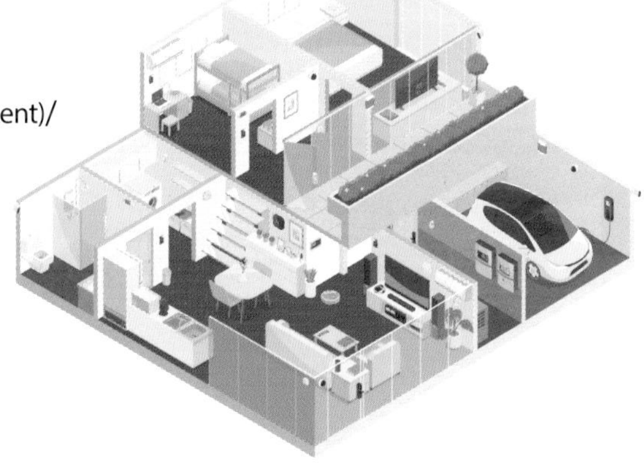

SENTENCES TO USE

그들의 집은 107평방미터고, 셋이 살기에 충분해요.
Their house is 107 square meters and spacious enough for the three of them.

우리 아파트는 베란다가 없어서 햇빛을 즐길 야외 공간이 없어요.
Our apartment has no balcony, so we don't have an outdoor space to enjoy sunlight.

그녀의 집은 거실 천장이 높았던 게 기억에 남아요.
I remember that her house had a high ceiling in the living room.

내 침실은 창이 동쪽으로 나 있어서 아침에 햇빛이 일찍 들어와요.
My bedroom's window faces east, so sunlight comes in early in the morning.

그의 원룸은 필요한 가구와 가전제품이 갖춰진 풀옵션이에요.
His studio apartment is fully furnished with the necessary furniture and appliances.

집에 햇빛이 잘 들다 get[have] a lot of[good] sunlight

환기가[통풍이] 잘 되다
be well ventilated

에어컨 시설이 돼 있다, 냉방 장치가 돼 있다
be air-conditioned, have air conditioning

냉방이 잘 되다 have good air conditioning

난방이 되다 be heated

단열이 잘 되다
be well insulated

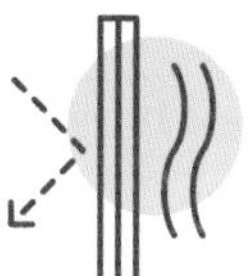

내진 설계가 돼 있다 be designed to be earthquake-resistant

집/건물 벽으로 빗물이 새다 rainwater leaks through the walls of a house/building
cf) rainwater leaks in a house/building 빗물이 집/건물 안으로 새어 들어가다

내화 재료로 마감하다 be finished with fire-resistant materials

조명이 어둡다 be poorly lit

집 인테리어를 새로 하다(상태) be redecorated, be renovated

SENTENCES TO USE

그의 집은 남향이라 햇빛이 잘 듭니다.
His house faces south, so it gets a lot of sunlight.

그의 집은 창문이 마주보고 있어서 환기가 잘 돼요.
His house has windows on opposite sides, so it is well ventilated.

우리 사무실은 냉방이 돼서 여름에 시원해요.
Our office is air-conditioned, so it's cool in the summer.

우리 아파트 건물은 내진 설계가 돼 있습니다.
Our apartment building is designed to be earthquake-resistant.

그 집은 인테리어를 새로 했고 정리도 잘 돼 있었어요.
The house had been redecorated and was well organized.

벽에 그림이 걸려 있다 there is a picture[painting] hanging on the wall, a picture[painting] is hanging on the wall

책/화분이 많다 there are a lot of[many] books/flower pots

집에 물건이 많다 one's house has a lot of things[stuff], there are a lot of things[there is a lot of stuff] at one's house

집에 물건이 별로 없다 one's house doesn't have many things[much stuff], there aren't many things[there isn't much stuff] at one's house

(집이) 정리가 잘 돼 있다, 깔끔하다 be tidy[well organized, in good order]

(집이) 청소가 돼서 깨끗하다 be clean

(집이) 지저분하다, 어질러져 있다 be messy, be in a mess

(집이) 먼지가 쌓여 있다 be dusty, be covered with dust

~에 곰팡이가 피어 있다 there is mold in[on] ~, ~ be moldy

SENTENCES TO USE

그 집 거실 벽에 그림이 몇 점 걸려 있었어요.
There were several paintings hanging on the living room wall of the house.

그 작가의 집에는 다양한 분야의 책이 아주 많습니다.
There are so many books from various fields in the writer's house.

그의 집은 물건이 별로 없고 정리도 잘 돼 있어요.
His house doesn't have many things and is well organized.

그녀의 집은 깔끔한 그녀의 겉모습과 대조되게 항상 지저분하게 어질러져 있습니다.
Her house is always messy, in contrast to her neat appearance.

욕실 청소를 몇 달 안 했더니 욕조에 곰팡이가 피어 있어요.
I haven't cleaned the bathroom for a few months and the tub is moldy.

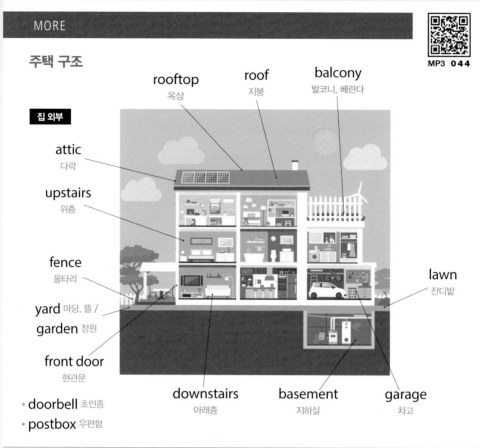

MORE

MP3 044

주택 구조

집 외부

rooftop 옥상

roof 지붕

balcony 발코니, 베란다

attic 다락

upstairs 위층

fence 울타리

yard 마당, 뜰 / garden 정원

front door 현관문

lawn 잔디밭

downstairs 아래층

basement 지하실

garage 차고

* doorbell 초인종
* postbox 우편함

집 내부

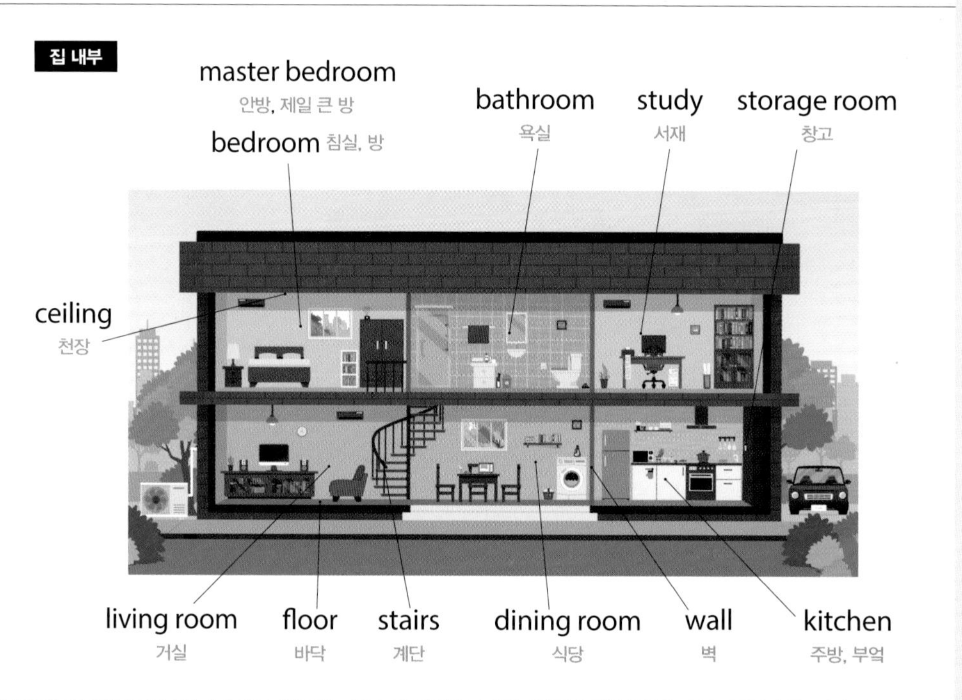

UNIT

3 가구, 가전제품, 각종 물건, 차량

MP3 045

가구

MP3 045-1

붙박이다 be built-in

조립식이다 be prefabricated

수제다, 손으로 만들었다 be handmade

목재다 be made of wood

원목이다 be made of hardwood[solid wood]

철제다 be made of iron

가죽으로 돼 있다 be made of leather

어린이용이다 be for children

사무용이다 be for office use

SENTENCES TO USE

이 옷장은 붙박이라서 이사 나갈 때 가져가실 수 없어요.
This wardrobe is built-in so you can't take it when you move out.

그 상점의 가구들은 많은 수가 조립식이에요.
Much of the store's furniture is prefabricated.

이 의자는 수제품으로, 70년도 넘은 거예요.
This chair is handmade and is over 70 years old.

이 책상은 원목이고 내구성이 아주 좋아요.
This desk is made of solid wood and is very durable.

이 2층 침대는 어린이용입니다.
These bunk beds are for children.

품질이 좋다
be of good quality,
the quality (of ~) is good

견고하다, 튼튼하다
be sturdy[solid]

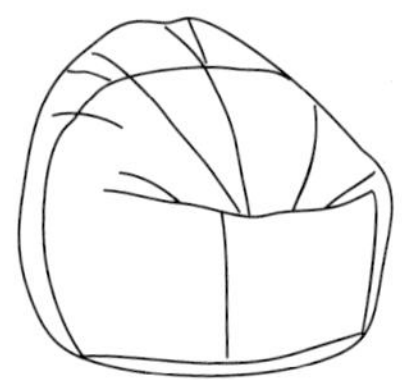

저렴하다
be cheap

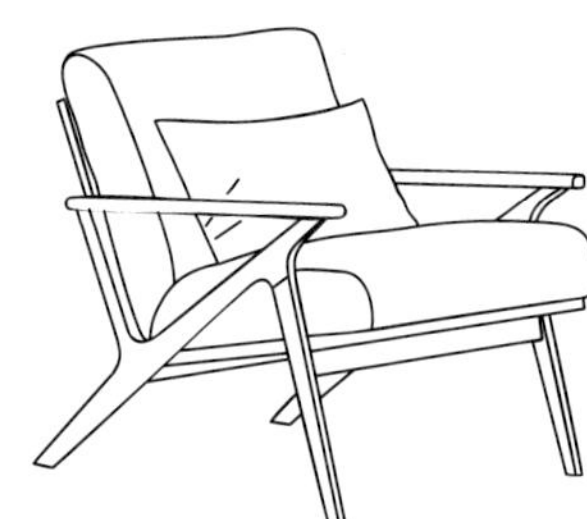

가성비가 좋다
be good value for money,
be cost-effective

* good value for money는 주로 가격에 비해 품질이 좋은 물건에 대해 쓰고, cost-effective는 서비스나 운영에 들어가는 비용 대비 효율이 높은 상황에 씀

값이 비싸다 be expensive[high-priced]

고급이다 be of high quality, be a quality product

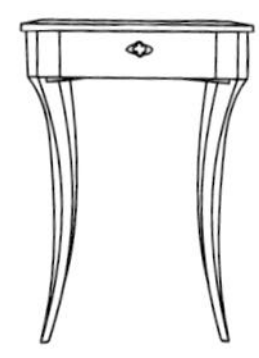

디자인이 단순하다
be simple in design, have a simple design,
the design (of ~) is simple

화려하다 be fancy

장식이 많다 have a lot of decoration

SENTENCES TO USE

이 침대는 값은 비싸지만 품질이 좋아요.
This bed is expensive, but the quality is good.

이 탁자는 그가 직접 만든 건데, 무척 견고해요.
He made this table himself, and it is very sturdy.

이 소파는 가성비가 좋아요. 구입을 강추합니다.
This sofa is good value for money. I highly recommend you buy it.

내 방 옷장은 디자인이 단순해요. 그래서 질리지 않아요.
The wardrobe in my room has a simple design. That's why I don't get tired of it.

요즘 가구들과 비교해서 그 시절 가구들은 장식이 많았어요.
Compared to today's furniture, the furniture in those days had a lot of decoration.

광이 나다 be shiny, shine, glow

~에 손때가[손자국이] 묻었다 there are hand stains[handprints] on ~

~에 흠이 있다 there is a blemish on ~

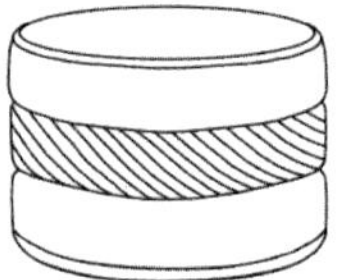

침대가/소파가/의자가 편하다 the bed/sofa/chair is comfortable

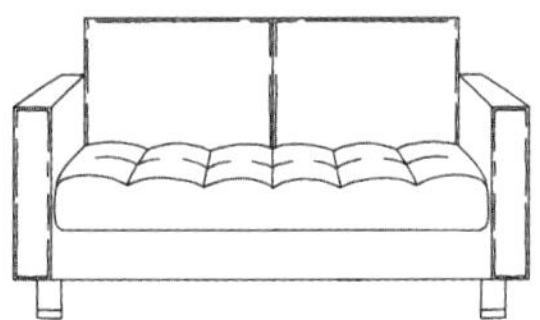

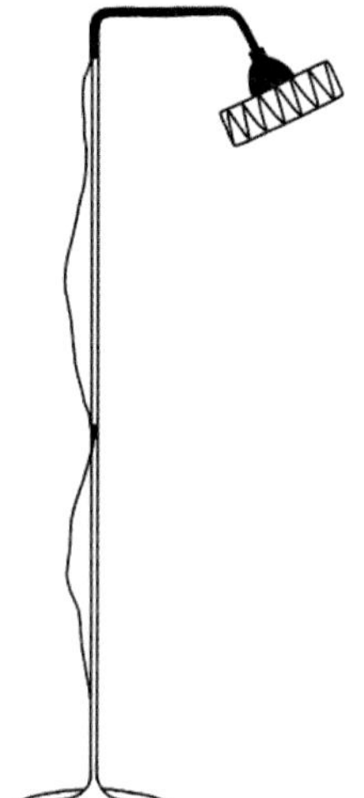

소파가/의자가 푹신하다 the sofa/chair is soft

책상이/탁자가 (폭이) 넓다 the desk/table is wide

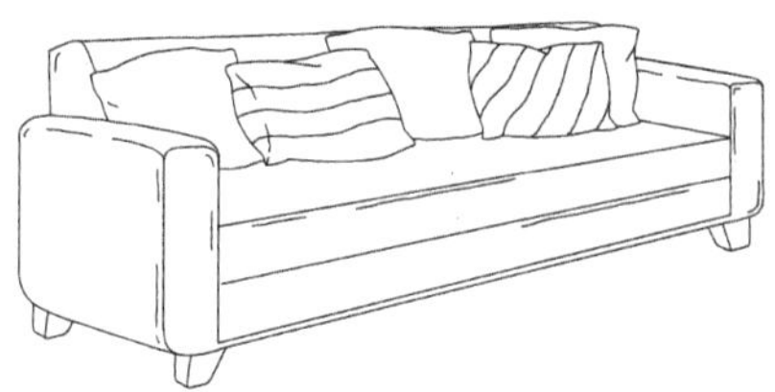

자리를 많이 차지하다 take up a lot of space

남는 공간에 놓을 수 있다 can be placed in any spare space

유행하다 be popular, be a popular product

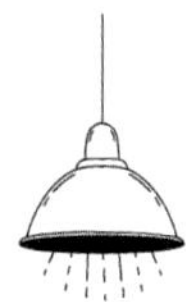

SENTENCES TO USE

할머니께 나전칠기 장을 물려받았는데, 광이 나요.
I inherited the mother-of-pearl lacquerware cabinet from my grandma, and it is shiny.

새로 산 침대는 편해서 허리가 아프지 않아요.
The new bed is comfortable and my back doesn't hurt.

그 소파가 너무 푹신하고 편해서 휴일에는 온종일 소파에 누워 지냅니다.
The sofa is so soft and comfortable that I lie on it all day on holidays.

이 책상은 폭이 넓어서 두 사람이 작업할 수 있어요.
This desk is wide, so two people can work at it.

그 안락의자는 요즘 유행하는 제품이에요.
The armchair is a popular product these days.

MORE

MP3 045

여러 가지 가구 MP3 045-2

싱글 침대 single bed
더블 침대 double bed, full-sized bed
퀸사이즈 침대 queen-size bed
킹사이즈 침대 king-size bed
2층 침대 bunk bed

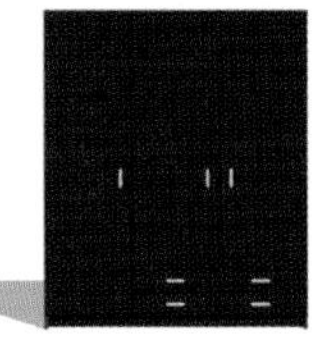

옷장 wardrobe
붙박이장 built-in closet
서랍 chest of drawers, dresser
화장대 dressing table, vanity

책상 desk
책상 의자 desk chair
접는 의자 folding chair
책장, 책꽂이 bookshelf, bookcase

TV장 TV stand
소파 sofa
안락의자 arm chair
흔들의자 rocking chair
안마의자 massage chair
진열장 display cabinet

싱크대 sink
싱크대 장 kitchen cabinet
싱크대 상부장 upper cabinet, wall cabinet
싱크대 하부장 base cabinet, lower cabinet
식탁 table
유아의 식사용 의자 high chair
등받이 없는 의자 stool

욕실장 bathroom cabinet

가전제품

MP3 045-3

소형 가전이다 be a small home appliance

대형 가전이다 be a large home appliance

소형화되다 become smaller

경량화되다 become lighter

절전형이다 be energy-saving[power-saving], be an energy-saving[a power-saving] appliance

에너지 소비 효율이 높다 be energy-efficient

에너지 소비 효율이 낮다 be energy-inefficient, be not energy-efficient

붙박이형이다 be built-in

신제품이다 be a new product

최신 기술 제품이다 be a cutting-edge product, be the latest technology

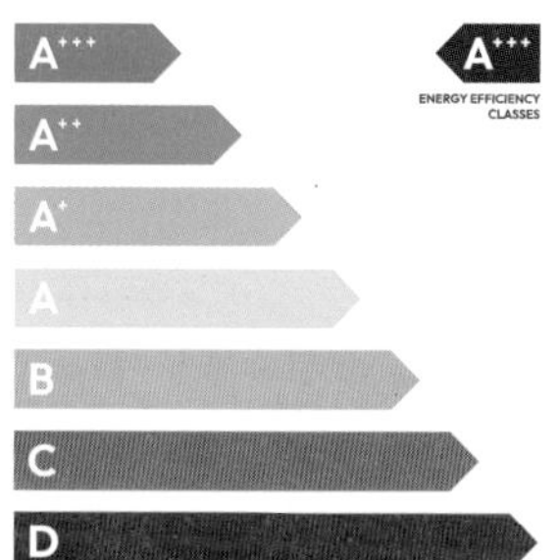

SENTENCES TO USE

많은 가전제품이 과거보다 소형화되었습니다.
Many home appliances have become smaller than in the past.

이 전기 난로는 절전형이라서 전기 요금이 적게 나와요.
This electric stove is energy-saving, so it lowers the household's electricity bill.

이 냉장고는 에너지 소비 효율이 높아요.
This refrigerator is energy-efficient.

우리 집 냉장고는 붙박이형이에요.
The refrigerator in my house is built-in.

에어 프라이어는 당시 그 회사의 신제품이었어요.
The air fryer was a new product from the company at the time.

UNIT 3

인기 있는[유행하는] 제품이다 be a popular[trendy] product

고급 제품이다 be a high-end product

가성비가 좋다 be good value for money, be cost-effective

* good value for money는 주로 가격에 비해 품질이 좋은 물건에 대해 쓰고, cost-effective는 서비스나 운영에 들어가는 비용 대비 효율이 높은 상황에 씀

성능이 뛰어나다 have excellent performance

작동이 잘 되다/잘 안 되다 work well/don't work well

리모컨으로/스마트폰으로 조작할 수 있다 can be operated with a remote control/a smartphone

고장 나다 be broken, break down, die, be out of order

* be broken과 break down이 가전제품/전자제품이 고장 났다고 표현할 때 전반적으로 쓸 수 있는 표현이고, die는 갑자기 작동이 안 되고 먹통이 된 느낌, be out of order는 자판기나 복사기 같은 것이 고장 났을 때 씀

고장이 잘 안 나다 don't break easily, rarely break down

디자인이 예쁘다 have a good[nice] design

크기가 작다/크다 be small/large in size

SENTENCES TO USE

의류 건조기는 요즘 인기 있는 제품으로, 대부분의 신혼부부들이 장만해요.
Clothes dryers are a popular product these days, and most newlyweds buy one.

이 공기청정기는 고급 제품입니다.
This air purifier is a high-end product.

이 전자레인지는 이제 작동이 잘 안 돼요. 하긴, 15년 동안 썼으니까요.
This microwave doesn't work well anymore. Well, I've used it for 15 years.

그 회사의 TV는 고장이 잘 안 나요.
The TVs from that company don't break down easily.

이 냉장고 디자인이 예쁘네요. 어느 회사 제품이에요?
This refrigerator has a good design. Which company's product is it?

MORE

MP3 045

여러 가지 가전제품 MP3 045-4

냉장고 refrigerator, fridge(회화체)

김치냉장고 kimchi refrigerator[fridge]

냉동고 freezer

전기밥솥 rice cooker

가스레인지 gas stove

인덕션 induction stove, induction cooktop

전자레인지 microwave

오븐 토스터 toaster oven

전기 주전자 electric kettle

정수기 water purifier

식기세척기 dishwasher

세탁기 washing machine, washer

의류 건조기 clothes dryer

전동 칫솔 electric toothbrush

전기면도기 electric razor

에어컨 air conditioner * 미국에서는 주로 AC라고 표현

선풍기 (electric) fan

가습기 humidifier

제습기 dehumidifier

공기청정기 air purifier

환풍기 ventilation[ventilating] fan, ventilator

전기장판 heating pad, electric pad

전기난로 electric heater

청소기 vacuum (cleaner) * vacuum으로만 쓰는 것이 더 일반적

로봇 청소기 robot vaccum, robot cleaner, Roomba(아이로봇사에서 만든 제품명으로, 미국에서 로봇 청소기를 대표하는 단어)

스타일러 clothing care system, garment steamer, steam closet

각종 물건

MP3 045-5

품질이 좋다/안 좋다 be of good/poor[bad, low] quality

내구성이 있다/없다 be durable/short-lived[not durable]

가격이 비싸다/싸다[저렴하다] be expensive/cheap[inexpensive]

가격이 적당하다 be affordable[reasonably priced]

가성비가 좋다 be good value for money

친환경 제품이다 be an eco-friendly[environmentally friendly] product

유행하다 be popular, be in fashion

고급이다 be of high quality, be high-end (명품에 가격도 높다는 의미를 내포)

싸구려다 be cheap

국산이다 be domestic

외제다 be foreign-made

(나라)산이다[제다] be from 나라 이름,
be made in 나라 이름,
be 나라 형용사 made

SENTENCES TO USE

이 칫솔은 품질이 좋고 내구성도 있어요.
This toothbrush is of good quality and also durable.

이 노트북은 가격이 적당해서 샀어요.
I bought this laptop because it was reasonably priced.

그 브랜드 제품들은 디자인도 예쁘고 품질도 괜찮은데 가격이 비싸요.
The brand's products have a nice design and good quality, but they're expensive.

그 주방세제는 친환경 제품이에요.
The dish detergent is an eco-friendly product.

그 커피는 베트남산인데 맛과 향이 괜찮아요.
The coffee is from Vietnam, and it tastes and smells good.

디자인이 예쁘다 have a good[nice] design, the design is good[nice]

디자인이 촌스럽다 be tacky[old-fashioned]

* tacky는 취향이 촌스러운 것, old-fashioned는 요즘 스타일이 아니어서 촌스러운 것을 의미

디자인이 시대에 뒤처지다 be outdated in terms of design, be out of date in terms of design, the design is outdated[out of date]

디자인이 깔끔하다 have a neat design, the design is neat

디자인이 단순하다[소박하다] have a simple design, the design is simple

디자인이 평범하다 have a plain design, the design is plain

디자인이 흔하다 have a common design, the design is common

디자인이 독특하다 have a unique design, the design is unique

SENTENCES TO USE

진열된 신발 중에서 이 샌들 디자인이 제일 예뻐요.
These sandals have the best design among the shoes displayed.

걔가 들고 다니는 가방 봤어? 되게 촌스러워.
Did you see the bag she had with her? It is very tacky.

그 회사 로고 디자인은 시대에 뒤처졌잖아요.
The company's logo is outdated in terms of design.

나는 이 자동차가 디자인이 단순해서 마음에 들어요.
I like this car because it has a simple design.

이 모자는 디자인이 독특하네요. 이걸로 할게요.
This hat has a unique design. I'll take this one.

UNIT 3

(디자인이) 감각적이다 have a stylish design, be stylish

(디자인이) 고전적이다 have a classic design, be classic

(디자인이) 복고풍이다 have a retro design, be retro

(디자인이) 대담하다 have a bold design, be bold

최신 유행 디자인이다 have a trendy design, be trendy

(디자인이) 유행을 타지 않는다 don't go out of style[fashion]

(디자인이) 인체공학적이다 have an ergonomic design

(디자인이) 환경친화적이다 have an eco-friendly[environmentally friendly] design, be eco-friendly[environmentally friendly]

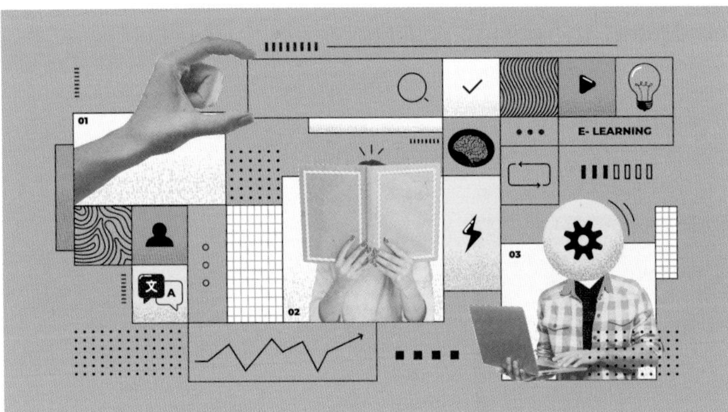

SENTENCES TO USE

그 회사 가구는 디자인이 감각적이야. 네 마음에 들 거야.
The company's furniture has a stylish design. I think you'll like it.

오늘 그녀가 입은 원피스는 복고풍이라 1960년대 패션을 연상시키네요.
The dress she is wearing today is retro, and it reminds me of 1960s fashion.

그 브랜드의 옷은 유행을 타지 않아요. 10년 후에도 입을 수 있을 거예요.
That brand's clothes don't go out of style. I'll be able to wear them 10 years from now.

이 키보드와 마우스는 인체공학적 디자인이라 손목에 무리가 가는 걸 방지합니다.
This keyboard and mouse have an ergonomic design that prevents wrist strain.

그 카페의 인테리어 디자인은 환경친화적이에요.
The cafe's interior design is eco-friendly.

차량

MP3 045-6

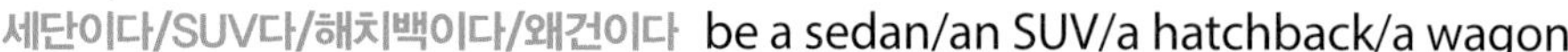

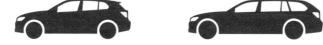

세단이다/SUV다/해치백이다/왜건이다 be a sedan/an SUV/a hatchback/a wagon

* 해치백은 객실과 트렁크의 구분이 없고 트렁크 문이 뒷좌석 위로 열리는 차종. 세단이 객실과 트렁크가 나뉘어 있는 것과 구별됨. 왜건은 트렁크 공간이 긴 차종

대형차다/중형차다/소형차다 be a full-size[large] car/a mid-size car/a compact[small] car

화물차다/승합차다/트레일러다/캠핑카다 be a truck/a van/a trailer/a camper (van)

이륜차다/전동 자전거다 be a two-wheeled vehicle/an electric bicycle

(차가) 5인승이다 be a 5 seater, seat 5 people * 5 자리에 숫자를 바꿔서 활용

국산 차다 be domestic, be a domestic car

외제[수입] 차다 be foreign-made[imported], be a foreign[an imported] car

독일제/미국제/일본제다 be made in Germany/the United States/Japan

SENTENCES TO USE

내 첫 번째 차는 은색 세단이었는데, 매일 출퇴근용으로 이용했어요.
My first car was a silver sedan, which I used for my daily commute.

그 사람 차는 중형 SUV로, 도심 주행과 비포장 도로 주행에 모두 적합해요.
His car is a mid-size SUV, suitable for both city driving and off-roading.

그 식당 앞에 주차돼 있던 차는 검정색 승합차였어요.
The car parked in front of the restaurant was a black van.

내 차는 5인승으로, 장거리 여행에도 가족들이 편안하게 이용할 수 있어요.
My car is a 5-seater, comfortably accommodating my family even on longer trips.

그 고객의 차는 외제 차였어요.
The customer's car was foreign-made.

UNIT 3

배기량이 ~cc다
have an engine displacement of ~ cc[cubic centimeters],
have a ~ cc engine displacement

승차감이 좋다/안 좋다 have a good/bad ride

성능이 좋다 perform well

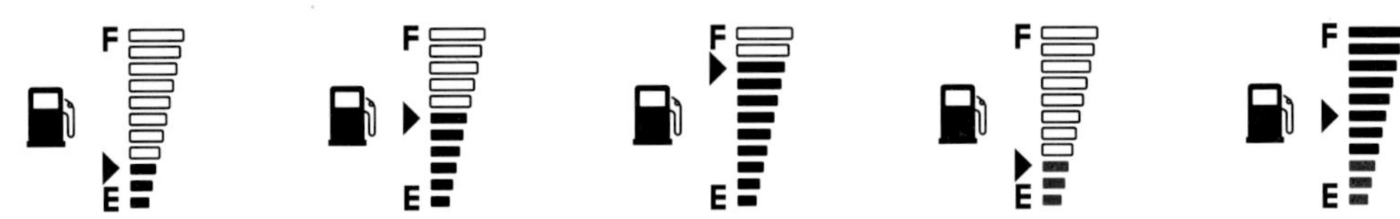

연비가 좋다 have good fuel efficiency[gas mileage, fuel mileage]

연비가 안 좋다 have poor fuel efficiency[gas mileage, fuel mileage]

차 내부가 더럽다 be dirty inside

차 내부에 쓰레기가 많다 have a lot of garbage inside

차체가[차 외부가] 더럽다 be dirty outside, be dusty

새 차 냄새가 나다
have that new-car smell

차에서 좋은 냄새가 나다
the car smells good

내부에서 악취가 나다
stink inside

SENTENCES TO USE

내 차는 배기량이 1,600cc예요.
My car has an engine displacement of 1,600 cubic centimeters.

제 차는 국산 세단인데 승차감이 좋아요.
My car is a domestic sedan, and it has a good ride.

연비가 좋아서 국산 중형차를 선택했어요.
I chose a domestic mid-size car because it has good fuel efficiency.

그녀의 차는 수입 대형차인데, 연비가 안 좋아요.
Her car is an imported full-size car, and it has poor fuel efficiency.

그의 차 내부에는 늘 쓰레기가 많아서 그 차는 타기가 싫어요.
His car always has a lot of garbage inside, so I don't want to get in it.

차량 고장, 정비 관련

MP3 045-7

(차가) 고장 나다 break down

시동이 걸리지 않다 don't start

배터리가 방전되다 the car battery is dead[discharged]

타이어가 펑크가 나다 사람 have a flat tire

차에서 이상한 소리가 나다 there is a strange noise[sound] coming from the[one's] car, hear strange noises from the[one's] car

창문/문이 안 열리다 car windows/doors do not open

전조등/방향 지시등에 불이 들어오지 않다 the headlights/the turn signals don't work[aren't working]

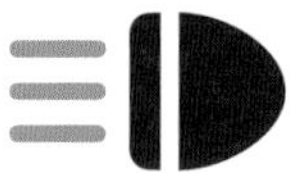

엔진 오일이 새다 the (car) engine oil[motor oil] is leaking

* 미국에서는 engine oil을 압도적으로 많이 사용

정비를 받다 have[get] the[one's] car serviced, the[one's] car has been serviced

SENTENCES TO USE

다리 위에서 차가 고장 나서 그는 너무 당황했어요.
He panicked when his car broke down on the bridge.

출근하려는데 차가 시동이 걸리지 않았어요.
I was going to work, but my car didn't start.

타이어에 펑크가 나서 보험회사의 긴급 서비스를 호출했어요.
I had a flat tire, so I called the insurance company's emergency service.

아침부터 차에서 이상한 소리가 나서 걱정돼요.
I'm worried because I've been hearing strange noises from my car since earlier today.

내 차 전조등에 불이 안 들어와서 수리를 받아야 해요.
The headlights on my car don't work, so they need to be fixed.

PART 4

일과 생활

CHAPTER

1

일과 업무

UNIT 1

일, 업무

일에 적응하다 adjust[adapt] to a job[work]

회사에 적응하다 adjust[adapt] to a company

일에 만족하다 be satisfied with one's work

일에 만족하지 못하다 be dissatisfied with one's work

업무 만족도가 높다 have high job satisfaction(격식체), be highly satisfied with one's work(회화체)

업무 만족도가 낮다 have low job satisfaction(격식체), be not satisfied with one's work(회화체)

일이 적성에 맞다 일 match one's aptitude, 사람 be cut out for the job

일이 적성에 맞지 않다 일 do not match one's aptitude, 사람 be not cut out for the job

SENTENCES TO USE

그녀는 새로 입사한 회사에 적응하는 중이에요.
She is adjusting to her new company.

나는 대체로 내가 하는 일에 만족합니다.
In general, I am satisfied with what I do.

그 사람은 자기 일에 만족 못해서 늘 불평해요.
He's dissatisfied with his work, so he always complains about it.

그 부서 직원들은 잦은 초과근무 때문에 업무 만족도가 낮아요.
Employees in that department have low job satisfaction due to frequent overtime.

그녀는 일이 적성에 맞지 않아서 고민이에요.
She is frustrated because the job does not match her aptitude.

MP3 046

일이 바쁘다 be busy with work

일이[업무량이] 많다 have a lot of work

과중한 업무에 시달리다
suffer from a heavy workload

일이 너무 바빠 정신없다
be swamped[overwhelmed] with work

~ 때문에 업무가 지장을 받다 one's work is hampered[hindered, disrupted] by[due to] ~

업무량이 적당하다 one's workload is moderate[decent, reasonable], have a moderate[decent, reasonable] workload

일이[업무량이] 많지 않다 don't have much[a lot of] work

~ 업무를 맡다[담당하다] be in charge of ~

~을 책임지고 있다 be responsible for ~

업무를 총괄하다 oversee[manage, supervise] the work

~ 부서/팀의 책임자다 be the head of the ~ department/team

중요한 업무를 부여받다 be assigned[given] an important task
* assigned가 더 격식체

SENTENCES TO USE

그 회사에 다닐 때는 과중한 업무에 시달렸죠.
When I worked for that company, I suffered from a heavy workload.

그 회사 직원들은 업무량이 적당한 것 같습니다.
The company's employees seem to have a moderate workload.

저는 회사에서 마케팅 업무를 맡고 있어요.
I am in charge of marketing for our company.

루이스 씨가 인사부 책임자예요.
Mr. Lewis is the head of the human resources department.

그녀는 최근에 중요한 업무를 부여받았는데, 자신의 가치를 입증할 기회입니다.
She has recently been given an important task, which is a chance to prove her worth.

UNIT 2 팀워크, 사내 관계

리더십이 있다
have leadership skills[qualities, abilities]

리더십이 없다
lack[have no] leadership skills[qualities, abilities]
* have no는 캐주얼한 느낌

팀워크가 좋다 have good[fine] teamwork

팀워크가 탄탄하다 have strong teamwork

팀워크가 좋지 않다 have poor teamwork

팀워크가 무너지다
one's teamwork fails, a team falls apart

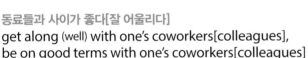

동료들과 사이가 좋다[잘 어울리다]
get along (well) with one's coworkers[colleagues],
be on good terms with one's coworkers[colleagues]

동료들과 사이가 좋지 않다[잘 어울리지 못하다]
don't get along (well) with one's coworkers[colleagues],
be on bad terms with one's coworkers[colleagues]

~에게 동료애를 느끼다 feel camaraderie with ~

SENTENCES TO USE

그 팀장은 리더십이 있어서 팀을 잘 이끌어요.
The team leader has leadership skills and leads his team well.

그 팀 팀원들은 팀워크가 별로 좋지 않아요. 일이 잘못되면 서로 비난해요.
The team members have poor teamwork. They blame each other when things go wrong.

그는 동료들과 사이가 좋아요.
He is on good terms with his coworkers.

그 신입사원은 아직 동료들과 잘 어울리지 못해요.
The new employee does not get along well with his colleagues yet.

그녀는 10년간 함께 일해 온 팀원들에게 동료애를 느낍니다.
She feels camaraderie with the team members she has worked with for 10 years.

동료 때문에 스트레스를 받다
feel stressed (out) because of one's coworkers[colleagues],
experience stress due to one's coworkers[colleagues]

동료들과 거리를 두다
keep[maintain] one's distance from one's coworkers[colleagues]

동료들과 경쟁하다
compete with one's coworkers[colleagues],
engage in competition with one's coworkers[colleagues]

동료들에 대해 경쟁심이 강하다
be very competitive with one's coworkers[colleagues]

상사에게서 많이 배우다
learn a lot from one's boss

상사/부하 직원 때문에 스트레스가 심하다
be under a lot of stress because of one's boss/subordinate,
feel very stressed (out) because of one's boss/subordinate

상사가 꼰대다
one's boss is a Boomer[an old-fashioned person]

부하 직원이 버릇이 없다
one's subordinate is rude[disrespectful]

SENTENCES TO USE

그는 회사에서 동료들과 거리를 두고 지냅니다.
He keeps his distance from his coworkers at work.

우리는 동료들과 경쟁할 수밖에 없어요.
We have no choice but to engage in competition with our colleagues.

나는 첫 번째 회사의 상사에게서 많은 것을 배웠어요.
I learned a lot from my boss at my first company.

그녀는 부하 직원 때문에 스트레스가 심해요.
She is under a lot of stress because of her subordinate.

내 상사는 나이도 많지 않은데 완전 꼰대라니까요.
My boss is not old, but he is such a Boomer.

직업 소개

나는 ~다. **I am a[an] ~.**
내 직업은 ~다. **My job is a[an] ~.**

가수 singer

가톨릭 수녀 nun

가톨릭 신부, 사제 (Catholic) priest

가톨릭 주교 bishop

가톨릭 추기경 cardinal

간호사 nurse

건축가 architect

검사 prosecutor

경비원 (security) guard(보안 담당), janitor(건물의 청소와 유지 담당)

경찰관 police officer * 집합적 의미의 '경찰'은 police

계산원(상점) cashier

공무원 civil servant, public official, government official

공장 노동자 factory worker

과학자 scientist

광부 miner, mine worker(영국)

교사 teacher

교수 professor

구급대원 paramedic

국회의원 member of the National Assembly(한국), member of Congress(미국), Congressperson(미국), member of Parliament(영국)

군인 장교 (military) officer

군인(사병) soldier

기술자, 엔지니어 engineer

기자 reporter, journalist

내과 의사, 의사 physician
농부 farmer
뉴스 진행자 (news) anchor, newscaster
도서관 사서 librarian
(도서) 편집자 (book) editor
드라마 작가 dramatist, playwright
만화가 cartoonist
만화영화 제작자 animator
메이크업 아티스트 make-up artist
목사 minister, pastor, rector(성공회의 교구 목사)
무용수, 댄서 dancer
물리치료사 physical therapist
미용사 hairdresser
발명가 inventor
방송(TV) 연출자 television director
방송(TV) 제작자 television producer

배달 기사, 택배 기사 delivery person[driver], courier
배우 actor(남자), actress(여자) * 요즘은 남녀 불문 actor로 칭하는 분위기
버스 기사 bus driver
번역가 translator
변호사 lawyer
사업가 businessperson, businessman
사진작가 photographer
사회복지사 social worker

소방관 firefighter
소설가 novelist
수의사 vet, veterinarian
승려 Buddhist monk, Buddhist priest
시나리오 작가 screenwriter

MORE

시인 poet

신문 기자 newspaper reporter, journalist

아나운서 announcer

약사 pharmacist

어부 fisherman

영양사 nutritionist

영화감독 movie[film] director

외과 의사 surgeon

외교관 diplomat * 대사: ambassador 영사: consul

영업사원 sales representative(더 격식체), salesperson

요리사 cook, chef(고급스런 환경에서 일하는 전문 요리사)

용접 기사 welder

웹툰 작가 webtoonist

유튜버 YouTuber, YouTube creator, content creator, influencer(영향력 있는 유튜버)

은행원 bank teller

음악가, 뮤지션 musician

의사 doctor

작가 writer

정치가 politician

제빵사 baker

조각가 sculptor

조리사 cook

주부 stay-at-home mother[mom], housewife, homemaker(가장 중립적이고 포괄적인 단어)

청소부 cleaner

치과 의사 dentist

택시 기사 taxi driver

통역가 interpreter

트럭 기사 truck driver

판사 judge

패션 디자이너 fashion designer

프로게이머 progamer

프로그래머 programmer

피부 관리사 aesthetician

한의사 doctor of oriental medicine, doctor of Korean medicine

화가 artist, painter

회계사 accountant

회사원 (company) employee, company worker, office worker, nine-to-fiver (회화체)

CHAPTER

2

관계, 소속

UNIT 1

친구

~을 알다, ~와 아는 사이다 know ~, be acquainted with ~

~을 모르다, ~와 일면식도 없다 don't know ~, be not acquainted with ~

~의 소개로 알게 되다 be introduced by ~

~의 소개로 …을 알게 되다
get to know … through someone's introduction

~와 친하다[사이가 가깝다] be close to ~

~와 사이가 좋다 get along with ~, be on good terms with ~

~와 친구다 be friends with ~

~와 단짝이다[절친이다, 베프다] be best friends with ~

SENTENCES TO USE

그 만화 좋아해요? 내가 그 만화가와 아는 사이거든요.
Do you like that cartoon? I know the cartoonist.

그는 하이드 씨와 일면식도 없어요.
He doesn't know Mr. Hyde. / He is not acquainted with Mr. Hyde.

나는 송년 파티에서 베이커 씨 소개로 그녀를 알게 되었죠.
I got to know her through Ms. Baker's introduction at the year-end party.

그녀는 동네 사람들과 사이가 좋아요.
She gets along with the people in the neighborhood.

제니는 키이라와 단짝이에요. 둘은 항상 붙어 다녀요.
Jenny is best friends with Keira. They always hang out together.

호형호제하다 be like brothers, be good friends with ~

~가 둘 다 아는 친구다 be one's mutual friend(s)

~와 사이가 멀어지다[소원해지다] become estranged from ~

사이가 나빠지다 one's[the] relationship gets worse

~와 사이가 나쁘다 be on bad terms with ~, don't get along with ~

~와 절교하다[손절하다]
end one's friendship[a relationship] with ~, cut ties with ~, be through with ~

~와 같은 학교 친구다 go to the same school as ~, be in the same school as ~

중학교/고등학교/대학교 동창이다 be middle school/high school/college[university] alumni

* alumni는 여러 사람을 뜻하는 단어이며, 한 사람일 때 남자면 alumnus, 여자면 alumna

SENTENCES TO USE

제시카는 우리가 둘 다 아는 친구예요.
Jessica is our mutual friend.

언제부터인지는 모르겠는데 나는 그녀와 사이가 멀어졌어요.
I don't know since when, but I've become estranged from her.

나는 작년에 그를 손절했어요. 제 뒤통수를 쳤더라고요.
I cut ties with him last year. He stabbed me in the back.

마이크와 제임스는 같은 학교 친구예요.
Mike and James go to the same school.

그 두 사람은 고등학교 동창이자 사돈이에요.
The two are high school alumni and in-laws.

UNIT 2

연인, 부부

MP3 050

~와 썸을 타다 have something going on with ~, be in a situationship with ~

~와 알아 가는 중이다 see ~, get to know ~

~을 어장 관리하다 keep ~ on the hook

~와 사귀다 date ~, go out with ~

천생연분이다 be a match made in heaven

~와 헤어지다 break up with ~

~와 약혼하다(상태) be engaged to ~

~와 파혼하다 break off one's engagement with ~

~와 결혼하다(상태) be married to ~

싱글이다, 임자가 없다 be single[on the market]

* on the market은 비격식체

품절남/품절녀다 be taken[off the market]

* off the market은 비격식체

돌싱이다 be back on the market

* 비격식체

SENTENCES TO USE

너 그 여자애랑 썸 타는 거 아니야?
Don't you have something going on with that girl?

사람을 어장 관리하는 건 옳지 못하다고.
It's not right to keep someone on the hook.

저 두 사람은 정말 천생연분이네요.
Those two are truly a match made in heaven.

이제 크리스티나는 품절녀예요.
Now Christina is off the market.

저도 이제 돌싱이랍니다.
I'm back on the market, too.

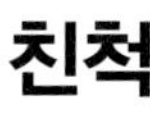 3 친척

MP3 051

친척이다/~와 친척이다 be relatives/be a relative of ~

사촌이다/~와 사촌이다 be cousins/be a cousin of ~

외가 쪽 사촌이다 be one's maternal cousin, be one's cousin on the mother's side

친가 쪽 사촌이다 be one's paternal cousin, be one's cousin on the father's side

오촌이다 be one's cousin's child (사촌의 자녀들), be one's father's/mother's cousin (부모님의 사촌)

육촌이다 be a second cousin

사돈지간이다/~와 사돈이다 be in-laws/be in-laws with ~

시가/처가 식구들이다 be one's in-laws, be one's husband's/wife's family

* one's in-laws라고 하면 주로 시부모나 장인, 장모를 가리킴

먼 친척이다 be a distant relative

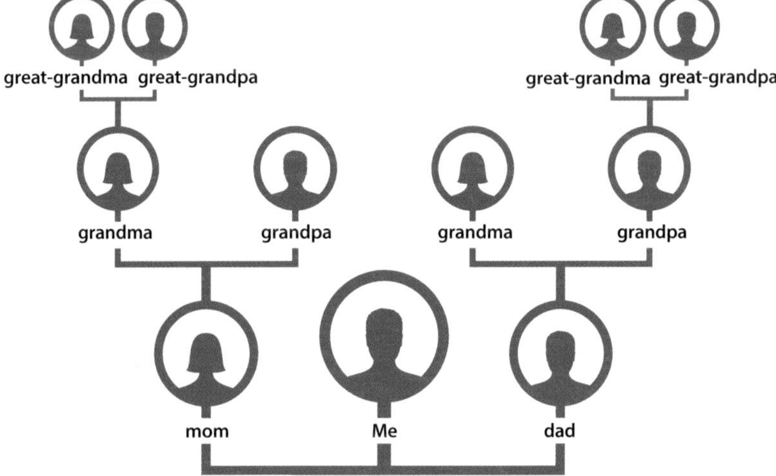

SENTENCES TO USE

나와 사라는 사촌인데, 서로 일 년에 한 번 정도 얼굴을 봐요.
Sara and I are cousins, and we see each other about once a year.

유진은 내 외가 쪽 사촌이에요. 그러니까, 엄마 언니의 아들이에요.
Eugene is my maternal cousin. In other words, he is the son of my mother's sister.

존과 나는 육촌 사이인데, 어려서부터 친해요.
John and I are second cousins, and we've been close since we were young.

저분들은 제 처가 식구들이에요. 시카고에서 어제 도착했어요.
Those are my wife's family. They arrived from Chicago yesterday.

나는 그 배우의 먼 친척이에요. 집안 행사에서 몇 번 봤어요.
I am a distant relative of that actor. I've seen him a few times at family events.

MORE

MP3 052

친척 관계

고조할아버지 great-great-grandfather
고조할머니 great-great-grandmother
증조할아버지 great-grandfather
증조할머니 great-grandmother
할아버지 grandfather
할머니 grandmother
친할아버지 grandfather on one's father's side, paternal grandfather
친할머니 grandmother on one's father's side, paternal grandmother
외할아버지 grandfather on one's mother's side, maternal grandfather
외할머니 grandmother on one's mother's side, maternal grandmother
아버지 father
어머니 mother
아들 son
딸 daughter
손주, 손자 손녀 통칭 grandchild
손자 grandson
손녀 granddaughter
삼촌, 백부, 숙부, 고모부, 이모부 uncle
고모, 이모, 백모, 숙모 aunt
사촌 cousin
오촌 one's cousin's child, one's father's/mother's cousin
육촌 second cousin
남자 조카 nephew
여자 조카 niece
시아버지, 장인 father-in-law
시어머니, 장모 mother-in-law
사위 son-in-law
며느리 daughter-in-law
시누이, 올케, 형수, 제수, 처형, 처제 등 sister-in-law
시동생, 처남, 자형, 매형, 자부, 매부 등 brother-in-law

4 회사 동료 & 기타

MP3 053

회사 동료

MP3 053-1

회사 동료다 be coworkers[colleagues, fellow workers], work for the same company

같은 부서/팀 소속이다
belong to the same department/team

같은 팀 동료다
be one's teammate, be one's colleague on the same team

내 옆 부서/팀 사람이다
be from the department/team next to mine

~와 입사 동기다
join the company the same year as 주어 did

상사다 be one's supervisor[boss, manager]

직속 상사다 be one's immediate supervisor[boss, manager]

부하 직원이다 be one's subordinate

직속 부하다 be one's direct report

회사 선배다 be a senior employee at one's company

회사 후배다 be one's junior colleague

거래처 사람이다 be one's client[business partner]

업무상 아는 사이다 know through work

SENTENCES TO USE

아까 마주친 그 남자와 저는 회사 동료예요.
The man we ran into earlier and I are coworkers.

마이클은 제 입사 동기입니다.
Michael joined the company the same year as I did.

파커 씨가 제 직속 상사라서 제가 그분께 직접 보고합니다.
Ms. Parker is my immediate supervisor, so I report to her directly.

그 친구는 제 회사 후배예요.
He is my junior colleague.

남편은 업무상 저랑 아는 사람이었는데, 저에게 도움을 많이 줬죠.
My husband knew me through our work, and he helped me a lot.

기타

MP3 053-2

~에 속하다, ~ 소속이다 belong to ~

~의 회원이다 be a member of ~

~ 동호회 회원이다 be a member of ~ club

~ 팬클럽 회원이다 be a member of someone's fan club, be a fan club member of ~

SENTENCES TO USE

그 사람은 우리 출판사 편집팀 소속이에요.
He belongs to the editorial team at our publishing company.

나는 소설 창작 모임 회원이에요.
I am a member of a novel writing club.

그는 회사 테니스 동호회 회원이에요.
He's a member of the company's tennis club.

그녀는 인기 K-pop 그룹 팬클럽 회원이라고 했어요.
She said she's a member of a popular K-pop group's fan club.

MORE

회사 직급, 직책

회장 chairperson, chairman
* 성별이 남성에 국한되는 느낌을 피하기 위해 chairperson을 쓰는 게 바람직함

부회장 vice chairperson, vice chairman

사장, 대표 president

부사장, 부대표 vice president

최고경영자 CEO (chief executive officer)

최고재무책임자 CFO (chief financial officer)

최고운영책임자 COO (chief operating officer)

고문 adviser, advisor

임원 executive, board member

전무 executive director

상무, 국장 director

이사 board member, member of the board of directors

본부장 head of headquarters, headquarters manager

지점장 branch manager

팀장 team manager[leader]

부장 general manager

차장 deputy general manager

과장 manager

대리 assistant manager

사원 staff member, employee

신입 사원 new employee, new hire

인턴 사원 intern

정규직 노동자 full-time worker

계약직 노동자 contract worker

일용직 노동자 day laborer

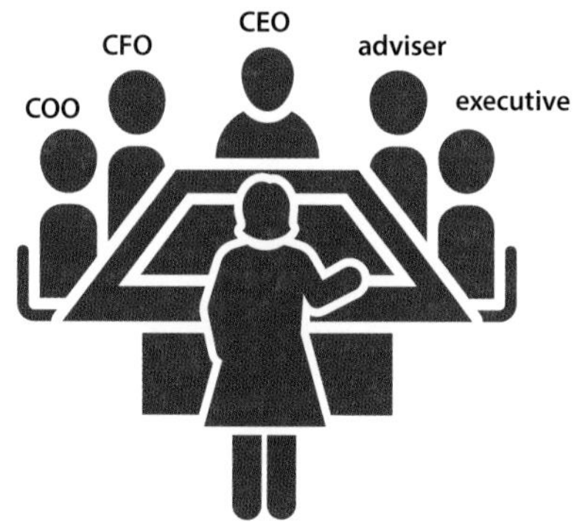

CHAPTER

3

분위기

UNIT 1

분위기 일반

화기애애하다
be friendly[cordial]
* cordial은 격식체

따뜻하다
be warm

편안하다
be comfortable

차분하다
be calm

들떠 있다
be excited

활기차다
be lively

열기가 달아오르다 heat up

열광적이다 be electric

열띠다 be heated
* 토론 등에서 의견이 달라서 열기를 띠는 것

소란스럽다 be noisy

산만하다 be distracted

SENTENCES TO USE

송년 모임 분위기는 화기애애했어요.
The mood at the year-end party was cordial.

이 카페는 분위기가 따뜻하고 아늑해서 참 편안하네요.
The atmosphere in this cafe is warm and cozy, making it very comfortable.

이 도서관은 분위기가 차분해서 여기 오면 긴장이 풀리고 편안해져요.
The atmosphere in this library is calm, so coming here helps me feel relaxed.

패스트푸드 식당에 여자아이들이 모여 있었는데, 분위기가 활기차더라고요.
A group of girls gathered at a fast-food restaurant, and the atmosphere was lively.

그 록 콘서트의 분위기는 다들 흥분해서 열광적이었어요.
The atmosphere at the rock concert was electric with excitement.

어색하다
be awkward

냉랭하다
be cold[chilly]

싸하다, 썰렁하다
be awkward[uncomfortable]

슬프다
be sad

우울하다
be gloomy

엄숙하다
be solemn

험악하다
be harsh[grim]

살얼음판이다
feel like walking on thin ice

무겁다
be heavy

SENTENCES TO USE

그날 모임은 분위기가 어색하고 냉랭했어요.
The mood at the meeting that day was awkward and cold.

그 젊은이의 장례식장 분위기는 유독 슬펐습니다.
The atmosphere at the young man's funeral was particularly sad.

사제 서품식은 엄숙했습니다.
The rite of priestly ordination was solemn.

잭이 저지른 실수 때문에 오늘 회의 분위기가 험악했어요.
The tone of today's meeting was harsh because of Jack's blunder.

분위기가 너무 무거워서 그녀가 애써 분위기를 띄워 보려고 했죠.
The atmosphere was so heavy that she tried to lighten it.

UNIT 2 사람의 분위기

밝다
be bright
* 똑똑하다는 뜻도 있음

여유 있다
have a relaxed attitude

편안하다 be comfortable, have a comfortable attitude

따뜻하다, 푸근하다 be warm

인간미가 넘치다 be full of humanity

기품 있다 be dignified

우아하다 be elegant

지적이다 be intelligent

SENTENCES TO USE

그녀는 언제나 밝아서 주변 사람들을 기분 좋게 만들어요.
She is always bright, and makes people around her feel good.

그 남자는 태도에 여유가 있는데, 그런 태도에서 힘이 느껴져요.
The man has a relaxed attitude, and I can feel his strength in it.

그 사람은 함께 있으면 편안해서 언제 만나도 기분이 좋아요.
I feel good whenever I meet that person because he is comfortable to be around.

심플하지만 우아한 옷차림의 그 노부인은 기품이 있었어요.
The old lady, dressed in simple yet elegant attire, was dignified.

그녀는 우아하고 지적이지만, 그런 모습이 다른 이들에게 항상 편한 건 아닐 수 있어요.
She is elegant and intelligent, but that may not always be comfortable for others.

야무지다
be on the ball
* 유능하고 똑부러지고 빈틈없다는 뜻

당당하다
be confident

강인하다 be tough[strong]

세련되다 be refined[sophisticated, polished]

근엄하다
be solemn[stern]
* solemn은 근엄하고 엄숙한 태도, stern은 엄격하고 다소 가혹한 태도

촌스럽다 be out of style[old-fashioned, countrified]

산만하다 be scatterbrained
* 침착하지 못하고 정신이 산만한 것

거만하다 be arrogant[stuck-up, conceited]
* stuck-up은 비격식체

속물적이다 be a snob, be snobbish[snobby]

도도하다, 콧대가 높다 be haughty

SENTENCES TO USE

그는 처음에는 야무져 보이지 않았거든요. 그런데 그 일을 완벽하게 처리했더라고요.
At first, he didn't seem on the ball. However, he handled the task perfectly.

그녀는 늘 당당한 모습이 매력적이에요.
She always looks confident, and that's what's attractive.

그 남자는 옷차림이나 행동이나 말투나 모든 게 다 세련됐어요.
The man is sophisticated in everything: his clothes, his actions, and his way of speaking.

그분은 근엄해 보이지만 사실은 친근하고 유머러스한 분이에요.
Although he looks solemn, he is actually a friendly and humorous person.

존을 처음 봤을 때는 속물인 줄 알았는데, 그렇지 않더라고요.
When I first saw John, I thought he was a snob, but it turned out he wasn't.

UNIT 2

차갑다 be cold

거칠다, 난폭하다 be rough[tough, aggressive]

천박하다, 상스럽다 be vulgar[crude]

음울하다
be gloomy

음흉하다
be sneaky

요상하다
be strange

SENTENCES TO USE

그 사람의 태도가 너무 차가워서 모임에 있던 사람들 모두가 불편했어요.
His attitude was so cold that it made everyone at the meeting uncomfortable.

그 남자는 너무 거칠어 보여서 다가가기가 겁이 나요.
The man looks so rough that it's intimidating to approach him.

나는 그 사람이 말투랑 행동이 상스러워서 싫어요.
I don't like him because his way of speaking and acting are vulgar.

그는 처음 만났을 때부터 좀 음흉한 느낌이 들었어요.
He seemed somewhat sneaky from the first time I met him.

UNIT 3

장소, 건물의 분위기

편안하다 be comfortable

아늑하다 be cozy

힐링되다 be therapeutic

차분하다 be calm

조용하다 be quiet

모던하다, 현대적이다 be modern

고풍스럽다 have a traditional style, look like an antique

고급스럽다 be luxurious

도시적이다 be urban

전원풍이다 be country-styled, have a country-style atmosphere

이국적이다 be exotic

SENTENCES TO USE

그 카페는 편안하고 아늑합니다.
The cafe is comfortable and cozy.

그 공원은 언제 가도 힐링이 돼요.
The park is therapeutic no matter when I visit.

그 대학교 건물은 고풍스러워요. 1800년대에 지어졌어요.
The university building has a traditional style. It was built in the 1800s.

그 호텔은 내부가 무척 고급스러웠어요.
The interior of the hotel was very luxurious.

그 마을은 꽤 이국적이어서 관광객들을 많이 끌어들였죠.
The town was quite exotic, so it attracted a lot of tourists.

CHAPTER

4

날씨, 계절, 시간, 위치, 방향

UNIT 1

날씨

MP3 058

맑다
it is sunny

흐리다
it is cloudy

비가 오다
it is raining(지금 비가 오고 있다),
it is rainy(비가 오는 날이다: 전반적인 날씨 표현)

눈이 오다 it is snowing(지금 눈이 오고 있다),
it is snowy(눈이 오는 날이다: 전반적인 날씨 표현)

날이 개다 it clears up

바람이 불다
it is windy

안개가 끼다 it is foggy

습하다 it is humid

건조하다 it is dry

SENTENCES TO USE

지금 날이 흐린데, 내일은 비가 올 것 같아요.
It's cloudy now, and it looks like it's going to rain tomorrow.

며칠 동안 비가 오다가 오늘 드디어 날이 갰어요.
After a few days of rain, it finally cleared up today.

오늘, 기온은 낮지 않은데 바람이 많이 불어서 춥네요.
The temperature isn't low today, but it feels cold because it's very windy.

오늘 이 도시는 안개가 심하게 끼었어요.
It's very foggy in this city today.

오늘은 비가 오고 있어서 날이 무척 습해요.
It's raining today, so it's very humid.

UNIT 2 계절

MP3 059

봄

MP3 059-1

추위가 가시다 the cold has gone

조금 쌀쌀하다 it is a little chilly

기온이 오르다
the temperature rises

따뜻해지다
it gets warm[warmer]

따뜻하다
it is warm

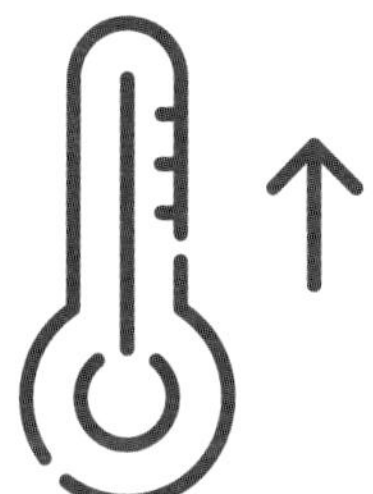

꽃샘추위가 찾아오다 the last cold snap has come

춥지도 덥지도 않다 it is neither cold nor hot

꽃이 피기 시작하다
flowers begin to bloom

꽃이 활짝 피다[만개하다]
the flowers are in full bloom

봄비가 내리다 spring rain falls

황사가 심하다 the yellow dust is bad[severe],
we have a lot of yellow dust

(초)미세먼지가 심하다 the (ultra)fine dust is bad[severe],
the (ultra)fine dust level is high,
we have a lot of (ultra)fine dust

SENTENCES TO USE

이제 추위가 가셔서 살 것 같아요.
Now that the cold has gone, I think I will survive.

좀 따뜻해지더니, 꽃샘추위가 찾아왔어요.
It got a little warmer, but then the last cold snap has come.

우리 동네에도 드디어 벚꽃이 만개했어요.
Cherry blossoms are finally in full bloom in our neighborhood.

중국의 영향으로 한국은 봄이면 황사가 심합니다.
Due to the influence of China, the yellow dust is bad in Korea in spring.

오늘이 이번 봄 들어서 미세먼지가 가장 심해요.
Today, the fine dust is the worst it's been this spring.

UNIT 2

여름

MP3 059-2

덥다 it is hot

무더위가[폭염이] 심하다, 불볕더위가 기승을 부리다
be particularly[severely, incredibly] hot,
there is a heat wave, a heat wave hits(폭염이 강타하다),
have[experience] a heat wave

습하다 it is humid

장마다 it is the rainy season

장마가 시작되다 the rainy season begins

장마가 계속되다 the rainy season continues[goes on]

장마가 끝나다 the rainy season ends[is over]

소나기가 쏟아지다 there is a rain shower

폭우[집중호우]가 쏟아지다 heavy rain falls,
there is torrential rain

홍수가 나다 there is a flood

불쾌지수가 높다
the discomfort index[temperature-humidity index] is high

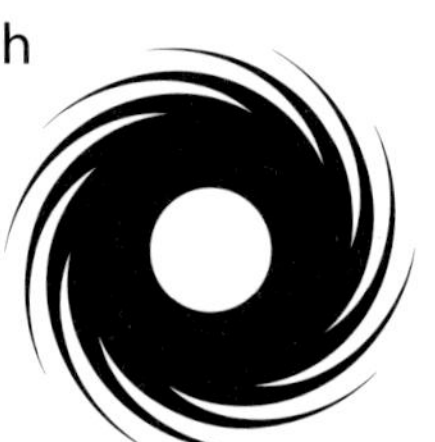

열대야가 지속되다 the tropical night continues

태풍이 오다/강타하다 a typhoon comes/hits

낮이 밤보다 더 길다 the days are longer than the nights

SENTENCES TO USE

올여름은 무더위가 특히 심할 거라는 전망입니다.
This summer is expected to be particularly hot.

7월 첫 주에 이 지역에도 장마가 시작되었죠.
In the first week of July, the rainy season began in this region too.

이 도시에 어젯밤 몇 시간 동안 폭우가 쏟아졌어요.
Heavy rain fell in this city for several hours last night.

오늘 불쾌지수가 무척 높으니 서로 배려합시다.
The discomfort index is very high today, so let's be considerate with each other.

10일 넘게 열대야가 지속되고 있어요.
The tropical nights have been continuing for over 10 days.

가을

MP3 059-3

선선하다, 서늘하다 it is cool

날씨가 쾌적하다 the weather is pleasant

날이 맑다 it is clear

하늘이 맑다/푸르다 the sky is clear/blue

일교차가 크다
the daily temperature difference is large[big],
there is a large[big] daily temperature difference

건조하다 it is dry

안개가 끼다 it is foggy

단풍이 들다 autumn leaves change colors,
the leaves turn red/yellow

서리가 내리다 it is frosty

SENTENCES TO USE

9월 중순이 되니 드디어 날씨가 선선하네요.
It's mid-September, and it is finally cool.

날씨가 쾌적해서 나는 가을이 좋아요.
I like autumn because the weather is pleasant.

초가을에는 일교차가 큽니다.
In early fall, the daily temperature difference is large.

10월 하순이 되면서 단풍이 들기 시작했어요.
Autumn leaves have begun to change colors in late October.

오늘 새벽에 서리가 내렸더라고요. 곧 겨울이 오겠어요.
It was frosty early this morning. Winter will come soon.

UNIT 2

겨울

MP3 059-4

춥다 it is cold

얼어붙을 듯이 춥다 it is freezing (cold)

한파가 심하다 be particularly[severely, incredibly] cold, there is a cold wave, a cold wave hits(한파가 강타하다), have[experience] a cold wave

일조량이 적다[줄다] there is less sunlight

밤이 낮보다 더 길다 the nights are longer than the days

눈이 내리다 it snows

폭설이 내리다 there is heavy snow

도로가 얼다[빙판이다]/미끄럽다 the road is icy/slippery

건조하다 it is dry

SENTENCES TO USE

어제는 날씨가 얼어붙을 듯이 추워서 외출을 안 했어요.
It was freezing cold yesterday, so I didn't go out.

겨울에는 밤이 낮보다 더 길고 일조량이 적어요.
In winter, the nights are longer than the days, and there is less sunlight.

크리스마스이브인데, 밖에 눈이 내리고 있어요.
It's Christmas Eve, and it's snowing outside.

어제 눈이 와서 오늘 도로가 빙판이고 미끄럽네요.
It snowed yesterday, and the roads are icy and slippery today.

겨울에는 건조해서 가습기를 틀어야 해요.
In winter, it is dry, so you need to use a humidifier.

Cherry
blossoms
are finally
in full
bloom
in our neighborhood.

시간

MP3 060

시간이 (너무) 이르다 it is (too) early

시간이 (너무) 늦다 it is (too) late

~에 일찍 오다[가다] 사람 be early for ~

~에 늦다 사람 be late for ~

시간이 많다
have a lot of time,
there is a lot of time
* 캐주얼한 대화에서는 much나 many보다 a lot of가 더 자연스러움

시간이 넉넉하다
have plenty of time,
there is plenty of time

시간이 충분하다
have enough time,
there is enough time

시간이 별로 없다
don't have much time,
there isn't much time

시간이 없다
have no time,
there is no time

SENTENCES TO USE

시간이 너무 일러서 행사장에는 사람이 거의 없었어요.
It was so early that there were few people at the venue.

어젯밤에는 시간이 너무 늦어서 세탁기를 돌리지 못했어요.
I couldn't run the washing machine last night because it was too late.

나는 약속에 일찍 가 있었어요. 늦는 걸 싫어하거든요.
I was early for the appointment. I hate being late.

오늘은 시간이 많으니까 재미있게 놀아 보자.
We have a lot of time today, so let's have some fun.

오늘은 그 문제에 대해 논의할 시간이 충분합니다.
We have enough time to discuss the matter today.

MORE

시간 관련 속담을 영어로

세월이 유수(流水)와 같다.
Time flies.
Time goes by so fast.

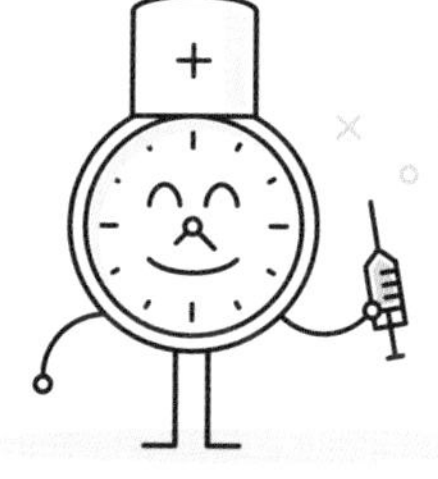

세월이 약이다.
Time heals all wounds.

세월 앞에 장사 없다.
All things yield to time.
Nothing escapes time.
Time changes everything.
Everyone gets old.

십 년이면 강산도 변한다.
Time changes everything.
Nothing escapes time.
A lot can happen in ten years.

세월은 사람을 기다려 주지 않는다.
Time waits for no man.

일각(一刻)이 여삼추(如三秋)다.
A minute seems like a lifetime.

사람 팔자 시간문제다.
You never know what's going to happen.

UNIT 4 위치, 방향

(붙어서) ~ 위에 있다
be on ~,
be on top of ~

~ 위에 있다
be above ~

* above와 over는 모두 '~ 위에'라는 뜻이지만, above는 정적인 느낌, over는 움직임을 나타내는 동적인 느낌이 있음

~ 위에 있다
be over ~

* 이동해 가는 움직임을 나타낼 수 있고, 위로 무엇을 덮는 것을 나타냄

~ 아래[밑]에 있다
be under[below] ~

~ 앞에[정면에] 있다
be in front of ~

~ 뒤에 있다
be behind ~

~ 옆에 있다 be beside[next to] ~

* next to는 바로 옆, beside는 바로 옆은 아님

~ 맞은편에 있다 be across from ~,
be on the opposite side of ~

~와 대각선 방향이다 be diagonally across from ~,
be in a diagonal direction with ~

A와 B 사이에 있다 be between A and B

SENTENCES TO USE

소나기가 내린 후에 그 고층 빌딩 위에 쌍무지개가 걸려 있었어요.
A double rainbow was above the tall building after a rain shower.

그 대학교 정문 앞에 횡단보도가 있습니다.
A crosswalk is in front of the main entrance of the university.

우리 아파트 뒤에는 등산로가 있어서 나는 주말에 자주 거기로 하이킹을 가요.
A hiking trail is behind our apartment, so I often go hiking there on weekends.

그 우체국은 그 대형 서점에서 대각선 방향이에요. 찾기 쉬워요.
The post office is diagonally across from the large bookstore. You can't miss it.

그 천주교회와 방송국 사이에 6차선 도로가 있습니다.
There is a six-lane road between the Catholic church and the broadcasting station.

~ 가까이에 있다
be near ~

~에서 엎어지면 코 닿을 거리에 있다
be within a stone's throw of ~

~에서 멀다 be far from ~

~의 오른쪽에/왼쪽에 있다
be to the right/left of ~

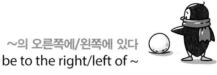

모퉁이에 있다 be on the corner

~의 동쪽/서쪽/남쪽/북쪽에 있다
be to the east/west/south/north of ~

~에서부터 ~미터/킬로미터 거리에 있다
be ~ meters/kilometers from ~

~에서부터 ~분/시간 거리에 있다
be ~ minute(s)/hour(s) away from ~

버스로/지하철로/차로/기차로/비행기로 ~분/~시간 거리에 있다
be ~ minute(s)/hour(s) away by bus/subway/car/train/plane

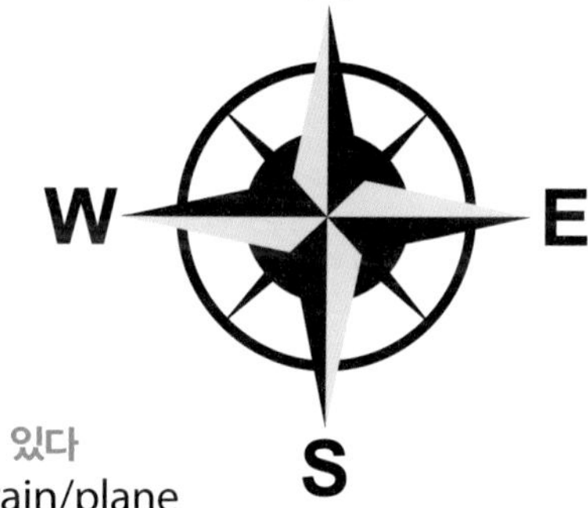

걸어서 ~분/시간 거리에 있다
be a ~-minute/hour walk away

걸어갈 수 있는 거리에 있다
be within walking distance

SENTENCES TO USE

그가 이사 간 집은 지하철역에서 멀어요.
The house he moved to is far from the subway station.

뉴욕시는 필라델피아 북쪽에 있어요.
New York City is to the north of Philadelphia.

그 도시는 여기서 약 200킬로미터 거리에 있고, 차로 세 시간 정도 걸려요.
The city is about 200 kilometers from here, and it takes about three hours by car.

그의 사무실은 집에서 지하철로 약 50분 거리에 있어요.
His office is about 50 minutes away from his home by subway.

시장과 은행이 걸어서 갈 수 있는 거리에 있어서 생활하기 편리해요.
The market and bank are within walking distance, making it a convenient place to live.

CHAPTER

5

개인의 경제 생활

UNIT 1

개인 경제 전반

부자다, 부유하다 be rich[wealthy, well off]

벼락부자(가 되)다 become suddenly rich,
suddenly become a part of new rich,
be a part of the nouveau riche(경멸적 의미)

준재벌이다
have an enormous amount of money,
be a quasi-conglomerate

금수저다(부잣집에 태어났다)
be born with a silver spoon in one's mouth,
be born into a rich family

돈 여유가 있다 have some money to spare,
have extra money(앞의 표현보다 더 상당한 여유가 있음을 의미)

먹고살 만하다 make[earn] a living, earn a crust

SENTENCES TO USE

그 사람은 비트코인에 투자해서 벼락부자가 됐어요.
That person became suddenly rich by investing in Bitcoin.

그녀는 사업이 성공해서 준재벌이 됐다고 하네요.
It is said that her business was successful, and she became a quasi-conglomerate.

그 남자는 금수저라 우리 같은 사람들 심정을 몰라요.
He was born into a rich family and doesn't know how people like us feel.

나는 직장생활을 시작하고 몇 년이 지나서야 돈 여유가 좀 생겼어요.
It wasn't until a few years after I started working that I had some money to spare.

우리 집은 이제 좀 먹고살 만해요.
Our family can now make a living.

가난하다 be poor

돈에 쪼들리다 be pressed for money, be short of money

금전적으로 여유가 없다 have no money to spare, have no financial resources

---

재산이 ~(금액)이다 have a fortune of[worth] ~, have assets of[worth] ~

저축액이 ~(금액)이다 have ~ in savings, one's savings amount is ~

투자액이 ~(금액)이다 have an investment of ~

현금이 ~(금액) 있다 have ~ in cash

~(금액)의 부동산을 갖고 있다 have real estate worth ~

(부동산 가치가) ~(금액)이다 be worth ~, cost ~

SENTENCES TO USE

그는 열심히 일하는데도 늘 돈에 쪼들려요.
He works hard, but he is always pressed for money.

나는 나이 40에 재산이 5백만 달러였어요.
I had a fortune worth 5 million dollars at the age of 40.

그 스물두 살 청년은 저축액이 만 달러예요. 대단한 것 같아요.
The 22-year-old has 10,000 dollars in savings. I think it's amazing.

그녀는 집은 있는데 현금은 몇 천 달러밖에 없어요.
She has a house but only a few thousand dollars in cash.

킴벌리 씨는 백만 달러 상당의 부동산을 가지고 있습니다.
Ms. Kimberly has real estate worth 1 million dollars.

UNIT 2

임금, 연금

MP3 064

연봉이 ~(금액)이다
have an annual salary of ~,
one's annual salary is ~

연 수입이 ~(금액)이다
have an annual income of ~,
one's annual income is ~

월급이 ~(금액)이다
have a (monthly) salary of ~,
one's (monthly) salary is ~

주급이 ~(금액)이다 the[one's] weekly wage is ~

일당이 ~(금액)이다 the[one's] daily wage is ~

시급이 ~(금액)이다 the[one's] hourly wage is ~

최저임금이 ~(금액)이다 the minimum wage is ~

국민연금을 매달 ~(금액) 받다
receive[get] a national pension of ~ every month,
receive[get] ~ of national pension every month,
receive[get] ~ per[a] month from the national pension

노령연금을 매달 ~(금액) 받다
receive[get] an old-age pension of ~ every month,
receive[get] ~ of old-age pension every month,
receive[get] ~ per[a] month from the old-age pension

SENTENCES TO USE

그 교수는 연봉이 십만 달러가 넘어요.
The professor has an annual salary of more than one hundred thousand dollars.

그 시인은 연 수입이 2만 달러도 안 된다네요.
It is said that the poet's annual income is less than twenty thousand dollars.

2009년 대학 졸업 후 내 첫 월급이 2,500달러였어요.
When I graduated from college in 2009, my initial monthly salary was 2,500 dollars.

2024년 기준, 미국 연방 최저임금은 시간당 7.25달러입니다.
As of 2024, the federal minimum wage in the U.S. is $7.25 per hour.

우리 할머니는 노령연금을 매달 300파운드 받으세요.
My grandmother receives an old-age pension of 300 pounds every month.

UNIT 3

예금, 대출, 투자

정기 예금을 들고 있다 have a time deposit

정기 적금을 들고 있다 have an installment savings account

매달 정기 적금에 ~(금액)을 붓다
put ~ into one's installment savings every month

정기 예금에 ~(금액)이 있다 have ~ in one's time deposit

~(금액)짜리 정기 적금을 들고 있다
have a ~ installment savings account,
have an installment savings account of[worth] ~

금리가 (연) ~퍼센트다
the interest rate is ~ percent (per annum),
have an interest rate of ~ percent (per annum)

정기 예금이 만기가 되다 a time deposit has matured

정기 적금이 만기가 되다 an installment savings account has matured

(예금/적금이) 비과세 상품이다 be a tax-free[tax-exempt] product

SENTENCES TO USE

나는 매달 정기 적금에 400달러를 붓고 있어요.
I am putting $400 into my installment savings every month.

그녀는 정기 예금에 십만 달러 정도가 있어요.
She has about $100,000 in her time deposits.

이 예금은 금리가 연 4.5퍼센트입니다.
This deposit has an interest rate of 4.5 percent per annum.

정기 적금이 만기가 돼서 은행에 가야 해요.
I have to go to the bank because my installment savings account has matured.

이 정기 예금은 비과세 상품입니다.
This time deposit is a tax-exempt product.

UNIT 3

부채가[빚이] ~(금액)이다[있다] have a debt of ~, owe ~

(개인) 대출이 ~(금액)이다[있다] have a (personal) loan of ~, have ~ on loan

주택 담보 대출이 ~(금액)이다[있다] have a mortgage of ~, have ~ on a mortgage

대출 이율이 (연) ~퍼센트다 the loan interest rate is ~ percent (per annum), the interest rate on one's loan is ~ percent (per annum)

대출 이율 한도가 ~퍼센트다 the loan interest rate can be up to ~ percent

대출 이자가 매달 ~(금액)이다 one's loan interest[the interest on one's loan] is ~ per month, have a loan interest of ~ per month

대출 이자가 연체되다 the interest on the loan is overdue

대출/주택 담보 대출 상환이 끝나다, 대출금을/주택 담보 대출금을 다 갚다
one's loan/mortgage is paid off[is done]

대출이 막히다 have no way to get a loan

SENTENCES TO USE

그는 사업으로 진 빚을 거의 갚고 지금 빚이 십만 달러 있어요.
He has almost paid off his business debt and now owes $100,000.

나는 대출이 30만 달러 정도 있어요. 이 집을 사느라 받았죠.
I have a loan of about $300,000. I took it out to buy this house.

그녀는 주택 담보 대출이 20만 달러 있는데, 20년 안에 갚아야 해요.
She has a mortgage of $200,000, and needs to pay it off in 20 years.

그는 대출 이자가 매달 1,000달러예요.
The interest on his loan is $1,000 per month.

내 주택 담보 대출은 지난달에 상환이 끝났어요. 나는 이제 빚이 없어요.
My mortgage was done last month. I'm debt-free now.

주식을 가지고 있다 have[own] stocks

주식에 투자하다 invest in stocks

~(금액) 어치 주식을 보유하고 있다
have[own] stocks worth ~,
have[own] stocks valued at ~

주식으로 이익을 보다[돈을 벌다]
make a profit on stocks, make money on stocks[in the stock market]

주식으로 손해를 보다[돈을 잃다] lose money on stocks[in the stock market]

펀드에 투자하다 invest in a fund

~(금액) 어치 펀드를 보유하고 있다 have[own] a fund worth ~, have[own] a fund valued at ~

펀드로 이익을 보다[돈을 벌다] make a profit on the fund, make money with the fund

펀드로 손해를 보다[돈을 잃다] lose money on[with] the fund

암호화폐를[가상자산을] 보유하고 있다 have[own] cryptocurrency

암호화폐에[가상자산에] 투자하다 invest in cryptocurrency

암호화폐로[가상자산으로] 이익을 보다[돈을 벌다]
make a profit on cryptocurrency, make money with cryptocurrency

암호화폐로[가상자산으로] 손해를 보다[돈을 잃다] lose money on cryptocurrency

SENTENCES TO USE

매트는 만 달러어치 주식을 갖고 있어요. 20살 생일에 아버지가 주신 거예요.
Matt owns stocks worth $10,000, which his father gave him on his 20th birthday.

나는 대학에 다닐 때부터 주식에 조금 투자해 왔어요.
I have been investing a little in stocks since I was in college.

일부 소식통에 따르면 그녀가 주식으로 큰돈을 벌었다고 합니다.
It is said by some sources that she made a great deal of money from stocks.

그녀는 주식 투자는 안 하지만 펀드에는 조금 투자하고 있어요.
She doesn't invest in stocks but invests a little in funds.

그는 암호화폐에 투자해서 큰 이익을 봤다고 해요.
He is said to have made a large profit on cryptocurrency.

UNIT

4 보험, 세금

4대 보험에 가입되어 있다 have[be enrolled in] four major social insurance programs

* be enrolled in이 더 격식체
* 4대 보험: health insurance(건강보험), national pension(국민연금), workers' compensation insurance(산재보험), unemployment insurance(고용보험)

Insurance

Financial Insurance

Life Insurance

Family Insurance

Home Insurance

Health Insurance

Car Insurance

Safety

Secure

Risk

사설[개인] 보험에 몇 개 가입해 있다 have several private insurance policies

보험료가 매달 (금액) 나가다 one's insurance premium costs ~ every month, pay ~ in various insurance premiums every month, have insurance premiums of ~ per month

연금보험을/퇴직연금보험을 들고 있다 have an annuity/a retirement plan

세금을 해마다 ~(금액) 내다 pay ~ in taxes every year[per year, a year]

올해는 소득세가 ~(금액)다 this year, income tax is ~

해마다 재산세/자동차세를 ~(금액) 내다
pay ~ in property tax/car tax every year[per year, a year],
pay property tax/car tax of ~ every year[per year, a year]

SENTENCES TO USE

여기 아르바이트생들도 4대 보험에 가입돼 있습니다.
Part-timers here are also enrolled in four major social insurance programs.

내 건강보험료는 매달 300달러 정도 나가요.
My health insurance premium costs about $300 every month.

나는 국민연금 외에 퇴직연금보험을 들고 있어요.
In addition to the national pension, I have a retirement plan.

그녀는 해마다 세금을 1만 달러 정도 냅니다.
She pays about $10,000 in taxes every year.

나는 재산세를 해마다 1천 달러 정도 냅니다.
I pay about $1,000 in property tax every year.

공과금이 한 달 평균 ~(금액)다 the average utility bill is ~ per month

이번 달 전기료가 ~(금액)다 one's electricity bill is ~ this month, the electricity bill for one's house is ~ this month

이번 달 수도료가 ~(금액)다 one's water bill is ~ this month, the water bill for one's house is ~ this month

이번 달 가스 요금이 ~(금액)다 one's gas bill is ~ this month, the gas bill for one's house is ~ this month

아파트 관리비가 매달 ~(금액)쯤 되다 one's apartment maintenance fee is about ~ per month, the maintenance fee for one's apartment is about ~ per month

공과금을 자동이체로 납부하다 pay one's utility bills by automatic withdrawal

공과금이 자동이체로 납부되다 one's utility bills are paid by automatic withdrawal

공과금을 ~(기간)째 밀리다[체납하다] be behind on one's utility bills for ~, one's utility bills have been overdue for ~

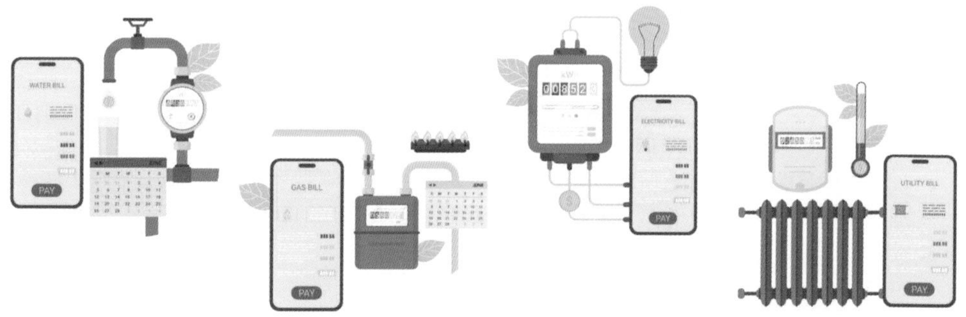

SENTENCES TO USE

이번 달 우리 집 전기료가 100달러가 넘어요.
The electricity bill for my house is more than $100 this month.

가스 요금이 꽤 올라서 이번 달에는 400달러 넘게 나왔어요.
The gas rate has risen significantly, and the gas bill was over $400 this month.

그녀의 아파트 관리비는 매달 200달러쯤 됩니다.
The maintenance fee for her apartment is about $200 per month.

나는 모든 공과금을 자동이체로 납부하고 있어요.
I pay all my utility bills by automatic withdrawal.

보도에 의하면 그 가족은 7개월째 공과금이 밀린 상태였다고 합니다.
It is reported that the family had been behind on their utility bills for seven months.

MORE

여러 가지 보험

~ 보험을 갖고 있다/ ~ 보험에 들어 있다
have ~ / be enrolled in ~

생명보험 life insurance
종신보험 whole life insurance
연금보험 national pension(국민연금, 공적 연금보험), annuity(사적 연금보험)
퇴직연금보험 retirement plan * 미국의 경우 401(k) insurance
변액보험 variable life insurance
변액연금보험 variable annuity (insurance)
건강보험 health insurance
실비보험(실손의료비보험) medical reimbursement insurance
암보험 cancer insurance
치아보험 dental insurance
자동차보험 car insurance, auto insurance
운전자보험 driver's legal protection insurance
화재보험 fire insurance
여행(자)보험 travel insurance
간병보험 long-term care insurance
반려동물보험 pet insurance
고용보험 unemployment insurance
산재보험 workers' compensation insurance

여러 가지 세금

~(세금)을 내다 **pay ~**
~(세금)이 (금액)가 나오다 (세금) **is** (액수)

국세 national taxes * 미국에서는 federal taxes(연방세)

소득세 income tax
법인세 corporate tax
종합부동산세 comprehensive real estate holding tax

MP3 067

상속세 inheritance tax
증여세 gift tax
양도세 transfer tax

부가가치세 VAT (= value-added tax) * 미국에서는 sales tax(판매세)
개별소비세 special[specific, individual] consumption tax
* 미국에서는 excise tax(국내 소비세)

주세 liquor tax
인지세 stamp tax, stamp duty * 법률 문서에서는 stamp duty라고 표현하는 게 일반적
증권거래세 securities transaction tax
교육세 education tax
교통세 traffic tax
에너지세 energy tax
환경세 environmental tax, green tax
농어촌특별세 special tax for rural development

지방세 local taxes

주민세 residence tax
재산세 property tax
자동차세 car tax, automobile tax, vehicle tax
취득세 acquisition tax
지방소득세 local income tax
담배소비세 tobacco consumption tax, tobacco tax

여러 가지 공과금

전기 요금 electricity bill, power bill
상수도 요금 water bill
하수도 요금 sewer bill

가스 요금 gas bill
아파트 관리비 apartment maintenance fee
휴대전화 사용료 mobile phone bill, cell phone bill

인터넷 사용료 Internet bill
케이블 TV 수신료 cable TV bill
위성 TV 수신료 satellite TV bill
TV 수신료 TV license fee

CHAPTER

6

취미, 종교

UNIT 1

취미

취미가 ~이다 one's hobby is ~

취미가 많다 have a lot of[many] hobbies

취미가 없다 have no hobbies

취미로 ~을 시작하다 take up[start] ~ as a hobby

취미를 살려서[취미로] ~을 하다 do something as a hobby

~에 취미가 없다 have no interest in ~,
don't have much interest in ~ (~에 별 취미가 없다)

~을 좋아하다 like ~

~하는 것을 좋아하다 like 동사ing[to 동사원형]

~을/하는 것을 즐기다 enjoy 명사/동사ing

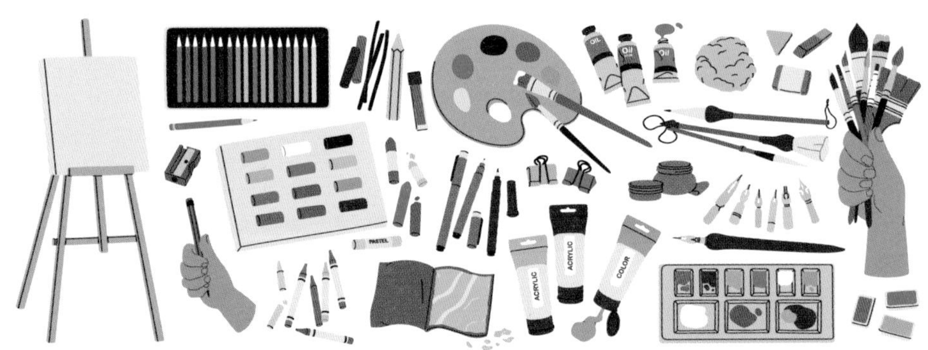

SENTENCES TO USE

내 취미는 좋아하는 책을 필사하는 거예요.
My hobby is transcribing my favorite books.

그는 취미가 없어서 취미가 많은 사람들이 궁금하고 흥미롭죠.
He has no hobbies, so he finds people who have many hobbies fascinating.

나는 최근에 취미로 요리를 하게 되었는데, 하면 할수록 더 재미를 느껴요.
I have recently taken up cooking as a hobby, and the more I cook, the more I enjoy it.

그녀는 취미를 살려서 가족과 친구들 초상화를 그립니다.
As a hobby, she draws portraits of her family and friends.

그녀는 시간이 될 때마다 캠핑 가는 걸 즐깁니다.
She enjoys going camping whenever time allows.

MP3 068

~의 팬이다, ~ 덕후다 be a fan of ~

~의 열성 팬이다 be a big fan of ~

~의 덕질을 하다 dig ~ (조금 예스러운 표현),
fanboy[fangirl] over ~ (대중문화 관련 덕질에 유머러스하게 사용하는 표현으로, fanboy는 주어가 남자일 때, fangirl은 주어가 여자일 때 씀)

~(취미)가 돈이 많이 들다/돈이 안 들다
~ cost money/
~ don't cost money

~(취미)가 시간이 많이 들다/시간이 별로 안 들다
~ take a lot of[much] time/
~ don't take much time

~(취미)을 혼자 하다/남들과 함께 하다
do one's hobbies alone/with others[other people]

~(취미)는 배우기가 쉽다/어렵다
~ be easy/difficult to learn

~ 재료를 구하기가 쉽다/어렵다
it is easy/difficult to obtain ~ materials

SENTENCES TO USE

우리 아빠는 그 추리소설가의 팬이세요.
My father is a fan of that mystery novelist.

나는 예전에 그 록밴드의 열성 팬이어서 콘서트에 빼놓지 않고 갔지요.
I used to be a big fan of that rock band, so I never missed their concerts.

그녀는 요즘 그 한국인 배우 덕질을 하고 있어요.
She is fangirling over that Korean actor these days.

그의 취미는 뮤지컬 관람인데, 돈이 꽤 듭니다.
His hobby, watching musicals, costs quite a bit of money.

각종 취미들

내 취미는 ~다
My hobby is ~

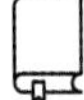
책 읽기[독서] reading (books)
오디오북 듣기 listening to audiobooks

글 쓰기 writing
(클래식) 음악 감상 listening to (classical) music
영화 보기 watching movies, going to the movies
TV 드라마 보기 watching TV series[TV dramas, TV shows]
TV 예능 프로/코미디 프로/토크쇼/리얼리티쇼 보기 watching variety shows/comedy shows/talk shows/reality shows
연극 보기 watching plays
뮤지컬 보기 watching musicals
콘서트 가기 going to concerts

노래 부르기 singing
노래방 가기 going to karaoke, singing karaoke

피아노/기타/드럼 연주하기 playing the piano/guitar/drums
춤추기 dancing
미술 전시 관람 going to[viewing] art exhibitions

사진 찍기 taking pictures(캐주얼한 느낌), photography(좀 더 전문가적인 느낌)

그림 그리기 drawing[painting] pictures
만화 그리기 drawing cartoons
공예 doing[making] crafts
다이어리 꾸미기 decorating a[one's] diary
캘리그래피 calligraphy
붓글씨 쓰기 ink brush calligraphy

SNS 활동 using social media
요리 cooking
제빵 baking
제과 making cookies

뜨개질 knitting

옷 만들기 making clothes

인형 만들기 making dolls

반려동물 돌보기 taking care of pets, caring for pets

음반 수집 collecting LPs[CDs]

화폐 수집 collecting coins and banknotes

우표 수집 collecting stamps

모바일/온라인/컴퓨터 게임 playing mobile/online/computer games

보드게임/카드 게임 playing board games/card games

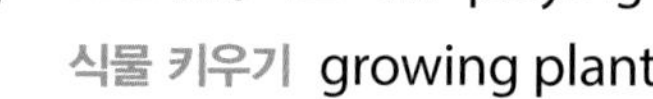
식물 키우기 growing plants

정원 가꾸기 gardening

텃밭 가꾸기 vegetable gardening

천체 관측 stargazing, observing celestial bodies

산책 taking a walk, going for a walk

드라이브 going for a drive, taking a drive

등산 hiking, mountain climbing

* hiking은 둘레길을 걷거나 가볍게 등산하는 것, mountain climbing은 전문 장비를 갖추고 등산하는 것

여행 travel

국내 여행 domestic travel

해외 여행 traveling abroad

배낭여행 backpacking

유람선 여행 going on a cruise

캠핑 going camping

낚시 fishing

축구/야구/농구/배구 하기
playing soccer/baseball/basketball/volleyball

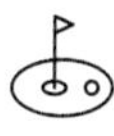
배드민턴/테니스/탁구/당구/골프 치기 playing badminton/tennis/table tennis/billiards/golf

볼링 치기 going bowling

마라톤 running marathons, marathon running

자전거 타기 cycling

요가 doing yoga

태권도 practicing taekwondo

서핑 surfing

UNIT

2 종교

MP3 070

종교가 있다 have a religion

종교가 없다 have no religion

종교를 가진 적이 없다 have never had a religion

(독실한) 기독교/불교/천주교[가톨릭]/개신교 신자다
be a (devout) Christian/Buddhist/Catholic/Protestant
* 기독교는 천주교와 개신교를 포함하는 명칭

성당/교회/절에 다니다
go to[attend] Catholic church/church/Buddhist temple
* attend가 더 격식체

유신론자다 be a theist

무신론자다 be an atheist

유일신을 믿다 believe in one (and only) God

신앙심이 깊다 be (very) religious

신앙심이 얕다 have shallow faith

(가톨릭) 세례를 받다 be baptized (a Catholic)

사이비 종교에 빠지다
get into[fall for] a cult [pseudo-religion]
* fall for는 회화에서 주로 쓰이고, get into는 다소 중립적 느낌

SENTENCES TO USE

우리 엄마는 불교 신자로, 주말마다 절에 다녀요.
My mother is a Buddhist and goes to temple every weekend.

정신분석학자 프로이트가 무신론자였다는 거 알았어요?
Did you know that the psychoanalyst Freud was an atheist?

나는 (예전엔) 유일신을 믿는 사람들이 신기했어요.
I used to be amazed at people who believed in one God.

그녀는 50이 넘어서 가톨릭 세례를 받고 성당에 다니기 시작했어요.
When she was over 50, she was baptized a Catholic and began attending Catholic church.

그 남자가 사이비 종교에 빠져서 집을 나갔다고 해요.
The man is said to have fallen for a cult and left home.

종교 관련 용어

종교 일반

신앙(심) faith
믿음 belief
영성 spirituality
종파, 교파 religious group, (religious) sect, denomination
신학 theology
교리 doctrine
유신론 theism
유신론자 theist
유일신교, 일신론 monotheism
다신론, 다신교 polytheism
범신론, 만유신교 pantheism
이신론(理神論), 자연신교 deism
* 신이 세계를 창조한 후에는 관여하지 않고 세계가 자체의 법칙에 따라 움직인다는 사상
무신론 atheism
무신론자 atheist
불가지론 agnosticism * 인간은 신의 존재에 대해 알 수 없다는 사상

주요 종교

기독교 Christianity
기독교도 Christian
천주교, 가톨릭 Catholicism
천주교도 Catholic
개신교 Protestantism
개신교도 Protestant

(동방) 정교회 Eastern Orthodoxy,
Eastern Orthodox Christianity, Byzantine Christianity
정교회 교도 Eastern Orthodox Christian
성공회 Anglicanism
성공회 교도 Anglican

유대교 Judaism
유대교도 Jew
불교 Buddhism
불교도 Buddhist
이슬람교 Islam
이슬람교도 Muslim
힌두교 Hinduism
힌두교도 Hinduist

개신교 교파

장로회 Presbyterianism * 장로교회 Presbyterian church
감리회 Methodism * 감리교회 Methodist church
침례회 Baptists * 침례교회 Baptist church
성결교회 Holiness Movement[Church]
* Holiness Movement가 좀 더 포괄적이고 넓은 개념으로 쓰임
복음주의 Evangelicalism, Evangelical Christianity, Evangelical Protestantism
구세군 Salvation Army
퀘이커 Quakers, Religious Society of Friends

종교 관련 인칭 명사

하느님(천주교), 하나님(개신교), 신 God
주, 주님 Lord
성모 마리아 the Virgin Mary, Saint Mary
성인 saint
예언자 prophet
사제, 신부 priest
수녀 nun
목사 minister, pastor
수도자, 수도승 monk
승려 Buddhist monk
여승, 비구니 Buddhist nun, bhikkhuni
이맘 imam * 이슬람교에서 예배를 인도하는 성직자

랍비 rabbi * 유대교의 지도자, 율법학자
구루 guru * 힌두교의 스승, 지도자
신자 believer
성직자(사제, 목사, 랍비 등) the clergy(집합적, 복수), clergyman, clergywoman
평신도 layperson
개종자 convert

종교 경전

성경 (기독교) Bible
불경 (불교) Buddhist scriptures

꾸란 (이슬람) Quran
토라 (유대교) Torah
베다 (힌두교) Vedas
탈무드 (유대교) Talmud

종교 행위와 주요 개념

기도 prayer
묵상 meditation
미사 (천주교) Mass * 소문자로 쓰기도 함
예배 (개신교) worship

찬송, 찬양 praise
성가, 찬송가 hymn
성가대 choir
강론, 설교 sermon
세례 baptism
영성체, 성찬 communion

순례 pilgrimage
순례자 pilgrim
단식 fasting
고해 confession
삼위일체 the (Holy) Trinity
(그리스도의) 부활 the Resurrection
구원 salvation, redemption

(불교의) 깨달음, 득도 enlightenment
업보, 카르마 karma
열반, 해탈 nirvana
환생 reincarnation
내세 afterlife
선교, 전도 mission work
개종 conversion

예배 및 수행 장소

성당, 천주교회 Catholic church
대성당 cathedral * 주교가 관장하는 교구 내 중심 성당
교회 church
절, 사찰 Buddhist temple
모스크 (이슬람) mosque
시너고그 (유대교) synagogue
수도원 monastery
수녀원 convent
성지(聖地), (성인의 유골·유물을 모신) 성당·묘 shrine

기타

이교 heathenry * 자기가 믿는 종교 이외의 종교
이교도 heathen, pagan
이단 heresy
* 자기가 믿는 종교의 교리에 어긋나는 이론이나 행동, 또는 그런 종교
성화(聖畫), 성상(聖像) icon
순교자 martyr
신성한, 성스러운 holy, sacred
불경스러운, 신성 모독적인 profane
신성 모독 blasphemy
배교 apostasy * 믿던 종교를 배반함
사이비 종교 집단 cult

CHAPTER

7

언어, 교육

UNIT 1

언어

~(언어)가 모국어다
~ is one's mother tongue[native language, first language]

~(언어)가 두 번째 언어다
~ is one's second language

2개 언어를 사용하다
be bilingual (in[of] ~)

3개 언어를 사용하다
be trilingual (in[of] ~)

여러 언어를 사용하다
be multilingual

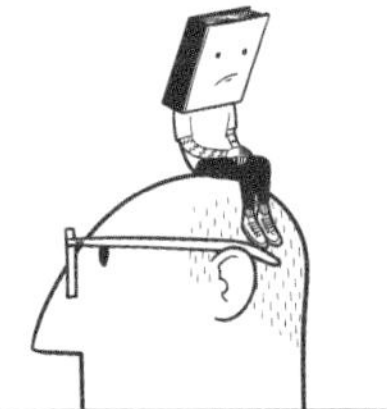

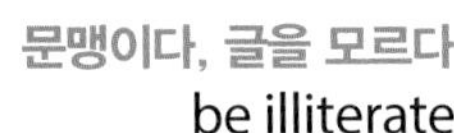

문맹이다, 글을 모르다
be illiterate

글을 읽고 쓸 줄 알다
be literate, can read and write

언어에 재능이 있다
have a talent for language

언어 감각이 좋다
have a good sense of language

SENTENCES TO USE

마이클의 모국어는 영어고 독일어가 두 번째 언어입니다.
Michael's mother tongue is English, and German is his second language.

그 여성은 2개 언어를 사용하는데, 영어와 이탈리아어를 합니다.
The woman is bilingual in English and Italian.

그의 할머니는 문맹으로, 자신의 이름도 쓸 줄 모르셨어요.
His grandmother was illiterate and couldn't even write her own name.

한국인의 99퍼센트 정도가 글을 읽고 쓸 줄 압니다.
About 99% of Koreans can read and write.

그녀는 언어 감각이 좋은데, 결국 작가가 되었어요.
She has a good sense of language and eventually became a writer.

~(언어)를 잘하다 can speak ~ well,
be good at ~,
be proficient at ~ (더 격식체)

~(언어)가 유창하다 be fluent in ~ (더 격식체),
speak ~ fluently

~(언어)에 익숙하다 be familiar with ~

~(언어)를 알아듣다 can understand ~

~(언어)를 조금 하다 speak a little ~,
speak ~ a little

~(언어)를 생존[기초] 수준으로 하다 speak basic ~

~(언어)를 잘 못하다 cannot speak ~ well,
be poor at ~

~(언어)를 못하다 cannot speak ~

~(언어)를 (전혀) 못 알아듣다
cannot[don't] understand ~ (at all)

SENTENCES TO USE

그는 상하이에 10년 넘게 살고 있어서 중국어가 유창합니다.
He is fluent in Chinese because he has lived in Shanghai for over 10 years.

부모님이 앨라배마주 출신이셔서 저는 남부 사투리에 익숙해요.
My parents are from Alabama, so I'm familiar with the Southern accent.

나는 영어를 알아듣기는 하지만 영어로 말은 잘 못해요.
I can understand English, but I can't speak it well.

그 남자는 영어를 생존 수준으로 합니다.
The man speaks basic English.

나는 프랑스어를 못 알아들어서 그에게 그녀가 하는 말을 통역해 달라고 부탁했어요.
I don't understand French, so I asked him to translate what she said.

UNIT 2

교육

유치원생이다 be a kindergartner, be in kindergarten, go to kindergarten

초등학생이다 be an elementary school student, be in elementary school, go to elementary school

중학생이다 be a middle school student, be in middle school, go to middle school

고등학생이다 be a high school student, be in high school, go to high school

ELEMENTARY SCHOOL

MIDDLE SCHOOL

HIGH SCHOOL

대학생이다 be a college[university] student, go to college[university], be an undergraduate

* an undergraduate는 대학원생(a graduate student)과 비교해 '학부생'을 가리킴

(고등학교, 대학교의) 신입생이다 be a freshman

대학원생이다 be a graduate student, attend graduate school

SENTENCES TO USE

그 부부의 아이들은 아직 유치원생이에요.
The couple's children are still in kindergarten.

그의 두 딸은 초등학생입니다.
His two daughters are elementary school students.

제 아들은 중학생인데, 소설가가 되는 게 꿈입니다.
My son is in middle school, and his dream is to become a novelist.

제 조카는 올해 대학 신입생이에요.
My niece is a freshman in college this year.

그녀는 대학원생이에요. 심리상담사가 되려고 공부를 하고 있죠.
She is a graduate student. She is studying to become a mental health counselor.

석사 과정에 있다
be in a master's program,
be enrolled in a master's program

(~의) 석사 학위가 있다
have a master's degree (in ~)

박사 과정에 있다
be in a Ph.D. program,
be in a doctoral program,
be enrolled in a Ph.D.[doctoral] program

박사 학위가 있다 have a Ph.D.[doctorate]

박사 후 연구원이다 be a postdoc,
be a postdoctoral fellow[researcher]

의무 교육을 받다
get[receive] compulsory education
* receive가 좀 더 격식체

대학 교육을 받다 be college-educated,
get[receive] a college education,
graduate from college,
have a college degree

고등 교육을 받다 get[receive] higher education,
be highly educated

SENTENCES TO USE

그녀는 미생물학을 공부하는데, 지금 석사 과정에 있습니다.
She's studying microbiology, and is currently enrolled in a master's program.

나는 영화학 석사 학위가 있어요. 석사 학위 논문 제목은 〈로드 무비의 인물 분석〉이에요.
I have a master's degree in film studies. The title of my master's thesis is "Analysis of Characters in Road Movies."

그는 미네소타 대학교에서 커뮤니케이션학 박사 후 연구원으로 있습니다.
He is a postdoctoral researcher in the Department of Communication Studies at the University of Minnesota.

그의 부모님은 의무 교육만 받으셨어요.
His parents received only compulsory education.

집안이 가난했음에도 그의 형제들은 모두 대학 교육을 받았어요.
Even though his family was poor, all of his siblings were college-educated.

UNIT 2

공교육을 받다 get[receive] public education

사교육을 받다
get[receive] tutoring[private education]
* 예체능 강습을 제외한 과외나 학원 교습을 의미

영재 교육을 받다
get[receive] education (designed)
for gifted children[the gifted]

무상 교육을 받다 get[receive] free education

정규 교육을 받다
get[receive] formal schooling[school education]

예체능 교육을 받다
get[receive] arts and
physical education

(~) 조기 교육을 받다 get[receive] early education (in ~)

(~) 선행 교육을 받다 get[receive] prior education (in ~)

가정 교육을 잘 받다 be well-brought-up
* 부모에게서 예절 교육 등을 잘 받다

가정 교육을 잘 못 받다 be poorly-brought-up

SENTENCES TO USE

그 나라의 아이들은 대부분 사교육을 받는다고 합니다.
It is said that most children in the country receive private education.

그 부부의 딸이 영재 교육을 받고 있다고 하네요.
The couple's daughter is said to be receiving education designed for gifted children.

그 나라 사람들은 고등학교까지 무상 교육을 받습니다.
People in the country receive free education through high school.

우리 할머니는 정규 학교 교육은 거의 받지 못하셨지만 책을 많이 읽으셨어요.
My grandmother got little formal schooling, but she read a lot of books.

그 사람은 가정 교육을 잘 받은 듯 보여요.
The person seems to be well-brought-up.

Buon giorno!
Long time no see.
Come sta?
Hello!
Buona sera.

ENGLISH
ITALIAN

The woman is bilingual in English and Italian.

PART 5

사회

CHAPTER

1

정치, 외교, 경제

UNIT 1 정치

민주 국가
a democratic country

독재 국가
a dictatorship, an autocracy, an autocratic country

전체주의 국가
a totalitarian country

자본주의 국가
a capitalist country

공산주의 국가
a communist country

사회주의 국가
a socialist country

공화국 a republic

민주공화국 a democratic republic

대통령제 국가[공화국] a presidential republic
* 주요 국가: 한국, 미국, 브라질, 인도네시아 등

의원내각제 공화국 a parliamentary republic
* 주요 국가: 독일, 이탈리아, 아일랜드, 인도, 이스라엘 등

SENTENCES TO USE

현재, 50개가 넘는 국가들이 독재 국가로 분류될 수 있습니다.
Currently, over 50 countries can be classified as dictatorships.

북한, 중국, 베트남, 라오스, 쿠바는 사회주의 국가입니다.
North Korea, China, Vietnam, Laos, and Cuba are socialist countries.

공화국은 정치 권력이 국민에게 있는 나라입니다.
A republic is a country where political power lies with the people.

대한민국 헌법 제1조에는 "대한민국은 민주공화국이다."라고 나와 있습니다.
Article 1 of the Constitution of the Republic of Korea states, "The Republic of Korea is a democratic republic."

인도네시아는 대통령제 국가로, 대통령의 임기는 5년입니다.
Indonesia is a presidential republic, and the president serves five years.

MP3 074

입헌군주국 a constitutional[limited] monarchy

* 주요 국가: 영국, 덴마크, 네덜란드, 일본 등

영세중립국 a (permanently) neutral country

* 주요 국가: 스위스, 오스트리아, 아일랜드 등

이원집정부제 국가
a semi-presidential republic,
a dual executive republic

* 주요 국가: 프랑스, 포르투갈, 이집트 등

영연방국가
a Commonwealth country

* 주요 국가: 영국, 캐나다, 호주, 뉴질랜드, 남아프리카공화국, 인도 등
* 영연방: Commonwealth of Nations

연방제 국가 a federal country

* 주요 국가: 미국, 캐나다, 브라질, 독일 등

선진국 a developed country, an advanced country,
a more economically developed country (= MEDC)

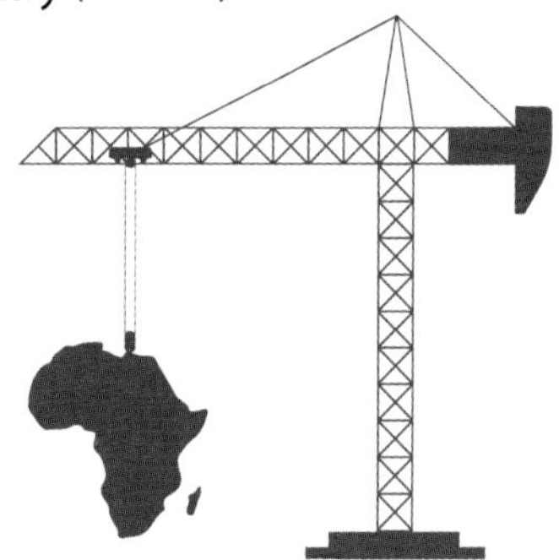

개발도상국, 발전도상국 a developing country,
a low and middle-income country

* 주요 국가: 중국, 인도, 베트남 등

후진국, 후발발전도상국 a least developed country

SENTENCES TO USE

영국과 일본은 입헌군주국입니다.
The U.K. and Japan are constitutional monarchies.

프랑스는 대통령과 총리가 있는 이원집정부제 국가입니다.
France is a semi-presidential republic with a president and a prime minister.

영연방 국가들의 대다수는 대영제국의 옛 영토예요.
The vast majority of the Commonwealth countries are former territories of the British Empire.

남아메리카의 브라질과 아르헨티나는 개발도상국입니다.
Brazil and Argentina in South America are developing countries.

불과 30년 전에 그 나라는 후진국이었습니다.
Just 30 years ago, the country was a least developed country.

UNIT 1

국가가 독립하다 become independent, gain independence

(두 나라가) 하나로 통일되다 be unified

정치적으로 안정되다/불안정하다 be politically stable/unstable

정치적으로 성숙하다/미성숙하다 be politically mature/immature

정치적으로 중립을 지키다 be[remain] politically neutral

정치 성향이 좌익이다 have left-wing political leanings(캐주얼한 대화에서 더 자주 사용), be left-wing in politics

정치 성향이 우익이다 have right-wing political leanings(캐주얼한 대화에서 더 자주 사용), be right-wing in politics

정치 성향이 중도다 have a moderate political orientation

정치 성향이 진보적이다 have progressive political inclinations(캐주얼한 대화에서 더 자주 사용), be progressive in political orientation

정치 성향이 보수적이다 have conservative political inclinations(캐주얼한 대화에서 더 자주 사용), be conservative in political orientation

여당이다/야당이다 be the ruling/opposition party

(당이) 집권하고 있다 be in power

~(공직)로 재직 중이다 be serving as ~

임기가 ~년이다 have a ~-year term, serve ~ years

임기가 ~년/달 남아 있다 have ~ years/months remaining in one's term, have ~ years/months remaining in office

SENTENCES TO USE

그 나라는 경제적으로는 발전했지만 정치적으로는 불안정합니다.
The country has developed economically but is politically unstable.

그 지역 주민들은 정치적으로 무척 성숙합니다.
The residents of that area are politically very mature.

그 여성은 정치 성향이 진보적입니다.
The woman has progressive political inclinations.

그 당이 집권하고 있어요. 즉, 여당이죠.
That party is in power. That is, it is the ruling party.

그 나라 대통령은 임기가 5년이므로, 지금 대통령은 임기가 2년 남아 있습니다.
The president of that country has a five-year term, so the current president has two years remaining in office.

POLITICS
VOTE

UNIT 2 외교

~와 우호 관계를 맺고 있다[유지하다]
have[maintain, enjoy] friendly relations
[a friendly relationship] with ~

(두 나라가) 우호 관계를 맺고 있다[유지하다]
have[maintain, enjoy] friendly relations
[a friendly relationship]

~와 협력 관계를 맺고 있다[유지하다]
have[maintain, enjoy] a cooperative relationship with ~

(두 나라가) 협력 관계를 유지하다
have[maintain, enjoy] a cooperative relationship

(~와) 갈등 관계에 있다 be in conflict (with ~)

(~와) 긴장 관계에 있다 have a tense relationship (with ~)

SENTENCES TO USE

한국과 튀르키예는 오랫동안 우호 관계를 유지해 왔습니다.
South Korea and Türkiye have long maintained friendly relations.

캐나다와 프랑스는 우호적이며 협력적인 관계를 유지하고 있습니다.
Canada and France maintain a friendly and cooperative relationship.

사우디아라비아와 이란은 많은 면에서 갈등 관계에 있습니다.
Saudi Arabia and Iran are in conflict in many respects.

미국은 그 나라와 20년 넘게 갈등 관계에 있습니다.
The United States has been in conflict with that country for over 20 years.

인도와 파키스탄은 1940년대부터 계속 긴장 관계에 있습니다.
India and Pakistan have had a tense relationship since the 1940s.

실리 외교를 펼치다
engage in[practice] practical diplomacy

~와 등거리 외교를 펼치다
engage in[practice] equidistant diplomacy with ~

~와 수교하다
establish diplomatic relations[ties] with ~

~와 단교하다
sever diplomatic relations[ties] with ~

~와의 외교를 강화하다
strengthen diplomacy with ~

~와의 외교를 중단하다
suspend diplomatic relations with ~,
suspend diplomacy with ~

다자 외교를 펼치다
engage in[practice] multilateral diplomacy

외교 관계가 수립되다
diplomatic relations are established

외교 관계가 확대되다
diplomatic relations expand

SENTENCES TO USE

그 나라는 주변 국가들과 등거리 외교를 펼치고 있습니다.
The country practices equidistant diplomacy with its neighbors.

니카라과는 대만과 단교한 상태입니다.
Nicaragua has severed diplomatic relations with Taiwan.

당시 행정부는 미국과의 외교를 강화했습니다.
The administration at the time strengthened diplomacy with the United States.

그 행정부는 다자 외교를 펼친 것으로 유명했습니다.
That administration was famous for engaging in multilateral diplomacy.

2024년에 한국과 쿠바의 외교 관계가 수립되었습니다.
Diplomatic relations between Korea and Cuba were established in 2024.

UNIT 3

경제 전반

MP3 076

경제 규모가 크다
have a large economy

~번째 경제 대국이다
be the ~th largest economy

경제적으로 발전하다
have developed economically, be economically developed

경제적으로 낙후되다
be economically underdeveloped[disadvantaged]

경제 성장률이 ~퍼센트다
the economic growth rate is ~ percent

경제 성장세가 빠르다
economic growth is fast[rapid]

경제 성장이 둔화되다 economic growth slows (down)

* slow가 좀 더 격식체, slow down은 회화체

산업화되다
become industrialized

산업화가 덜 되다
be less industrialized

산업화가 급속히 진행되다 industrialization progresses rapidly, 국가 undergo rapid industrialization

SENTENCES TO USE

캐나다는 2022년 기준 전 세계 8번째 경제 대국입니다.
Canada is the eighth largest economy in the world as of 2022.

그 대륙에 있는 국가들은 대부분 경제적으로 낙후되었습니다.
Most countries on the continent are economically underdeveloped.

1970년대에 그 나라는 경제 성장세가 빨랐어요.
In the 1970s, the country's economic growth was fast.

코로나19가 전 세계로 퍼진 2020년 이후로 경제 성장이 둔화돼 왔어요.
Economic growth has slowed since 2020 when COVID-19 spread worldwide.

그 나라는 인근 국가들에 비해 산업화가 덜 되었습니다.
The country is less industrialized than its neighbors.

UNIT 4 경기

경기가 좋다, 호황기이다
the economy is good[in good shape, in a boom period]

* be in good shape는 안정적인 경기 상태를 나타내는 중립적 의미, be in a boom period는 급속한 경제 성장으로 호황을 누리는 상태를 나타냄

불경기이다, 불황이다 be in a recession

경기가 살아나다[회복되다]
the economy recovers[picks up, revives]

경기가 과열되다 the economy gets overheated

경기가 침체되다 the economy is sluggish[stagnant]

* sluggish는 경제 활동의 둔화, stagnant는 성장과 변화가 없는 상태

경기 침체가 계속되다
the economic downturn continues[persists]

경기가 위축되다 the economy shrinks

인플레이션/디플레이션이 심하다
inflation/deflation is high[severe],
have high[severe] inflation/deflation

인플레이션이 둔화되다 inflation slows (down)

디플레이션이 완화되다 deflation eases

스태그플레이션에 빠지다 be in[fall into] stagflation

* 스태그플레이션: 경기 불황 중에 물가가 계속 오르는 현상

SENTENCES TO USE

그때는 경기가 좋아서 취업하기가 쉬웠어요.
At that time, the economy was good, making it easy to find a job.

불경기여서 우리 가게도 장사가 안 돼요.
Since the economy is in a recession, our store is also struggling.

올해 들어서 경기가 슬슬 살아나는 것 같아요.
The economy seems to be slowly recovering this year.

해가 여러 번 바뀌었음에도 경기 침체가 계속되고 있습니다.
Despite the passage of years, the economic downturn continues.

그 나라는 인플레이션이 심해서 금리를 더 빨리 인상할 가능성이 높습니다.
The country has high inflation and is likely to raise interest rates faster.

UNIT 5

무역, 외환

MP3 078

exports

imports

수출이 증가세다/감소세다
exports are on the rise/decline

수입이 증가세다/감소세다
imports are on the rise/decline

무역수지 흑자/적자가 계속되다
trade surplus/deficit continues[persists]

외환보유고가 증가하다/감소하다
foreign exchange[currency] reserves increase/decrease

외환 위기에 처하다
face a (foreign) currency crisis,
be in a (foreign) currency crisis

외환 위기에서 벗어나다
emerge from the (foreign) currency crisis

외환 위기를 극복하다
overcome the (foreign) currency crisis

외환 위기가 재발하다
the (foreign) currency crisis recurs

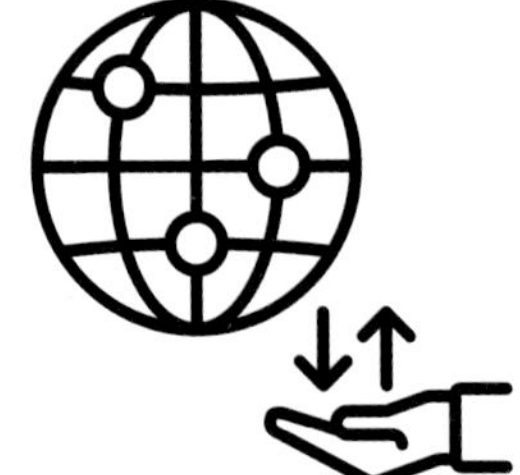

SENTENCES TO USE

그 나라는 3년째 수출이 증가세에 있습니다.
The country's exports have been on the rise for three years.

무역수지 적자가 11개월째 계속돼서 걱정이 커지고 있습니다.
Concern is mounting as the trade deficit has continued for 11 months.

코로나 정국에도 외환보유고는 지속해서 증가했습니다.
Foreign exchange reserves continued to increase even during the coronavirus pandemic.

그 나라는 1990년대 후반에 외환 위기에 처했는데, 그 위기는 광범위한 어려움을 초래했습니다.
The country faced a currency crisis in the late 1990s, causing widespread hardship.

온 국민이 함께 외환 위기를 극복할 수 있었습니다.
The entire nation was able to overcome the currency crisis together.

6 물가

* '물가'는 보통 복수형 prices로 씀

물가가 높다/낮다 prices are high/low

물가상승률이 ~퍼센트다 the inflation rate is ~ percent

물가상승률이 ~퍼센트를 웃돌다 the inflation rate exceeds ~ percent

소비자물가지수가 ~퍼센트다 the consumer price index (CPI) is ~ percent

물가가 안정적이다/불안정하다 prices are stable/unstable

물가가 오르다 prices rise[go up]

물가가 두 배로 뛰다
prices double, prices increase by double
* 3배/4배로 뛰다: triple/quadruple

물가가 폭등하다 prices skyrocket[soar]
* skyrocket이 더 극적인 느낌

물가가 내리다 prices fall[go down]

물가가 폭락하다 prices plummet

물가가 오르락내리락하다 prices rise and fall

SENTENCES TO USE

외식비를 생각하면 여기 물가가 높다는 걸 느낄 겁니다.
Considering the cost of dining out, you'll notice prices here are high.

지난해 물가상승률은 3퍼센트를 웃돌았습니다.
Last year, the inflation rate exceeded 3 percent.

지난 몇 달 사이에 물가가 너무 많이 올랐어요.
Prices have risen too much in the last few months.

물가가 지난 1년 사이에 두 배로 뛰었어요. 특히 과일과 채소가요.
Prices have doubled in the past year, especially for fruits and vegetables.

그 나라는 심각한 인플레이션으로 물가가 폭등했습니다.
The country's prices have skyrocketed due to severe inflation.

UNIT 7

금리

* 금리는 interest rate(s)

(금리가) 높다/낮다 be high/low

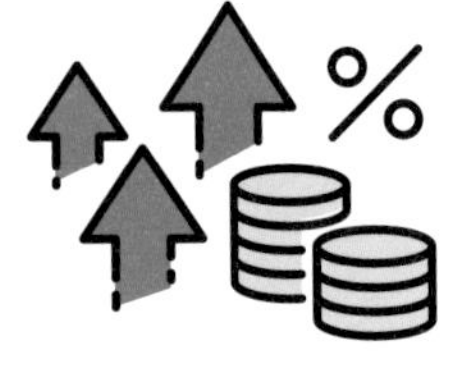

(금리가) 인상되다
go up, rise

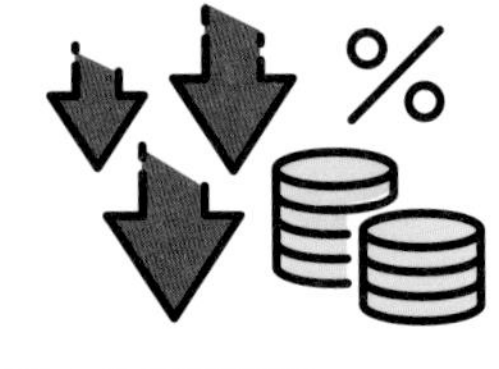

(금리가) 인하되다
go down, be lowered

(금리가) 안정적이다 be stable

(금리가) 유지되다 be maintained

(금리가) 심하게 변동되다 fluctuate wildly

(금리가) 동결되다 be frozen

(금리가) 자유화되다 be deregulated, undergo deregulation

(금리가) 확정되다 be fixed

(금리가) 0%대 진입을 눈앞에 두다 be on the verge of entering the 0% range, be about to enter the 0% range

SENTENCES TO USE

이 은행이 예금 금리가 더 높아요. 그래서 여기서 정기 예금을 들었어요.
Deposit interest rates are higher in this bank, so I signed up for a time deposit here.

이번 달에 기준 금리가 인하되었어요.
The benchmark interest rate was lowered this month.

6개월 연속 예금 금리가 유지되었습니다.
The deposit interest rate was maintained for six consecutive months.

그 주택담보대출 금리는 이번 달에 동결되었어요.
The interest rate on the mortgage was frozen this month.

이 나라 역시 금리가 0%대 진입을 눈앞에 두고 있습니다.
The interest rates in this country are also on the verge of entering the 0% range.

UNIT 8

주가, 주식

주가가 오르다[상승하다]
stock prices rise

주가가 폭등하다[급등하다]
stock prices skyrocket[soar]
* skyrocket이 더 극적인 느낌

주가가 떨어지다[하락하다]
stock prices fall

주가가 폭락하다[급락하다]
stock prices plummet

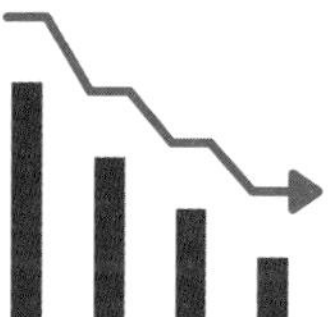

주가가 반등하다
stock prices rebound

주가지수 ~선이 무너지다[붕괴하다]
the stock index collapses[falls] below ~ level
* collapse가 더 극적인 느낌

주가가 최저치를 기록하다 stock prices hit a record low

주가가 회복세를 보이다 stock prices show signs of recovery

SENTENCES TO USE

주가가 계속 오르고 있어서 많은 투자자들이 주식 시장에 뛰어들고 있습니다.
As stock prices continue to rise, many investors are jumping into the stock market.

지난 몇 달 사이에 그 생명공학 기업의 주가가 폭등했습니다.
The biotech company's stock price has skyrocketed over the past few months.

그 전기차 제조업체의 주가가 최근에 급락했습니다.
The electric vehicle maker's stock price has recently plummeted.

지난 10개월 사이에 나스닥 지수 1900선이 붕괴되었습니다.
The NASDAQ Index collapsed below the 1900 level over the past 10 months.

주가가 얼마 전 최저치를 기록한 후 회복세를 보이고 있습니다.
Stock prices are showing signs of recovery after recently hitting a record low.

UNIT 8

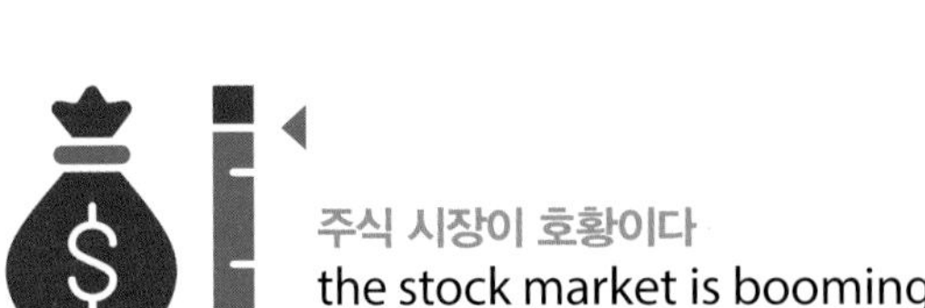

주식 시장이 호황이다
the stock market is booming

주식 시장이 불황이다
the stock market is down[declining]
* declining이 더 격식체

주식 시장이 반등하다
the stock market rebounds[bounces back]

주식 시장이 위축되다
the stock market shrinks

주식 시장이 불안정하다
the stock market is unstable

주식 시장이 과열되다
the stock market is overheated

주식 시장이 침체돼 있다
the stock market is stagnant[in a slump]
* stagnant가 더 격식체

주식 시장이 회복되다
the stock market recovers[picks up]
* recover가 더 격식체

SENTENCES TO USE

지난 2년간 주식 시장은 호황이었습니다.
The stock market has been booming for the past two years.

주식 시장이 반등하려는 신호들이 보입니다.
There are signs that the stock market is about to rebound.

대공황 직전에 미국 주식 시장은 지나치게 과열되어 있었습니다.
Just before the Great Depression, the U.S. stock market was extremely overheated.

주식 시장이 침체 상태라 그 회사는 상장하려던 계획을 철회했습니다.
The company withdrew its plan to go public because the stock market was in a slump.

침체되었던 주식 시장이 회복되기 시작했습니다.
The stock market, which had been in a slump, has begun to recover.

UNIT 9

부동산

MP3 082

부동산/주택 가격이 오르다[인상되다]
real estate/house prices rise

부동산/주택 가격이 폭등하다[급등하다]
real estate/house prices skyrocket[soar]

부동산/주택 가격이 떨어지다[하락하다] real estate/house prices decline[fall]

부동산/주택 가격이 폭락하다[급락하다] real estate/house prices plummet

부동산/주택 매물이 많다
there are many properties/houses for sale, there are many real estate listings

부동산/주택 매물이 없다
there are no properties/houses for sale, there are no real estate listings

부동산/주택이 (급)매물로 나오다 a property/house comes up for (a quick[an urgent]) sale, a property/house is put up for (a quick[an urgent]) sale

* '매물로 나오다'는 for sale로 관사 없이 쓰고, '급매물로 나오다'처럼 sale 앞에 quick이나 urgent 등의 형용사가 올 때는 for a quick [an urgent] sale로 앞에 관사를 씀

부동산으로 재산을 불리다[모으다]
make a fortune through real estate

부동산 투기가 심하다 real estate speculation is rampant[severe]

SENTENCES TO USE

투기 세력 때문에 부동산 가격이 급등했죠.
Real estate prices skyrocketed because of speculative forces.

작년 여름부터 부동산 가격이 하락하고 있어요.
Real estate prices have been declining since last summer.

대단지 아파트들이 있어서 이 지역에는 부동산 매물이 많아요.
With large apartment complexes, there are many properties for sale in this area.

주택 하나가 급매물로 나왔어요. 관심 있으세요?
A house has been put up for a quick sale. Are you interested?

그는 부동산으로 재산을 불려서 친구들이 부러워해요.
He made a fortune through real estate, so his friends are jealous of him.

UNIT 9

부동산 시장/주택 시장이 안정적이다
the real estate market/
the housing market
is stable

부동산 시장/주택 시장이 불안정하다
the real estate market/
the housing market
is unstable

부동산 시장/주택 시장이 호황이다
the real estate market/
the housing market
is booming

부동산 시장/주택 시장으로 돈이 유입되다
money flows into
the real estate market/
the housing market

부동산 시장/주택 시장이 불황이다 the real estate market/the housing market is in a recession

부동산 시장/주택 시장이 침체되다 the real estate market/the housing market is depressed

부동산 시장/주택 시장이 얼어붙다 the real estate market/the housing market is frozen

부동산 시장/주택 시장에 돈이 마르다
money dries up in the real estate market/the housing market

부동산 시장/주택 시장이 회복되다 the real estate market/the housing market recovers

SENTENCES TO USE

인플레이션이 계속되면서 부동산 시장이 불안정합니다.
The real estate market is unstable as inflation continues to rise.

그 나라는 몇 년째 부동산 시장이 호황입니다.
The country's real estate market has been booming for several years.

몇 달째 주택 시장으로 돈이 유입되고 있어요.
Money has been flowing into the housing market for months.

경기가 안 좋아서 부동산 시장도 침체돼 있어요.
The real estate market is also depressed due to the poor economy.

얼어붙었던 주택 시장이 지난봄 이후 회복되고 있습니다.
The frozen housing market has been recovering since last spring.

Prices have doubled
in the past year,
especially for fruits and vegetables.

CHAPTER

2

법, 범죄, 사건 사고

UNIT 1 법

준법정신이 투철하다 have a strong respect for the law, be very law-abiding

준법정신이 약하다 be less law-abiding

관련 법이 마련돼 있다 related laws are in place, there are relevant laws in place

법이 집행되다 laws are enforced

법이 느슨하다 laws are lax[loose]

법이 엄격하다 laws are strict

고소당하다 be sued

~로 기소되다 be charged with ~, be indicted for ~

불기소 처분을 받다 be not indicted, be given a non-prosecution, receive a non-prosecution decision

* 뒤의 두 표현은 격식체

재판에 넘겨지다, 재판을 받다 be put on trial, be brought to trial

SENTENCES TO USE

이곳 시민들은 준법정신이 매우 투철해요. 교통 법규 하나 어기는 걸 보질 못해요.
The citizens here are very law-abiding. I never see them even breaking traffic laws.

그 문제에 대해서는 관련 법이 마련돼 있으니 찾아보세요.
There are relevant laws in place for that matter, so look them up.

그 나라는 성범죄와 관련해서는 법이 느슨한 것 같아요.
I think the law is lax in that country when it comes to sex crimes.

그는 인터넷에 악플을 남겨서 한 연예인에게 고소당했습니다.
He was sued by a celebrity for writing malicious comments on the Internet.

비슷한 사안으로 한 명은 불기소 처분을 받고 한 명은 재판에 넘겨졌습니다.
In similar cases, one person was not indicted and another was put on trial.

MP3 083

~(금액) 벌금형을 선고받다
be fined ~, be sentenced to a ~ fine,
be sentenced to a fine of ~

징역형을 선고받다 be sentenced to prison

징역 ~월/년을 선고받다
be sentenced to ~ month(s)/year(s) in prison

집행유예 ~년을 선고받다
be given a ~-year suspended sentence

징역 ~월/년에 집행유예 ~년을 선고받다
be given a ~-month/year jail sentence,
be suspended for ~ year(s)

무기징역[종신형]을 선고받다
be sentenced to life imprisonment

사형을 선고받다
be sentenced to death

수감 중이다 be in jail[prison]

* jail은 비교적 구금 기간이 짧을 때, prison은 장기 구금될 때 사용

전과자다 be an ex-convict

전과가 있다/없다
have a criminal record/have no criminal record

SENTENCES TO USE

그는 법정 모욕죄로 벌금형을 선고받았습니다.
He was sentenced to a fine for contempt of court.

그 사람은 징역 1년에 집행유예 2년을 선고받았습니다.
He was given a one-year jail sentence, suspended for two years.

그 살인범은 1심에서 무기징역을 선고받았습니다.
The murderer was sentenced to life imprisonment in the first trial.

그 가수는 알고 봤더니 전과자인데, 폭행 전과가 있다고 해요.
The singer turned out to be an ex-convict, and he has a criminal record of assault.

결혼하기 전에 상대가 전과가 있는지 없는지 확인하는 게 상책이에요.
Before getting married, it's best to check if your partner has a criminal record.

2 범죄

도둑맞다 be stolen

강도를 당하다 be[get] robbed

소매치기를 당하다 be[get] pickpocketed

폭행을 당하다
be[get] assaulted[beaten up]

묻지마 폭행을 당하다 be[get] assaulted in an unprovoked attack

가정 폭력을 당하다 suffer domestic violence, be a victim of domestic violence

아동 학대를 당하다 suffer child abuse, be a victim of child abuse

학교 폭력을 당하다 suffer school violence, be a victim of school violence

괴롭힘[집단 따돌림]을 당하다
be bullied,
be a victim of bullying

데이트 폭력을 당하다 suffer dating violence[abuse], be a victim of dating violence[abuse]

스토킹을 당하다 be stalked, be a victim of stalking

SENTENCES TO USE

그 사람은 거리에서 묻지마 폭행을 당해서 크게 다쳤습니다.
The person was assaulted in an unprovoked attack on the street and suffered serious injuries.

가정 폭력을 당하는 남편들도 적지 않아요.
There are quite a few husbands who suffer domestic violence.

이 노래는 아동 학대를 당하는 소녀의 이야기를 들려 줍니다.
This song tells the story of a girl who suffers child abuse.

중학교 때 집단 따돌림을 당했던 일이 그녀에게 정신적 외상을 남겼어요.
Being bullied in middle school left her traumatized.

점점 더 많은 사람들이 데이트 폭력을 당하는 것 같아요.
It seems that more and more people are experiencing dating violence.

폭행/묻지마 폭행/가정 폭력/아동 학대/학교 폭력/괴롭힘[집단 따돌림]/데이트 폭력/스토킹 피해자다
be a victim of assault/assault in an unprovoked attack/domestic violence/child abuse/school violence/bullying/dating violence/stalking

미행을 당하다 be followed[tailed]

유괴[납치]를 당하다
be kidnapped

인질로 잡히다
be held hostage

마약에 중독되다 be[get, become] addicted to drugs
* be는 중독된 상태를, get과 become은 중독되지 않았다가 중독된 상태가 되는 변화를 나타냄

성범죄를 당하다 experience a sex crime, suffer a sex crime

성희롱을 당하다
be sexually harassed

성추행을 당하다
be sexually harassed, be molested
* be molested는 특히 아동에 대한 성추행을 뜻함

성폭행을 당하다
be sexually assaulted, be[get] raped

살해되다 be murdered

SENTENCES TO USE

그 작가가 학교 폭력 피해자였다고 해요. 그래서 피해자 캐릭터의 감정을 잘 묘사할 수 있었던 거죠.
It is said that the writer was a victim of school violence. That's why she could portray the emotions of the victim character well.

과거에는 아동이 이따금 유괴를 당했습니다.
In the past, children were sometimes kidnapped.

그 나라에서 점점 더 많은 사람들이 마약에 중독되고 있습니다.
More and more people are getting addicted to drugs in that country.

그녀는 성범죄를 겪은 후 트라우마에 대처하기 위해 치료를 받아 왔습니다.
She has been treated to cope with the trauma after suffering a sex crime.

그녀는 직장 상사로부터 성희롱을 당한 후 인사팀에 불만을 제기했습니다.
She filed a complaint with HR after being sexually harassed by her boss at work.

사건 사고

교통사고가 나다 there is a car accident, a car accident occurs

접촉 사고가 나다 there is a fender bender(비격식 회화체), there is a minor collision[car accident]

충돌 사고가 발생하다 there is a car crash, a car crash occurs

추돌 사고가 발생하다 there is a rear-end collision, a rear-end collision occurs

열차가 탈선하다
a train derails

비행기가 추락하다
a plane[an airplane] crashes

배가 침몰하다
a ship sinks

건물이/다리가 무너지다 a building/bridge collapses

가스가 폭발하다 there is a gas explosion, gas explodes

화재가 발생하다 a fire breaks out

방사능 누출 사고가 발생하다 there is a radioactive leak, a radioactive leak occurs

SENTENCES TO USE

교차로에서 4중 추돌 사고가 발생하여 차량이 정체되었습니다.
A four-car rear-end collision occurred at an intersection, stopping traffic.

열차가 탈선했는데 다행히 인명 피해는 없었습니다.
The train derailed, but fortunately there were no casualties.

비행기가 추락하여 탑승자 전원이 목숨을 잃었습니다.
The plane crashed, and all on board lost their lives.

그해에 다리가 무너지는 초유의 사고가 발생했습니다.
That year, an unprecedented accident of a bridge collapsing occured.

지진 해일로 인해 원전에서 방사능 누출 사고가 발생했습니다.
A radioactive leak occurred at a nuclear power plant due to a tsunami.

노사 갈등/분쟁이 발생하다 a labor-management conflict/dispute arises, there is a labor-management conflict/dispute

민주화 시위가 벌어지다 a pro-democracy protest occurs[takes place], there is a pro-democracy protest

반정부 시위가 일어나다 an anti-government protest occurs[takes place], there is an anti-government protest

총기 난사 사고가 발생하다
a shooting spree[a random shooting] occurs[takes place], there is a random shooting[a shooting spree]

테러가 발생하다 a terrorist attack occurs[takes place], there is a terrorist attack

전쟁이/내전이 발발하다
a war/a civil war breaks out

유행병이/전 세계적 유행병이 발생하다 an epidemic/a pandemic breaks out, there is an outbreak of an epidemic/a pandemic

* epidemic은 특정 지역이나 집단 내에서 질병이 갑작스럽게 유행하는 것을 뜻함

유행병이/전 세계적 유행병이 유행하다
an epidemic/a pandemic spreads[is widespread]

* 전국적으로 유행할 때는 nationwide, all over[around] the country를,
전 세계적으로 유행할 때는 worldwide, all over[around] the world를 추가할 수 있음

SENTENCES TO USE

그 도시에서 민주화 시위가 벌어졌지만 실패로 끝났습니다.
A pro-democracy protest took place in that city, but ended in failure.

미국에서는 총기 난사 사고가 자주 발생합니다.
Shooting sprees occur frequently in the U.S.

며칠 전, 그 공항에서 테러가 발생해 수십 명이 사망했습니다.
A terrorist attack occurred at the airport a few days ago, killing dozens of people.

전 세계 여러 나라에서 이따금 내전이 발발합니다.
Civil wars occasionally break out in different countries around the world.

2020년 초부터 코로나19가 전 세계적으로 유행해 왔습니다.
Since early 2020, COVID-19 has been widespread all over the world.

CHAPTER

3

미디어, 대중문화

UNIT 1 미디어, 언론, SNS

~가 화제다 be a hot topic, be the talk of the town

* the talk of the town은 회화체

~가 유행이다 be in fashion[in vogue]

* in vogue가 더 격식체에 우아한 느낌

~가 인기 있다 be popular

~가 트렌드다 be a trend

~가 대세다
be a general trend, be a thing, be trending

* be a thing, be trending은 회화체

반짝 유행이다 be a fad

트렌드에 민감하다 be sensitive to trends

트렌드[시대]에 뒤처지다 be[fall] behind the trends[times], be out of date

~라는 신조어가 유행이다 the newly-coined word ~ is in vogue

SENTENCES TO USE

지난 주말, 그 세계적인 야구 선수의 결혼이 화제였습니다.
Last weekend, the world-class baseball player's marriage was a hot topic.

요즘은 그런 인테리어 스타일이 유행이에요.
These days, that type of interior style is in fashion.

생활의 많은 측면이 비대면화되는 게 최근의 트렌드입니다.
It is a recent trend that many aspects of life are becoming contactless.

그는 트렌드에 무척 민감해요. 시대에 뒤처지는 걸 못 견디죠.
He is very sensitive to trends. He can't stand being behind the times.

코로나19 이후 '마기꾼'이라는 신조어가 유행입니다.
After COVID-19, the newly-coined word "maskfishing" is in vogue.

MP3 086

종이 신문의 시대는 갔다 the era of newspapers is over[gone], the days of newspapers are over[gone]

인터넷으로 뉴스를 접하다 access the news on the Internet, get news on the Internet

가짜뉴스가 성행하다
fake news is prevalent,
fake news prevails

(신문과 방송이) 편파적이다 be biased

친정부/반정부 성향이다 be pro-government/anti-government

공중파 TV 방송이 위기다 over-the-air television is in crisis

OTT 서비스가 인기다
OTT services are popular

* OTT: Over-the-top media service. 'top, 즉 셋톱박스를 넘어'라는 뜻으로, 케이블이나 위성 기반 공급자를 거치지 않고 공개 인터넷을 통해 제공되는 미디어 서비스를 뜻함

다양한 OTT 플랫폼이 있다
there are various OTT platforms

유튜브가 대세다 YouTube is popular, YouTube is a thing[a general trend]

1인 미디어가 발달하다
one-person media is on the rise, independent content creators are gaining popularity

SENTENCES TO USE

신문의 시대가 갔지만 우리 아버지는 여전히 종이 신문을 보세요.
The era of newspapers is over, but my father still reads them.

요즘 가짜뉴스가 성행하는데, 그게 심각한 문제예요.
These days, fake news is prevalent, and that's a serious problem.

그 방송국은 보수 정권이 들어서면 친정부 성향이 됩니다.
The broadcasting station becomes pro-government when a conservative administration comes into power.

유튜브와 OTT 서비스 때문에 공중파 TV 방송이 위기에 처해 있습니다.
Over-the-air television is in crisis due to YouTube and OTT services.

1인 미디어의 발달로 누구나 마음만 먹으면 방송을 할 수 있습니다.
With the rise of one-person media, anyone can broadcast if they want to.

UNIT 1

SNS(소셜 미디어)에서 화제다 be a hot topic[a big hit] on social media

(~ 사이에서) SNS(소셜 미디어)의 영향력이 크다 social media has a great influence (on ~), the influence of social media is great (among ~)

SNS(소셜 미디어)에 중독되다(상태) be addicted to social media

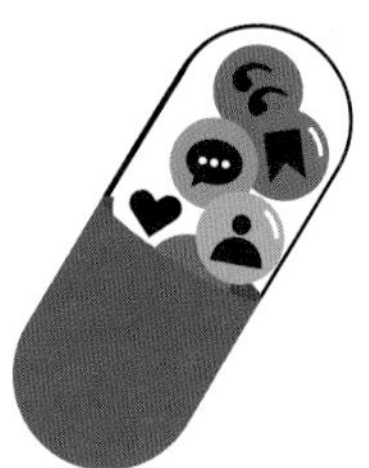

SNS(소셜 미디어) 마케팅이 중요하다 social media marketing is important

SNS(소셜 미디어)에서 입소문이 나다 go viral on social media

SENTENCES TO USE

그 음료가 최근에 SNS에서 큰 화제예요.
That drink has been a hot topic on social media recently.

요즘 젊은이들 사이에서는 SNS의 영향력이 큽니다.
Social media has a great influence on young people these days.

우리 아들은 SNS에 중독된 것 같아요. 하루 종일 SNS를 들여다보고 있어요.
I think my son is addicted to social media. He's looking at it all day.

요즘은 SNS 마케팅이 무척 중요하고 필수가 됐어요.
These days, social media marketing is very important and it has become a necessity.

UNIT 2 예술, 대중문화

MP3 087

예술 일반

MP3 087-1

인기 있다 be popular

선풍적인 인기를 끌다
be[become] sensationally popular, achieve sensational popularity (좀 더 격식체)

한 시대를 풍미하다 dominate an era

음악, 대중가요, 콘서트

(노래가) 듣기 좋다/감동적이다/신선하다/심금을 울리다/귀에 거슬리다
be good to listen to/be touching/sound fresh/touch one's heart/sound annoying

콘서트의 음향/조명이 훌륭하다/형편없다
the sound/lighting at the concert is great/poor

콘서트가 매진[만석]이다 the concert is sold out

노래를 잘하다 sing well, be good at singing

가창력이 뛰어나다 have good[great, excellent] singing skills

무대 매너가 좋다 have good stage manners

* stage manners는 '무대 매너'로 직업 가수나 연기자들에 대해 쓰고, stage presence는 '무대에서의 존재감'을 뜻하며 일반인에게도 쓸 수 있음

춤을 잘 추다 dance well

SENTENCES TO USE

그 영화가 요즘 선풍적 인기야. 보러 갈까?
That movie is sensationally popular these days. How about going to see it?

그 여가수는 한 시대를 풍미했고, 그의 노래는 오늘날에도 애창되고 있어요.
The female singer dominated an era, and her songs are still sung today.

그 록 밴드의 콘서트는 항상 매진이에요. 표 구하기가 정말 힘들어요.
The rock band's concerts are always sold out. It's really hard to get tickets.

그 가수는 생각보다 가창력이 무척 뛰어났어요.
The singer had much better singing skills than I had expected.

그 가수는 경력이 오래된 만큼 무대 매너가 좋아요.
The singer has good stage manners as he has had a long career.

UNIT 2

TV, 영화, 연극 등

MP3 087-2

재미있다/웃기다/감동적이다/새롭다/인상적이다
be interesting[fun]/funny/touching[moving]/new/impressive

재미없다/지루하다/진부하다
be not interesting[fun]/be boring/be corny

(다큐멘터리나 시사 프로그램이) 배울 점이 있다/시사점이 있다/시의적절하다
there is something to learn (from ~)/
there is an implication (in ~)/be timely

시청률이 높다/낮다 have high/low (viewer) ratings

(영화가) 흥행에 성공하다 be a success[a box office hit], succeed at the box office

(영화가) 흥행에 실패하다 be a box office failure, fail at the box office

(배우가) 연기를 잘하다 act well, be a good actor, be good at acting

(배우가) 연기를 못하다 can't act, be a bad actor, be poor at acting

~에서 상을 받다 win an award at ~

~ 상을 받다 win ~, be awarded ~

~ 후보에 오르다 be nominated for ~, be nominated in ~ category

* 최우수 작품상/감독상/각본상/남우주연상/여우주연상/남우조연상/여우조연상
Best Picture/Best Director/Best Original Screenplay/Best Actor/Best Actress/Best Supporting Actor/Best Supporting Actress

상을 석권하다 sweep the awards

SENTENCES TO USE

우연히 보았던 그 아이슬란드 영화는 인상적이었어요.
The Icelandic movie I accidentally watched was impressive.

외상 센터에 대한 그 드라마는 시청률이 높았습니다.
The drama about a trauma center had high viewer ratings.

그 형제 감독이 이번에 만든 영화는 흥행에 실패했습니다.
The movie the brothers directed this time was a box office failure.

그 영화는 7개 부문 후보에 올라 최우수 작품상과 각본상을 받았습니다.
The film was nominated in seven categories, winning Best Picture and Best Original Screenplay.

그 한국인 감독의 영화가 그해 아카데미상을 석권했지요.
The Korean director's film swept the Academy Awards that year.

That drink has been a hot topic
on social media recently.
LIKE
SPARKLING WATER
naturaleza
SPARKLING
WATER
Good

CHAPTER

4

지역 묘사

UNIT 1 국가

수도는 ~다 the capital (city) is ~

공용어는 ~다 the official language is ~

~에 (위치해) 있다 be located in ~

인구가 ~명이다 the population is ~, have a population of ~

인구밀도는 평방킬로미터당 ~명이다
the population density is ~ people per square kilometer

면적이 ~평방킬로미터다 cover (an area of) ~ square kilometers

역사는 ~년 됐다 one's history is ~ years old,
have a ~-year history, have a history of ~ years

기후는 ~다 the climate is ~, have ~ climate

정치 체제는 ~다 the political system is ~

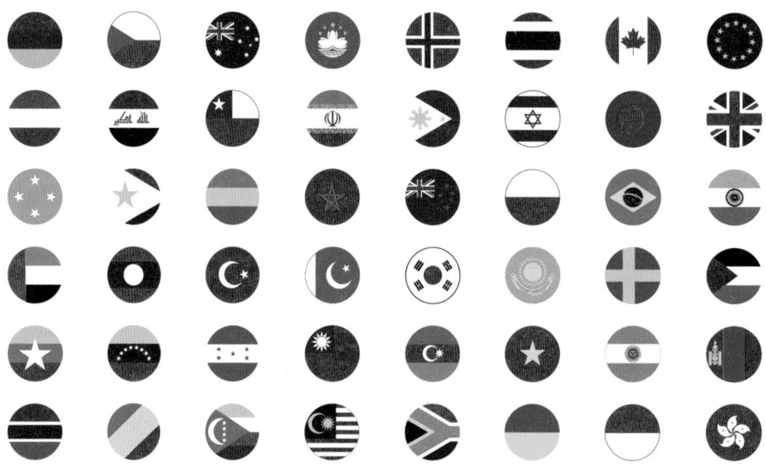

SENTENCES TO USE

모로코의 공용어는 아랍어와 베르베르어지만, 프랑스어도 쓰입니다.
The official languages of Morocco are Arabic and Berber, but French is also spoken.

아이슬란드는 인구가 39만 명 정도밖에 안 되며, 수도는 레이캬비크입니다.
Iceland has a population of only about 390,000, and its capital is Reykjavik.

세계에서 가장 넓은 나라인 러시아는 면적이 17,098,242평방킬로미터입니다.
Russia, the world's largest country, covers 17,098,242 square kilometers.

몽골의 기후는 여름은 짧고 겨울이 긴 대륙성 기후입니다.
Mongolia has a continental climate with short summers and long winters.

쿠바의 정치 체제는 사회주의 1당 독재 체제입니다.
Cuba's political system is a socialist one-party dictatorship.

(전화) 국가번호는 ~다 the country code is ~

국가 도메인은 ~다 the Internet country code[domain] is ~

* 인터넷 국가 도메인 정식 명칭: Country Code Top-Level Domain (ccTLD, 국가 코드 최상위 도메인)

통화는 ~다 the currency is ~

GDP(국내총생산)가 ~달러다 the GDP is ~ dollars, have a GDP of ~ dollars

1인당 GDP가 ~달러다 GDP per capita is ~ dollars

~로 유명하다 be famous for ~

주요 산업은 ~다 the main[major] industries are ~

국교는 ~다 the state religion is ~

주요 관광명소는 ~다 the main tourist attractions[destinations] are ~

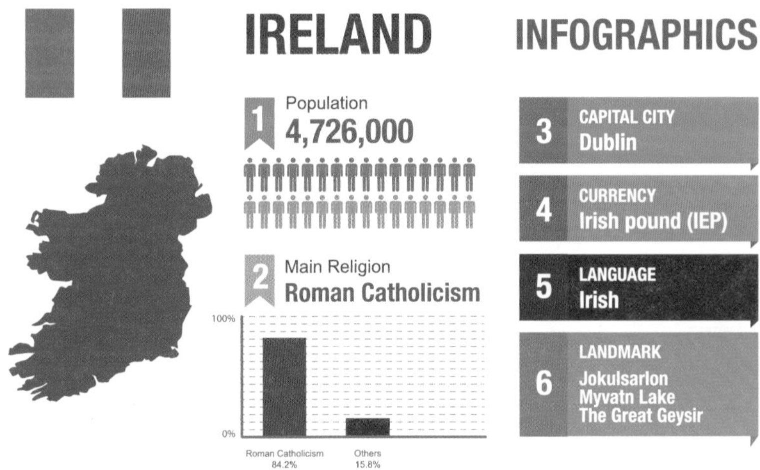

SENTENCES TO USE

멕시코의 통화는 멕시코 페소로, 약칭은 MXN입니다.
Mexico's currency is the Mexican peso, which is abbreviated as MXN.

2022년 대한민국의 GDP는 약 1조 7천억 달러였습니다.
South Korea's GDP in 2022 was about $1.7 trillion.

핀란드는 호수로 유명한데, 수만 개의 호수가 있습니다.
Finland is famous for its lakes, with tens of thousands of lakes.

칠레의 주요 산업은 농업, 수산업, 광업입니다.
Chile's main industries are agriculture, fisheries, and mining.

스위스의 주요 관광지는 알프스와 루체른, 취리히 등의 도시입니다.
Switzerland's main tourist destinations are the Alps and cities such as Lucerne and Zurich.

UNIT 2

도시, 지방

대도시다
be a big city

중간 규모 도시다
be a medium-sized city

소도시다
be a small town

농촌이다
be a rural area, be a farming village

어촌이다
be a fishing village

바닷가 마을이다
be a seaside town

섬마을이다
be an island village

산골 마을이다
be a mountain village

번화하다
be bustling[busy]

* bustling은 에너지 넘치고 활기찬 긍정적 의미 내포

외지다
be remote[isolated]

* remote는 거리가 멀어 접근이 힘든 것,
isolated는 단절되어 외로운 것

SENTENCES TO USE

그가 사는 도시는 인구 약 40만 명의 중간 규모 도시입니다.
The city where he lives is a medium-sized city with a population of about 400,000.

이곳은 예전엔 농촌이었지만, 지금은 거대한 산업 단지입니다.
This used to be a rural area, but now it is a huge industrial complex.

그 소설의 배경은 그림 같은 어촌 마을입니다.
The setting of the novel is a picturesque fishing village.

그 가수가 태어나 자란 곳은 섬마을이에요.
The place where the singer was born and raised is an island village.

그 사람은 산골 마을에 사는데, 그곳은 풍경이 아름답지만 무척 외집니다.
He lives in a mountain village, which has beautiful scenery but is very remote.

인구가 ~명이다 the population is ~, have a population of ~

면적이 ~평방킬로미터다 cover (an area of) ~ square kilometers

인구가 많다/적다 have a large/small population

인구가 조밀하다/희박하다 be densely/sparsely populated

면적이 넓다/좁다 have a large/narrow area

~에 (위치해) 있다 be located in[on] ~

~로 유명하다 be famous for ~

주요 산업은 ~다 the main[major] industries are ~

주요 관광명소는 ~다 the main tourist attractions[destinations] are ~

특산물은 ~다 the specialty[regional product] is ~

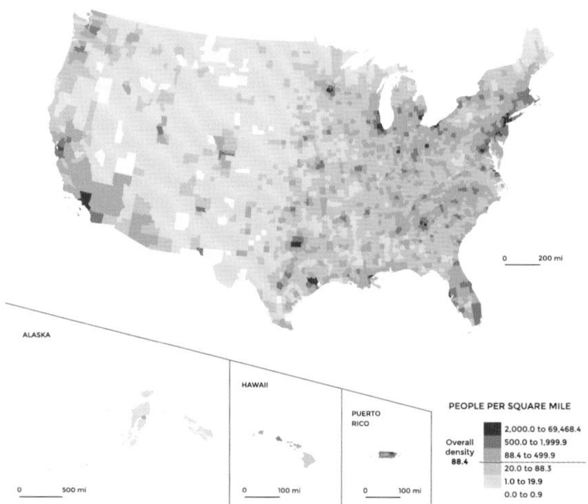

SENTENCES TO USE

그 도시는 인구가 10만 명인데, 25퍼센트가 그 산업 단지에서 근무합니다.
The city has a population of 100,000, and 25% of them work in the industrial complex.

일부 지방 도시들은 인구가 희박하여 공동체가 소멸할 위기에 처해 있습니다.
Some local cities are so sparsely populated that their communities are on the verge of extinction.

오리건주는 미국 서부 태평양 연안에 위치해 있으며, 주도는 세일럼입니다.
Oregon is located on the Pacific Coast of the western United States, and its capital city is Salem.

이탈리아 베네치아는 운하와 곤돌라 타기로 유명하지요.
Venice, Italy, is famous for its canals and gondola rides.

버몬트주에는 사과 과수원이 많고, 그곳 특산물은 사과입니다.
There are many apple orchards in Vermont, and its specialty is apples.

UNIT 3

동네

구시가지다, 구도심이다 be an old town

신도시다 be a new town

평지다 be flat

경사지에 있다 be situated on a slope

한적하다 be quiet

번화하다, 복작거리다 be bustling[busy]

* bustling은 에너지 넘치고 활기찬 긍정적 의미 내포

시끄럽다 be noisy

고급스럽다 be luxurious[upscale]

부유한 동네다 be a wealthy[rich] neighborhood

* wealthy는 격식체, rich는 캐주얼한 느낌

낙후되다 be underdeveloped, be in poor condition

* underdeveloped는 개발이 덜 되고 생활 수준이 떨어지는 것, in poor condition은 오래되고 관리가 안 된 것

향수를 불러일으키다 be nostalgic, evoke nostalgia

SENTENCES TO USE

우리 동네는 경사지에 있어서 어르신들이 다니기가 힘들어요.
My neighborhood is situated on a slope, making it difficult for the elderly to navigate.

그 동네는 깨끗하고 한적해서 산책하기 아주 그만이었어요.
The neighborhood was clean and quiet, so it was perfect for a walk.

우리 동네에는 지하철역이 있어서 번화하고 오가는 사람들도 많아요.
Our neighborhood has a subway station, so it's bustling and a lot of people come and go.

그 동네는 2000년 이후로 낙후되어 있어요.
The neighborhood has been underdeveloped since 2000.

이 도시는 70~80년대 모습을 간직하고 있어서 향수를 불러일으킵니다.
This city evokes nostalgia because it retains the look of the '70s and '80s.

MP3 090

주택가다 be a residential area

아파트 단지다 be an apartment complex

빌라촌이다 be a neighborhood with many town houses

원룸촌이다
be a neighborhood with many studios[studio apartments]

근처에 ~가 있다 ~ be (located) nearby, have ~ nearby

동네에 있는 시설들

재래시장 a traditional market
대형 마트 a major[large] supermarket
공원 a park
공공 도서관 a public library
우체국 a post office
은행 a bank
헬스클럽, 체육관 a gym[fitness club, fitness center]
생활 편의 시설 amenities

SENTENCES TO USE

우리 동네는 인구가 많은 대규모 아파트 단지예요.
My neighborhood is a large apartment complex with a large population.

이 지역은 대학이 근처에 있어서 원룸촌이에요.
This area is a neighborhood with many studio apartments because a college is nearby.

우리 동네는 재래시장과 대형 마트가 근처에 있습니다.
Our neighborhood has a traditional market and a large supermarket nearby.

이 동네는 다양한 생활 편의 시설들이 근처에 있어서 살기 편해요.
This neighborhood is convenient to live in because of its proximity to various amenities.

그녀의 동네는 근처에 공원이 있어서 산책하기 아주 좋은 곳입니다.
Her neighborhood, which has a park nearby, is a great place for a walk.

UNIT 3

~ 뒤에 (뒷)산이 있다 there is a hill[mountain] behind ~
* hill은 야트막한 산

근처에 개천이 흐르다 a stream flows nearby

지하철역이 가까이 있다 be close to the subway station, a subway station is nearby

역세권이다 be in the area near the subway station

버스 노선이 여러 개 있다 have several bus routes[lines], there are several bus routes[lines]

유명한 학군지(에 있)다
be (in) a famous school district

재개발로 사라지다
disappear due to redevelopment

동네가 새로 조성됐다
a new neighborhood has been created

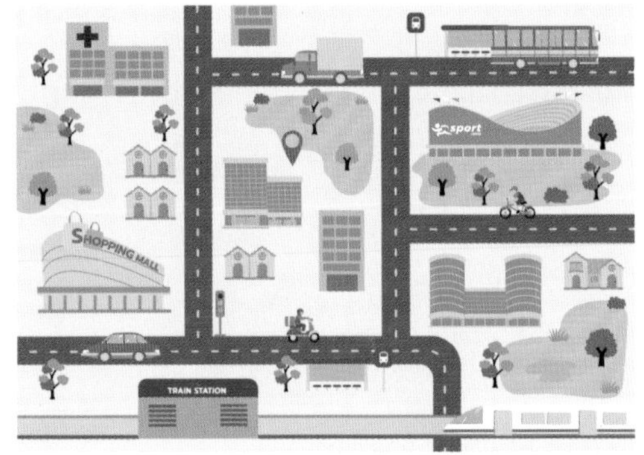

SENTENCES TO USE

우리 집 뒤에 산이 있어서 매일 거길 오릅니다.
There is a hill behind my house, so I hike it every day.

그 아파트는 지하철역이 가까워서 가격은 좀 비싸지만 인기가 있어요.
The apartment is close to the subway station, so it is a bit expensive but popular.

우리 동네는 버스 노선이 여러 개 있어서 출퇴근하기 용이해요.
My neighborhood has several bus lines, so it is easy to commute.

그들이 이사 간 동네는 유명한 학군지에 있어요.
The neighborhood they moved to is in a famous school district.

내가 태어나고 자란 동네가 재개발로 사라졌어요.
The neighborhood where I was born and raised has disappeared due to redevelopment.

UNIT 4 거리, 도로

MP3 091

거리

MP3 091-1

(거리가) 번화하다 be bustling[busy]

(거리가) 인파로 가득하다 be full of[filled with] people

거리에 인적이 드물다 there are few people on the street, the street is almost deserted

* 전자는 소수의 사람이 있는 것, 후자는 거의 없거나 아예 없어서 버려진 듯한 느낌

거리에 사람이 없다 there are no people on the street

(거리가) 한적하다 be quiet

(거리가) 깨끗하다 be clean

(거리가) 지저분하다 be dirty

거리에 가로수가 늘어서 있다 the street is lined with trees

거리에 낙엽이 쌓여 있다 fallen leaves are piled up on the street

SENTENCES TO USE

그 거리는 늘 번화하고 인파로 가득합니다.
The street is always bustling and full of people.

그 거리는 주말에는 인적이 드물어요.
The street is almost deserted on weekends.

그 도시는 거리가 한적하고 깨끗해요. 나는 그 거리를 돌아다니는 게 좋아요.
The streets of the city are quiet and clean. I enjoy exploring them.

그 도시는 거리가 지저분해서 모두가 그곳을 빨리 떠나고 싶어 했어요.
The streets in the city were dirty, so everyone wanted to get out of there quickly.

그 거리는 가로수가 늘어서 있어서 가을에는 낙엽이 쌓여 있어요.
The street is lined with trees, so fallen leaves are piled up in autumn.

UNIT 4

도로

MP3 091-2

도로가 넓다/좁다 the road is wide/narrow

(도로가) ~차선이다
be a ~-lane road, (the road) has ~ lanes

제한 속도가 시속 ~킬로미터[마일]이다
the speed limit is ~ kilometers[miles] per hour

교차로가 있다
there is an intersection

어린이 보호구역이다
be a school zone

고가도로가 있다
there is an overpass

(도로가) 사방으로 뚫려 있다 be open in all directions

(도로가) 확장되다 be expanded

(도로가) 새로 생기다 be newly opened[built]

(도로가) 얼어 있다, 빙판이다 be icy

SENTENCES TO USE

우리 아파트 앞 도로는 8차선 도로예요.
The road in front of our apartment is an eight-lane road.

시내 도로는 제한 속도가 시속 50킬로미터입니다.
The speed limit on city roads is 50 kilometers per hour.

여기서 1분 정도만 걸어가면 교차로가 있어요.
There is an intersection about one minute's walk from here.

우리 동네에는 고가도로가 있어서 동네가 낡은 느낌이 납니다.
There is an overpass in my neighborhood, which gives the area a run-down feel.

이곳은 어린이 보호구역이라 시속 30킬로미터 이하로 운전해야 합니다.
This is a school zone, so you must drive below 30 kilometers per hour.

UNIT 5

교통 상황

MP3 092

교통량이 많다, 길이 막히다 there is heavy[a lot of] traffic, there is a traffic jam, a road is congested

도로의 통행이 차단되다 a road is blocked

교통사고가 나서 due to[because of] a traffic accident

차량 정체의 원인들

도로 보수 road repairs
도로 공사 road construction
폭설 heavy snow
교통량 증가 increased traffic volume
불법 주차 illegal parking
차량 고장 vehicle breakdown

차들로 복잡하다 be crowded with cars

도로가 사방이 정체돼 있다 the traffic[road] is gridlocked[congested] everywhere

길에서 꼼짝 못하다 be stuck in traffic, be stuck on the road

차가 기어가다 a car crawls

출퇴근 시간이다, 막히는 시간이다 it's rush hour

길이 잘 뚫리다, 차가 안 막히다 traffic is smooth

(길에) 차가 거의 없다[한산하다] there are very few cars

(길에) 차가 하나도 없다 there is no traffic

SENTENCES TO USE

금요일 저녁이라 차가 많아 길이 막히네요. 모임에 늦겠어요.
It's Friday evening, so there's a lot of traffic. We'll be late for the gathering.

연휴 첫날이라 도로가 사방이 정체돼 있습니다.
Because it is the first day of the holiday, the roads are congested everywhere.

길이 막혀서 길에서 30분째 꼼짝 못하고 있어요.
The road is congested and I've been stuck in traffic for 30 minutes.

출퇴근 시간에 이 도로에서는 차가 기어다녀요.
During rush hour, the cars crawl along this stretch of road.

일요일 아침에는 길이 잘 뚫려요.
Traffic is smooth on Sunday mornings.

PART 6

자연과 환경

CHAPTER

1

자연

UNIT 1

자연 일반

숲이 울창하다 the forest is thick

나무가 키가 크다/작다 a tree is tall/short[small]

나무가 덩치가 크다/왜소하다 a tree is big/small

나무가 잎이 무성하다 be densely covered with leaves, be thick with leaves

나무가 앙상하다 a tree is bare of leaves

새싹이 돋다 sprouts come out[emerge]

(나무에) 새잎이 돋다 new leaves sprout on trees

신록이 아름답다 fresh greenery is beautiful

꽃봉오리가 맺히다 flower buds form

꽃이 만개하다 flowers are in full bloom

꽃이 지다[떨어지다] flowers fall

거리에 꽃잎이 떨어져 있다 petals litter the street, petals are on the street

거리에 낙엽이 쌓여 있다 fallen leaves are piled up on the street, the street is covered with fallen leaves

SENTENCES TO USE

7월이어서 숲이 무척 울창했어요.
It was July, so the forest was very thick.

그 마을 입구에 있던 나무는 나뭇잎이 무성했습니다.
The tree at the entrance to the village was densely covered with leaves.

4월 말이라 신록이 푸르고 아름다워요. 새잎들은 꽃보다 더 예쁜 것 같아요.
It is late April, so the fresh greenery is beautiful. I think new leaves are prettier than flowers.

남부 지방은 벚꽃이 만개했습니다.
Cherry blossoms are in full bloom in the southern region.

해마다 이맘때면 거리에 은행잎 낙엽이 쌓여 있습니다.
At this time of year, fallen ginkgo leaves are piled up on the streets.

MP3 093

산이/언덕이 높다/낮다
the mountain/hill is high[tall]/low

산세가 빼어나다 the mountain scenery is beautiful

산세가 험하다 the mountain is rugged[rough]

들판이 푸르다 the fields are green

풀이 무성하다 grass is lush[thick]

강이 넓다/좁다/깊다/얕다
the river is wide/narrow/deep/shallow

바다가/호수가 넓다/깊다
the sea/lake is wide/deep

강물이/호수가/바닷물이 반짝이다
the river/lake/sea water glistens[glitters]

강물이 출렁이다 the river is rolling

파도가 넘실대다
the waves are rolling[swelling, surging]

야생동물/새/벌레가 많다
there are a lot of[many] wild animals/birds/insects[bugs]

SENTENCES TO USE

그 도시 중앙에 있는 산은 300미터 정도로, 아주 높지는 않아요.
The mountain in the center of the city is about 300 meters, so it's not very tall.

산의 오솔길 양옆으로 풀이 무성하네요.
The grass is lush on both sides of the mountain path.

강물이 햇빛을 받아 반짝였어요.
The river glistened in the sunlight.

검푸른 바다에서 파도가 넘실대고 있었습니다.
The waves were surging in the dark blue sea.

나는 여름에 캠핑할 때 벌레가 많은 게 너무 싫어요.
I hate it when there are many bugs around while I'm camping in the summer.

UNIT **2**

자연 현상

해가/달이 뜨다 the sun/the moon rises[comes up]

해가/달이 지다 the sun/the moon sets[goes down]

밤하늘에 달이 떠 있다 the moon is in the night sky

다양한 달의 형태

보름달 a full moon **반달** a half moon
초승달 a new moon, a waxing crescent (moon)
그믐달 an old moon, a waning crescent (moon)
* a crescent moon(눈썹달)은 초승달과 그믐달을 모두 가리킴

노을이 지다 the sun sets

하늘이 노을로 물들다 the sky glows with the setting sun

무지개가/쌍무지개가 뜨다 a rainbow/a double rainbow appears, there is a rainbow/a double rainbow

오로라가 나타나다 the aurora (borealis) appears, the northern/southern lights appear
* 북반구에서는 the northern lights, 남반구에서는 the southern lights

달무리가 지다 there is a moon halo

일식/개기일식/부분일식이 일어나다 a solar eclipse/a total solar eclipse/a partial solar eclipse occurs, there is a solar eclipse/a total solar eclipse/a partial solar eclipse

SENTENCES TO USE

하늘을 올려다보니 예쁜 초승달이 떠 있었습니다.
When I looked up at the sky, there was a beautiful crescent moon.

서쪽 하늘이 노을로 물들어 있어요. 너무나 장관이에요.
The western sky glows with the setting sun. It's breathtaking.

소나기가 쏟아진 뒤에 쌍무지개가 떴습니다.
A double rainbow appeared after the rain shower.

달무리가 진 걸 보니 내일 비가 오려나 봐요.
Seeing that there is a moon halo, I think it might rain tomorrow.

일식이 일어나서 오후 3시인데 어둑어둑합니다.
There is a solar eclipse, so it's 3 p.m. but it feels a little dark.

월식/개기월식/부분월식이 일어나다 a lunar eclipse/a total lunar eclipse/a partial lunar eclipse occurs, there is a lunar eclipse/a total lunar eclipse/a partial lunar eclipse

백야다 this is the midnight sun[white night]

* white night은 시적인 느낌이자, '잠 못 드는 밤'이라는 뜻도 있으며, 러시아어에서 온 표현

백야가 계속되다 the midnight sun continues

썰물 때다 it is time for ebb tide, the tide is out

밀물 때다 it is time for high[flood] tide, the tide is in

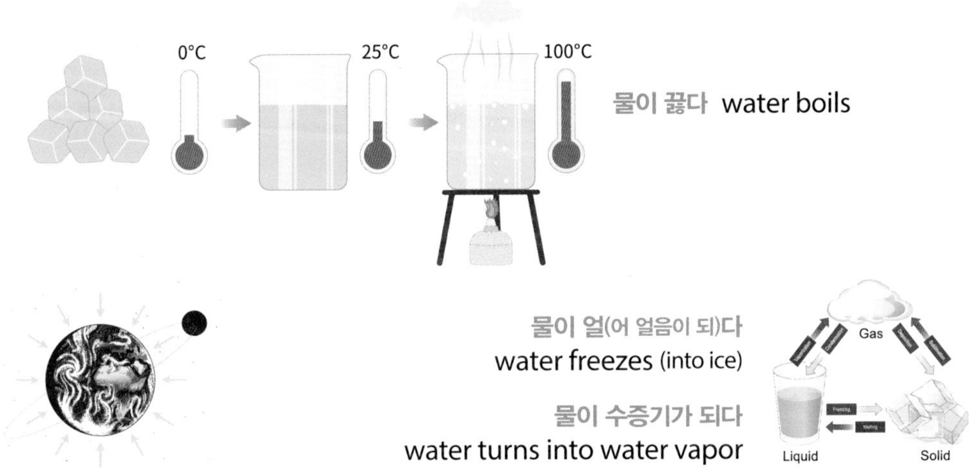

물이 끓다 water boils

물이 얼(어 얼음이 되)다 water freezes (into ice)

물이 수증기가 되다 water turns into water vapor

중력의 영향을 받다 be affected by gravity

빛보다 빠른 물질은 없다 nothing travels faster than light

SENTENCES TO USE

요즘 북유럽은 백야가 계속되고 있어 밤 10시에도 환합니다.
These days, the midnight sun continues in Northern Europe, so it is bright even at 10 p.m.

썰물일 때 육지와 그 섬 사이에 길이 생겨요.
When the tide is out, a path appears between the mainland and the island.

섭씨 0도에서 물이 얼어서 얼음이 되지요.
At 0 degrees Celsius, water freezes into ice.

지구상의 모든 물체는 중력의 영향을 받습니다.
All objects on Earth are affected by gravity.

빛보다 빠른 물질은 없다는 것이 정설입니다.
The established theory is that nothing travels faster than light.

UNIT 3

식물

광합성을 하다
photosynthesize,
perform photosynthesis

산소를 만들어 내다
produce[create] oxygen

상록수 an evergreen tree
* 형용사로 표현하면 be evergreen

낙엽수 a deciduous tree
* 형용사로 표현하면 be deciduous

활엽수 a broadleaf[broad-leaved] tree

침엽수 a coniferous[needleleaf] tree, a conifer

유실수 a fruit tree * 열매가 열리는 나무

(나무에) **열매가 열리다** bear fruit

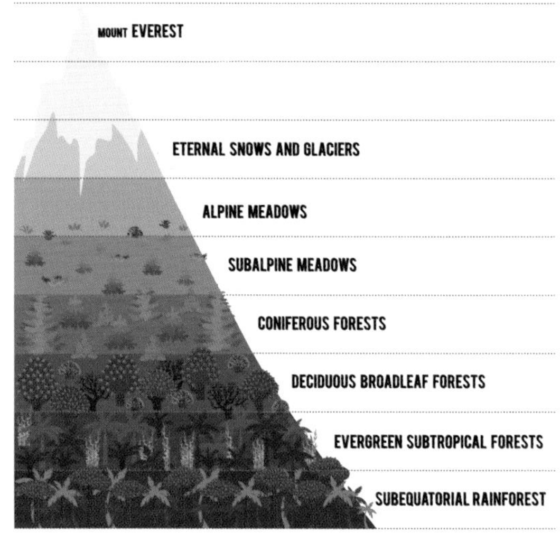

관엽식물 a foliage plant
* 잎을 보고 즐기기 위한 식물

다육식물 a succulent plant
* 선인장처럼 잎이나 줄기에 수분을 많이 함유한 식물

SENTENCES TO USE

식물은 광합성을 하는데, 그 과정에서 산소를 만들어 냅니다.
Plants perform photosynthesis, producing oxygen in the process.

그 나라를 대표하는 나무인 소나무는 상록 침엽수입니다.
Pine trees, the representative tree of the country, are evergreen conifers.

잎이 넓은 나무를 활엽수라고 하는데, 대부분 가을에 낙엽이 져요.
Trees with broad leaves are called broadleaf trees, and most lose their leaves in fall.

그녀의 집 마당에는 나무가 몇 그루 있는데, 유실수들입니다.
There are several trees in her yard, and they are fruit trees.

우리 어머니는 실내에서 식물을 많이 키우시는데, 모두 관엽식물이에요.
My mother grows a lot of plants indoors, and they are all foliage plants.

온대 식물 a temperate plant

아열대 식물 a subtropical plant

열대 식물 a tropical plant

고산 식물 an alpine plant

극지 식물 an arctic plant

습지 식물 a wetland plant

수중 식물 an aquatic plant

한해살이[일년생] 식물 an annual plant

두해살이[이년생] 식물 a biennial plant

여러해살이[다년생] 식물 a perennial plant

알뿌리 식물 a bulbous[bulb, root] plant

잡초 a weed

SENTENCES TO USE

파파야는 열대 식물이라 온대 기후 지역에서는 볼 수 없습니다.
Papayas are tropical plants, so we can't see them in the temperate climate regions.

수목한계선보다 고위도 지방에서 자라는 식물이 극지 식물입니다.
Plants that grow at higher latitudes than the tree line are arctic plants.

벼, 옥수수, 호박, 코스모스 등은 한해살이 식물입니다.
Rice, corn, pumpkins, cosmos, etc. are annual plants.

쑥, 국화, 감나무 등은 여러해살이 식물이에요.
Mugwort, chrysanthemums, persimmon trees, etc. are perennial plants.

양파, 튤립, 수선화가 대표적인 알뿌리 식물입니다.
Onions, tulips, and daffodils are representative bulbous plants.

UNIT 4

동물

척추동물이다/무척추동물이다 be a vertebrate/an invertebrate

포유류/조류/파충류/양서류/어류다 be a mammal/a bird/a reptile/an amphibian/a fish

육식동물/초식동물/잡식동물이다 be a carnivore/an herbivore/an omnivore

온혈[항온, 정온] 동물이다 be a warm-blooded[homoiothermal] animal

* homoiothermal은 과학 문헌, 기사 등에서 사용

체온이 일정하게 유지되다 maintain[have] a constant body temperature

냉혈[변온] 동물이다 be a cold-blooded[poikilothermal] animal

* poikilothermal은 과학 문헌, 기사 등에서 사용

스스로 체온을 조절할 수 없다
cannot regulate its own body temperature

온몸에 털과 땀샘이 있다
have hair and sweat glands all over one's body

새끼를 낳다
give birth to young

새끼를 젖을 먹여 키우다
raise one's young by breastfeeding

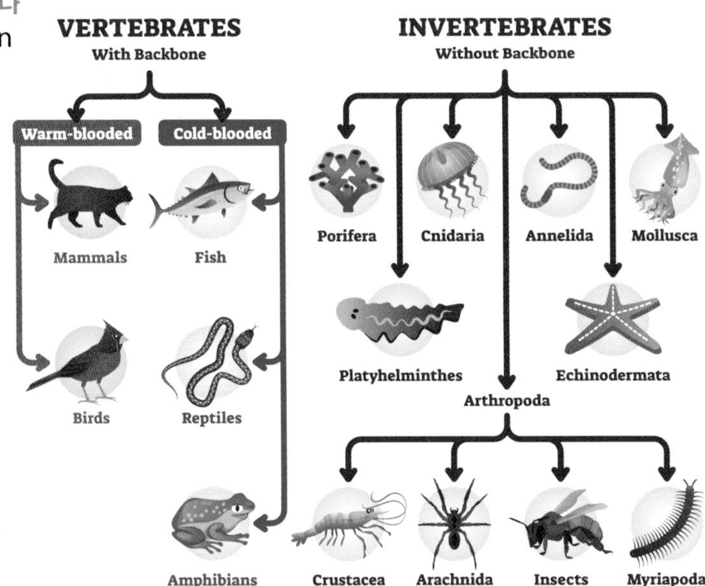

SENTENCES TO USE

보기와 달리 뱀은 척추동물이에요.
Contrary to what they look like, snakes are vertebrates.

코끼리, 하마, 기린 등은 초식동물인데, 초식동물은 대체로 육식동물보다 덩치가 큽니다.
Elephants, hippos, and giraffes are herbivores, and herbivores are generally larger than carnivores.

양서류는 변온동물로, 스스로 체온을 조절할 수 없습니다.
Amphibians are cold-blooded animals and cannot regulate their own body temperature.

거의 모든 포유류는 온몸에 털과 땀샘이 있습니다.
Almost all mammals have hair and sweat glands all over their bodies.

포유류는 새끼를 낳아 젖을 먹여 키웁니다.
Mammals give birth to young and raise them by breastfeeding.

알을 낳다
lay an egg

알에서 새끼가 부화하다
a baby hatches from an egg

앞다리가 날개로 변형되다 forelimbs are transformed into wings

시력이 매우 좋다 have very good eyesight

부리가 손 역할을 하다 the beak acts as a hand

깃털로 덮여 있다
be covered with feathers

딱딱한 각질로 덮여 있다
be covered with hard dead skin cells

피부가 건조하다/습하다
have dry/moist skin, one's skin is dry/moist

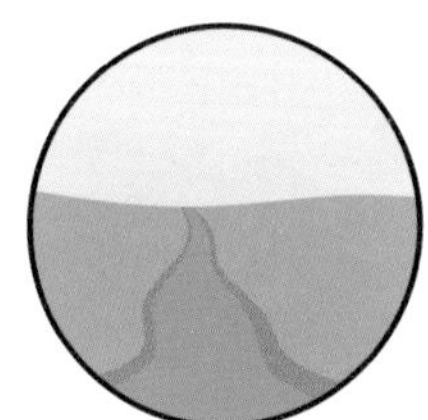

육지에/물속에서 살다
live on land/in the water

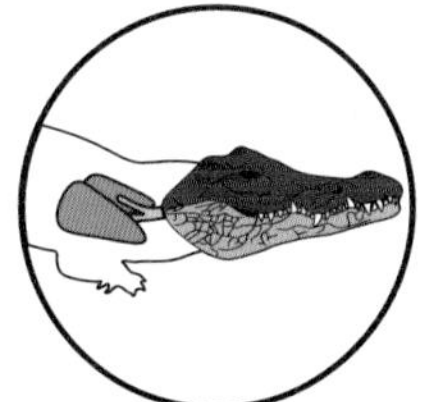

아가미로/폐로/피부로 숨을 쉬다
breathe through gills/lungs/the skin

SENTENCES TO USE

알을 낳는 동물들은 난생 동물이라고 합니다.
Animals that lay eggs are called oviparous animals.

조류는 다른 동물들에 비해 시력이 매우 좋습니다.
Birds have very good eyesight compared to other animals.

조류의 앞다리는 날개로 변형되었고, 부리가 손 역할을 합니다.
A bird's forelimbs have been transformed into wings, and its beak acts as a hand.

양서류는 어려서는 물속에 살고, 커서는 물속과 육지 양쪽에서 삽니다.
Amphibians live in the water when they are young, and when they grow up, they live both in the water and on land.

파충류는 폐로 숨을 쉬고 주로 육지에 삽니다.
Reptiles breathe through lungs and live mainly on land.

UNIT 5

지리, 지형

아시아에 (위치해) 있다 be (located) in Asia

태평양에 있다 be in the Pacific Ocean

5대양 6대주

태평양 the Pacific Ocean **대서양** the Atlantic Ocean **인도양** the Indian Ocean
북극해 the Arctic Ocean **남극해** the Southern Ocean, the Antarctic Ocean

아시아 Asia **유럽** Europe **북아메리카** North America
남아메리카 South[Latin] America **아프리카** Africa **오세아니아** Oceania

온대 지방에 (위치해) 있다 be (located) in the temperate region

온대 지방 the temperate region **열대 지방** the tropical region
아열대 지방 the subtropical region **적도 지방** the equatorial region
극지방 the polar region

대륙이다/대륙에 있다 be a continent/be on a continent

섬이다/섬에 있다 be an island/be on an island

내륙 국가다 be a landlocked country

바다를 접하고 있다 face the sea

~와 국경을 맞대고 있다 border ~

SENTENCES TO USE

튀니지는 아프리카 북부에 위치해 있으며, 수도는 튀니스입니다.
Tunisia is located in northern Africa and its capital is Tunis.

싱가포르는 적도 지방에 위치해 있어 연중 덥습니다.
Singapore is located in the equatorial region, so it is hot all year round.

인도는 아시아 대륙에 있지만, 스리랑카는 섬입니다.
India is on the Asian continent, but Sri Lanka is an island.

스위스는 내륙 국가라서 바다는 없지만 강과 호수가 많습니다.
Switzerland is a landlocked country, so there is no sea, but there are many rivers and lakes.

폴란드는 우크라이나와 국경을 맞대고 있어서 러시아-우크라이나 전쟁의 영향을 받고 있습니다.
Poland borders Ukraine and has been affected by the Russia-Ukraine War.

산악 지대다/산악 지대에 (위치해) 있다 be a mountainous area/
be (located) in a mountainous area

고산지대다/고산지대에 (위치해) 있다 be an alpine region/
be (located) in an alpine region

고원이다/고원에 (위치해) 있다 be a plateau/be (located) on a plateau

사막이다/사막에 (위치해) 있다 be a desert/be (located) in a desert

평지다/평지에 (위치해) 있다 be flat land/be (located) on flat land

경사지다/경사진 곳에 (위치해) 있다 be a slope/be (located) on a slope

내륙이다/내륙에 (위치해) 있다/~의 내륙에 (위치해) 있다
be inland/be (located) inland/be (located) in the inland of ~

해안(지대)에 (위치해) 있다
be (located) on the coast[in the coastal area]

빙산/빙하/유빙이 떠다니다
an iceberg/a glacier/floating ice[drift ice] floats

SENTENCES TO USE

에콰도르의 수도 키토는 고산지대에 위치해 있습니다.
Quito, the capital of Ecuador, is located in the alpine region.

'세계의 지붕'이라고 불리는 티베트는 중앙아시아 중심부에 위치한 고원입니다.
Tibet, called the "Roof of the World," is a plateau located in the heart of Central Asia.

아랍에미리트 최대 도시 두바이는 사막에 위치해 있습니다.
Dubai, the largest city in the United Arab Emirates, is located in the desert.

두브로브니크의 성벽은 아름다운 아드리아해의 해안에 있습니다.
Dubrovnik's city walls are on the coast of the beautiful Adriatic Sea.

빙하에서 떨어져 나온 빙산이 북극해에 떠다닙니다.
Icebergs, broken off from glaciers, float in the Arctic Ocean.

UNIT 5

산이 많다 have many mountains, there are many mountains, be mountainous (격식체)

* mountainous에는 '산이 많은'이라는 뜻 외에 '산지의, 산악의'라는 뜻도 있음

산이 없다 have no mountains, there are no mountains

산이 높다/낮다 the mountain is high[tall]/low

산이 험하다/완만하다
the mountain is rugged[rough]/gentle

강이/호수가 많다
have many rivers/lakes, there are many rivers/lakes

강이 넓다/좁다
the river is wide/narrow

강이/호수가/바다가 깊다/얕다
the river/lake/sea is deep/shallow

강이 굽이쳐 흐르다
a river meanders

강이 똑바로[곧게] 흐르다 a river flows straight[directly]

SENTENCES TO USE

그 나라에는 산이 많아요. 전체 영토의 70퍼센트쯤이 산지입니다.
There are many mountains in the country. About 70 percent of its territory is mountainous.

내가 기억하기로는 그 도시에는 산이 없어요.
As far as I remember, there are no mountains in the city.

그 산은 굉장히 험해서 등반하는 사람들이 가끔 목숨을 잃습니다.
The mountain is so rugged that people who climb it sometimes lose their lives.

도시를 지나는 지역에서는 센강이 템즈강보다 폭이 더 넓습니다.
The Seine is wider than the Thames in their respective urban areas.

그 강은 평원 사이를 굽이쳐 흐르면서 평원에 젖줄이 되어 주고 있습니다.
The river meanders through the plains, serving as a lifeline to them.

바다에 둘러싸여 있다
be surrounded by the sea

삼면이 바다다
be surrounded by the sea on three sides, have the sea on three sides, be a peninsula(반도라는 사실을 밝히는 표현)

고지대다 be an upland area, be a highland area, be on high ground

저지대다 be low-lying land[ground], be a low-lying area, be low-lying

구릉 지대다 be a hilly area, be hilly

* 구릉 지대는 완만한 기복을 이루는 산이나 언덕이 계속되는 지형

경사가 심하다
be steep, have a steep slope

경사가 완만하다
have a gentle slope

녹지가 많다
have a lot of green space

터널이 많다 have a lot of[many] tunnels, there are a lot of[many] tunnels

SENTENCES TO USE

남극 대륙은 남극해로 둘러싸여 있습니다.
Antarctica is surrounded by the Southern Ocean.

덴마크는 반도로, 삼면이 바다입니다.
Denmark is a peninsula, surrounded by the sea on three sides.

그 동네는 고지대여서 홍수 걱정은 없어요.
The neighborhood is on high ground, so there is no worry about flooding.

그 산은 경사가 완만해서 누구나 쉽게 등산할 수 있습니다.
The mountain has a gentle slope, so anyone can easily climb it.

그 고속도로에는 터널이 많은데, 총 30개쯤 있어요.
There are many tunnels on that highway—about 30 in total.

UNIT 6

기상

기온이 섭씨/화씨 ~도다
the temperature is ~ degrees Celsius/Fahrenheit

기온이 어제보다 ~도 높다/낮다
the temperature is ~ degrees higher/lower than yesterday

하늘이 맑다
the sky is clear

날이 맑다/흐리다 it is clear[sunny]/cloudy

구름이 조금 떠 있다
there are some clouds in the sky

구름이 잔뜩 끼다 it[the sky] is overcast

구름이 낮게 가라앉아 있다
the clouds are hanging low (in the sky)

바람이 불다
it is windy, the wind blows, there is wind

미풍이 불다
a breeze blows, there is a breeze

강풍이 불다
it is very windy, a strong wind blows, there is a strong wind

SENTENCES TO USE

오늘은 기온이 어제보다 6도나 낮아서 쌀쌀합니다.
The temperature today is 6 degrees lower than yesterday, so it is chilly.

이상하게도, 나는 하늘이 맑은 날에 기분이 우울해져요.
Strangely enough, I get depressed when the sky is clear.

구름이 잔뜩 낀 것이, 금방이라도 비가 올 것 같은데요.
Seeing as the sky is so overcast, it looks like it's going to rain any minute.

그녀는 구름이 낮게 가라앉은 날을 좋아해요.
She likes days when the clouds are hanging low.

오늘은 강풍이 부니 외출할 때 조심하세요.
There is a strong wind today, so be careful when you go out.

(예상) 강우량이 ~밀리미터다 the (projected[predicted]) rainfall[precipitation] is ~ millimeter(s)

비가/눈이 내리다
it rains/snows, rain/snow falls

폭우가 쏟아지다
it rains heavily, there is heavy rain, heavy rain falls

폭설이 쏟아지다
it snows heavily, there is heavy snow, heavy snow falls

번개가 치다[번쩍하다] lightning strikes[flashes]

천둥이 치다 thunder rumbles[crashes, booms]

천둥번개를 동반한 비가 쏟아지다
pour down during a thunderstorm

눈보라가 몰아치다 have a snowstorm[blizzard]

우박이 쏟아지다 it hails, hail falls, hailstones fall

안개가 끼다 it's foggy

태풍이/허리케인이/토네이도가 몰려오다[다가오다]
a typhoon/a hurricane/a tornado is coming[approaching]

모래폭풍이 불어오다/강타하다 a sandstorm is coming/hits

SENTENCES TO USE

오늘 예상 강수량은 20밀리미터로, 가뭄을 조금은 해소해 줄 거예요.
The projected rainfall today is 20 millimeters, which will ease the drought a bit.

이 지역은 해마다 여름이면 폭우가 한두 번은 쏟아집니다.
In this area, heavy rain falls once or twice every summer.

갑자기 번개가 번쩍하더니 몇 초 후에 천둥이 쳤습니다.
Suddenly, lightning flashed, followed by thunder rumbling a few seconds later.

오늘 오후에 갑자기 우박이 쏟아져 농작물에 피해를 입혔습니다.
Hail fell suddenly this afternoon, damaging the crops.

태풍이 남태평양에서 다가오고 있습니다.
A typhoon is approaching from the South Pacific.

UNIT 7

천체, 우주

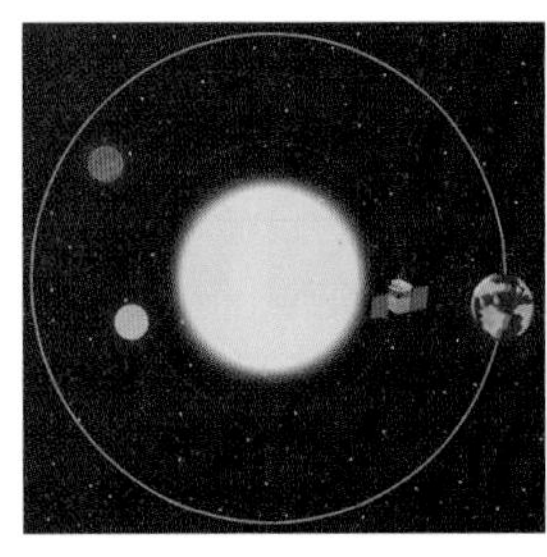

항성이다 be a star

~의 행성이다/~의 주위를 도는 행성이다
be a planet of ~/be a planet orbiting[moving around] ~

~의 위성이다/~의 주위를 도는 위성이다
be a satellite of ~/be a satellite orbiting[moving around] ~

~의 주위를 돌다 orbit ~, move around ~

* orbit ~은 '~의 주위를 궤도를 그리며 돌다'라는 뜻으로, move around보다 의미를 좀 더 명확히 표현

스스로 빛을 내다 emit[generate, produce] one's own light

혜성이다 be a comet

긴 꼬리가 있다 have a long tail

태양계에 속해 있다 belong to the solar system

태양과 행성들로 이루어져 있다 consist of[be made up of] the sun and planets

태양계의 행성들

Mercury(수성), Venus(금성), Earth(지구), Mars(화성), Jupiter(목성), Saturn(토성), Uranus(천왕성), Neptune(해왕성)

* 우주의 일부인 행성으로서 지구를 이야기할 때는 보통 Earth라고 쓰고, 우리가 사는 곳으로서 지구를 이야기할 때는 보통 the Earth라고 씀

SENTENCES TO USE

태양은 항성이고, 지구는 태양의 주위를 궤도를 그리며 도는 행성입니다.
The sun is a star, and Earth is a planet orbiting the sun.

달은 지구의 위성으로, 지구 주위를 돕니다.
The moon is Earth's natural satellite, which moves around Earth.

항성은 스스로 빛을 내지만, 행성은 스스로 빛을 내지 못합니다.
Stars emit their own light, while planets do not produce their own light.

혜성은 긴 꼬리를 가진 천체입니다. A comet is a celestial body which has a long tail.

토성은 태양의 주위를 도는 행성이며 태양계에 속해 있습니다.
Saturn is a planet orbiting the sun and belongs to the solar system.

태양계는 태양과 행성들, 기타 천체들로 이루어져 있습니다.
The solar system consists of the sun, planets, and other celestial bodies.

은하에 속해 있다 belong to the galaxy

은하수를 보기 힘들다 it's difficult[hard] to see the Milky Way

밤하늘에 별자리들이 있다 there are constellations in the night sky

봄/여름/가을/겨울을 대표하는 별자리로 유명하다
be famous as the constellation representing[of] spring/summer/autumn[fall]/winter
* representing을 쓰면 '대표하는'의 뜻으로 대표성이 강조되고, of를 쓰면 여러 개 중 하나라는 의미

별똥별이 떨어지다
a shooting star[a meteor] streaks across the sky,
a shooting star[a meteor] falls

대폭발로 탄생하다 originate from the Big Bang,
be born out of the Big Bang
* originate from이 더 격식체

팽창하다 expand

무중력 상태다
be weightless, be in a gravity-free state,
be in a zero-gravity state,
be in a state of weightlessness

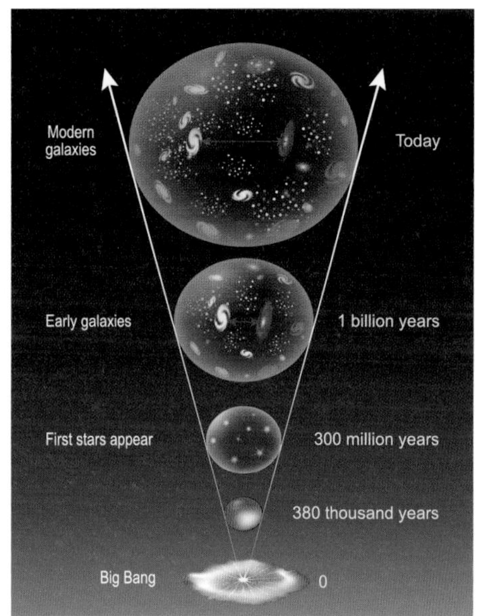

SENTENCES TO USE

우리 태양계도 거대한 은하에 속해 있습니다.
Our solar system also belongs to a vast galaxy.

대도시에서는 은하수를 보기가 힘듭니다.
It is difficult to see the Milky Way in a big city.

백조자리가 여름을 대표하는 별자리로 유명합니다.
Cygnus is famous as the constellation representing summer.

방금 저쪽 하늘에서 별똥별이 떨어졌어요.
A shooting star just streaked across the sky over there.

우주는 대폭발로 탄생하여 계속 팽창하고 있습니다.
The universe originated from the Big Bang and continues to expand.

우주 공간에서는 모든 것이 무중력이에요. 아무것도 중력의 영향을 받지 않죠.
In outer space, everything is weightless. Nothing is affected by gravity.

CHAPTER

2

자연재해와 환경

UNIT 1

각종 자연재해

폭우가 내리다[쏟아지다] there is heavy rain, it rains heavily, heavy rain falls[pours]

홍수가 나다 there is a flood

폭우로 침수되다 be flooded by[due to] heavy rain

폭설이 내리다[쏟아지다] there is heavy snow, it snows heavily, heavy snow falls

산사태가 일어나다 a landslide occurs

가뭄이 들다 experience a drought, there is a drought

폭염이 닥치다 a heat wave hits, experience a heat wave, have a heat wave, there is a heat wave

한파가 닥치다 a cold wave hits, experience a cold wave, have a cold wave, there is a cold wave

(~의 결과로) 사상자가 발생하다 ~ result in casualties

SENTENCES TO USE

3일째 폭우가 쏟아지고 있어요. 영영 그치지 않을 것 같아요.
Heavy rain has been pouring for three days. It feels like it's never going to end.

폭우로 많은 건물이 침수되었지만, 다행히도 인명 피해는 없었습니다.
A lot of buildings were flooded due to heavy rain, but fortunately, there were no casualties.

이 지역은 두 달 넘게 가뭄이에요.
This region has been experiencing a drought for over two months.

그 지역에 10년 만에 한파가 닥쳐서 수도관이 얼었어요.
The region experienced its first cold wave in 10 years, leading to frozen water pipes.

폭설이 쏟아져서 산사태가 일어났고, 사상자가 발생했습니다.
Heavy snowfall led to a landslide, resulting in casualties.

태풍/허리케인/토네이도가 발생하다/다가오다/덮치다
a typhoon/a hurricane/a tornado occurs/approaches/hits

지진이 발생하다 an earthquake occurs

지진 해일이[쓰나미가] 발생하다/덮치다 a tsunami strikes/hits

화산이 폭발하다
a volcano erupts

태풍/지진/지진 해일/화산 피해가 심각하다
a typhoon/an earthquake/a tsunami/a volcano causes severe damage,
the damage caused by a typhoon/an earthquake/a tsunami/a volcano is severe

싱크홀[땅꺼짐]이 발생하다
a sinkhole forms [emerges, appears]

황사가 심하다
the yellow dust is bad[severe],
we have a lot of yellow dust

(초)미세먼지가 심하다
the (ultra)fine dust is bad[severe],
the (ultra)fine dust level is high,
we have a lot of (ultra)fine dust

지구 온난화가 심하다/심각한 문제다
global warming is severe/a serious problem

SENTENCES TO USE

전 세계에서 발생하는 토네이도의 75퍼센트가 미국에서 발생합니다.
Seventy-five percent of tornadoes worldwide occur in the United States.

지진 자체보다 그로 인한 지진 해일의 피해가 더 심각한 경우들이 있습니다.
In some cases, a tsunami can cause more severe damage than the earthquake itself.

주택에서 싱크홀[땅꺼짐]이 발생하여 사람이 사망한 경우가 있었습니다.
There was a case where a sinkhole formed beneath a house, resulting in a fatality.

어제 예측된 바와 같이 오늘도 미세먼지가 심합니다.
As predicted yesterday, the fine dust level is still high today.

많은 이들이 생각하는 것 이상으로 지구 온난화는 심각합니다. 우리는 그것이 가져올 결과에 눈을 떠야 합니다.
Global warming is more severe than many think. We need to wake up to its consequences.

UNIT 2 지진, 화산

지진

지진이 발생하다 an earthquake occurs[strikes, happens]

진도가 ~이다 have a magnitude of ~

약한/강한 지진이다 experience[be] a weak/strong earthquake

여진이 계속되다 aftershocks continue[persist] * persist는 격식체

지진 해일이[쓰나미가] 우려되다
concerns arise regarding (the possibility of) a tsunami

지진 해일이[쓰나미가] 발생하다/덮치다
a tsunami strikes/hits

화산

활화산/휴화산/사화산이다
be (classified as) an active/a dormant[an inactive]/an extinct[a dead] volcano

* 과학 지문에서는 be classified as가 쓰임
* 요즘은 휴화산도 활화산에 포함시킴

화산이 폭발하다 a volcano erupts, eruption occurs

용암이 흘러나오다 lava emerges[flows out]

화산재가 날리다 volcanic ash scatters[flies]

용암/화산재에 덮이다
be covered[engulfed] in lava/volcanic ash

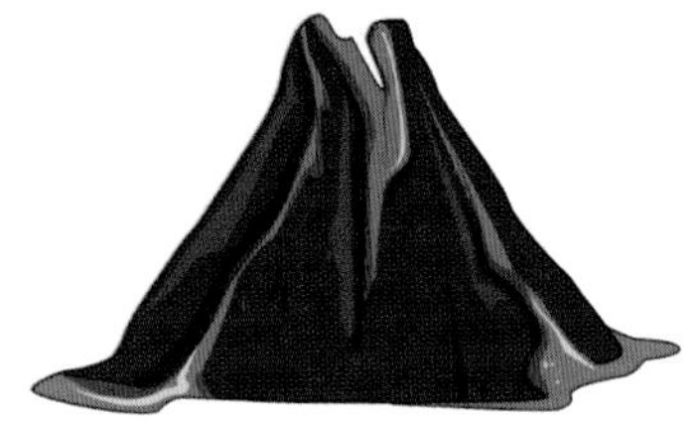

SENTENCES TO USE

어제 그 섬에서 발생한 지진은 강도가 6.0이었습니다.
The earthquake that occurred on that island yesterday had a magnitude of 6.0.

그 지진 이후 여진이 며칠째 계속되고 있습니다.
After the earthquake, aftershocks have continued for several days.

이번 지진으로 지진 해일 발생이 우려되고 있습니다.
Concerns arise regarding the possibility of a tsunami following this earthquake.

알래스카에 있는 포피크드산은 사화산으로 여겨졌으나, 2006년에 다시 분출하여 활화산이 되었습니다.
Fourpeaked Mountain in Alaska was considered an extinct volcano, but it erupted again in 2006 and became an active volcano.

폼페이는 서기 79년에 베수비오 화산이 폭발하여 화산재에 뒤덮였습니다.
Pompeii was covered in volcanic ash when Mount Vesuvius erupted in 79 AD.

Pompeii WAS COVERED IN VOLCANIC ASH

when Mount Vesuvius erupted in 79 AD.

UNIT 3

환경 일반

MP3 102

환경이 오염되다 the environment is polluted[damaged]

환경이 파괴되다 the environment is destroyed

환경 오염이 심하다
environmental pollution is severe, the environment is severely polluted

환경 보호 운동이 전개되다
the environmental (protection) movements take place[are underway]

대기/수질/토양 오염이 심하다
air/water/soil pollution is severe, have severe air/water/soil pollution

산성비가 내리다 acid rain falls[occurs]

(생물이) 멸종되다 become[go] extinct

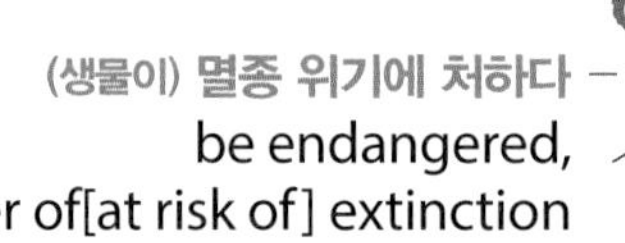

(생물이) 멸종 위기에 처하다
be endangered,
be in danger of[at risk of] extinction

(제품이) 환경친화적이다
be eco-friendly[environmentally friendly]

환경이 회복되다
the environment is restored

SENTENCES TO USE

환경 오염이 너무 심해져서 인류는 대비책을 마련하고 있습니다.
Environmental pollution has become so severe that humanity is preparing countermeasures.

전 세계의 많은 대도시가 대기 오염이 심합니다.
Many big cities around the world have severe air pollution.

바다의 수질 오염이 심한데, 특히 쓰레기로 인한 오염이 심각합니다.
Water pollution is severe in the sea, particularly due to garbage.

이 도시에서는 산성비가 자주 내려요. 비 안 맞게 조심하세요.
Acid rain often falls in this city. Be careful not to get caught in the rain.

환경 오염으로 인해 많은 동식물이 멸종 위기에 처해 있습니다.
Many plants and animals are endangered due to environmental pollution.

UNIT 4

지구 온난화

MP3 103

지구 온난화가 심각하다[심하다]
global warming is serious[severe]

빙하가 녹고 있다/줄고 있다
glaciers are melting/shrinking

해수면이 상승하고 있다
sea levels are rising

수온이 상승하고 있다
water temperatures are rising

자연재해 발생이 증가하고 있다 the frequency of natural disasters is increasing

사막화가 진행 중이다
desertification is underway[in progress]

온대 기후가 아열대 기후로 바뀌고 있다
temperate climates are changing to subtropical climates

이상 기후 현상이 (자주) 일어나고 있다
extreme weather events are occurring (frequently)

생물 다양성이 감소하고 있다 biodiversity[biological diversity] is decreasing
* 생물 다양성 감소 a decrease in biodiversity

SENTENCES TO USE

20세기 중반 이후 지구 온난화가 점점 더 심각해지고 있습니다.
Global warming has become increasingly serious since the mid-20th century.

지구 온난화로 빙하가 녹아서 해수면이 상승하고 있습니다.
Due to global warming, glaciers are melting, and sea levels are rising.

지구 곳곳에서 사막화가 진행 중이어서 여러 국가가 그 방지를 위해 노력하고 있습니다.
Desertification is underway worldwide, so many countries are working to prevent it.

지구 온난화로 인해 이상 기후 현상이 빈번히 발생하고 있습니다.
Due to global warming, extreme weather events are occurring frequently.

지구 온난화의 장기적 영향 중 하나는 생물 다양성의 감소입니다.
One of the long-term effects of global warming is a decrease in biodiversity.

INDEX

ㄱ

ㄲ

ㄴ

ㄷ

ㄸ

ㄹ

ㅁ

ㅂ

ㅃ

ㅅ

ㅆ

ㅈ

ㅉ

ㅊ

ㅋ

ㅌ

ㅍ

ㅎ

기타

More 부분 리스트